South Africa
in Southern Africa

South Africa in Southern Africa

Domestic Change and International Conflict

edited by
Edmond J. Keller
Louis A. Picard

Lynne Rienner Publishers • Boulder & London

Published in the United States of America in 1989 by
Lynne Rienner Publishers, Inc.
1800 30th Street, Boulder, Colorado 80301

and in the United Kingdom by
Lynne Rienner Publishers, Inc.
3 Henrietta Street, Covent Garden, London WC2E 8LU

Library of Congress Cataloging-in-Publication Data
South Africa in southern Africa : domestic change and international
  conflict / edited by Edmond J. Keller and Louis A. Picard.
      p. cm.
  Bibliography: p.
  Includes index.
  ISBN 1–55587–129–1 (alk. paper)
    1. South Africa—Politics and government—1978– 2. South Africa—
Foreign relations—1978– 3. South Africa—Foreign relations—
Africa, Southern. 4. Africa, Southern—Foreign relations—South
Africa. I. Keller, Edmond J. (Edmond Joseph), 1942–
II. Picard, Louis A.
DT779.952.S653 1989
327.68—dc20   89–3942
                                                                       CIP

British Cataloguing in Publication Data
A Cataloguing in Publication record for this book
is available from the British Library.

Printed and bound in the United States of America

The paper used in this publication meets the requirements of
the American National Standard for Permanence of Paper for
Printed Library Materials Z39.48–1984.

Educ

Contents

Acknowledgments

The editors would like to acknowledge the following individuals, who assisted in the preparation of this book: Kate Petersen, Office of the President, University of California, Berkeley; Jan Sallinger-McBride, Department of Political Science, University of California, Santa Barbara; and Paula Bilinsky, Graduate School of Public and International Affairs, University of Pittsburgh.

Partial financial support for this effort was provided by the Graduate School of Public and International Affairs and the University Center for International Studies of the University of Pittsburgh and the Department of Political Science, University of California, Santa Barbara.

Our thanks as well to the staff of Lynne Rienner Publishers, and in particular to Gia Hamilton, for their support and patience. Most importantly, we are grateful for the work Lorraine Gardner has put into this manuscript. Her organizational and editorial skills were critical in many ways to the successful completion of the book.

1

South African Patterns
of Change and Continuity

LOUIS A. PICARD & EDMOND J. KELLER

The demographics of South Africa tell the tale: in the year 2000, white South Africans, as a percentage of total population of the country, will fall to less than 10 percent, or slightly more than the current percentage of whites in Namibia. Over the past sixty years, the dominant white population has fallen from a high of 22 percent in 1921 to 15 percent in 1985. By the end of the century, the white population could be as low as 8 percent of the total population of the country.

Over the next twelve years, black professionals will come to dominate the South African economy. The shift has been and will be dramatic. In 1960, for example, only twenty-eight Africans obtained the matriculation exemption necessary for admission to the university. At that time, blacks (African, mixed-race, and Indian) constituted only 11 percent of all university students. By 1984, blacks had come to make up the majority of the matriculants, and they currently make up two-thirds of the college students in teacher training and one-third of all university students. By 1994, blacks will constitute the majority of all university graduates.[1] By the early 1990s, black South Africans will be the fastest growing segment of the country's professional, managerial, and business class. Given these demographics, it is not likely, twenty-five years after the dismantling of the colonial empires, that black elites

> will submit to being the only national bourgeoisie to remain dominated in their own state. As with every national bourgeoisie from Egypt to Zimbabwe, they will no longer seek to join the settler bourgeoisie, but to displace it: to enjoy the power and patronage of hegemony.[2]

The decade of the 1980s provides the backdrop to this demographic and managerial revolution. As such, it has been characterized by a number of both mutually reinforcing and contradictory themes as South Africa moves slowly toward a negotiated, majority rule, postapartheid state.

1

A first theme of South African politics in the past decade has been the development of a new strength and influence of both international and internal majority-rule forces, including the United Democratic Front (UDF), the African National Congress (ANC), and the National Forum (NF). Some coalition of these groups (and other "progressive" forces)[3] represents the likely successor regime to the present Nationalist Party (NP) government. The current state of emergency and the effective banning of the seventeen internal organizations[4] in February 1988 has in no way diminished the influence that both internal and external antiparliamentary groups have among black South Africans.

Ironically, and not surprisingly, the strength of the nonparliamentary forces in South Africa has been mirrored by the dramatic increase in the influence of the parliamentary and extra-parliamentary forces on the right. Spurred on by what it perceived to be unnecessary reforms of the Botha government, the right-wing Conservative Party, led by Adries Treurnicht, has been able to take control of a significant number of mid-level city councils in the Transvaal and the Orange Free State.

Along with the rise in influence of the extra-parliamentary groups, and no doubt because of it, there has developed, under the state of emergency, a system of militarized political control that is both all-encompassing and effective.[5] This includes the use of the military to control the forces of change in the black townships, the effective abolition of all political activity by internally based political forces, and the use of "hot pursuit" to attack guerrillas of the ANC and the Pan-Africanist Congress (PAC) inside South Africa's neighboring states. In the past four years South Africa has attacked Botswana, Mozambique, Zambia, Zimbabwe, Lesotho, Swaziland, and Angola (with its attacks against the guerrillas of the South West Africa People's Organization [SWAPO] and support for those of the National Union for the Total Independence of Angola [UNITA]).[6]

A third and somewhat ambiguous theme has become apparent in South Africa since the early 1980s: there has been a recognition by the ruling forces in the NP under the leadership of P. W. Botha that "Grand Apartheid"—the division of the country into ten African homelands—will not provide a satisfactory political dispensation for this rapidly industrializing and urbanizing society. The homelands are too small, too fragmented, and too politically flawed to provide a significant outlet for black political demands within the country.[7] Moreover, it is clear that most black South Africans will settle for nothing less than full citizenship and the rights that obtain to it.

This has led to a fourth pattern of events since 1979. The South African government has introduced a series of conservative but not inconsequential reforms designed to create a group-defined multiracial state in which market forces predominate within the context of a political "power-sharing" arrangement. The significance of these reforms is that they do indicate a real shift away from geographically based "Grand Apartheid." However, while some socioeconomic reforms—in particular the legalization of black trade unions and the end of influx control—are important, the Nationalist Party remains trapped in its group (or narrow apartheid) approach to political reform.

While the reforms of the Botha regime will not result in South Africa's final dispensation of forces, they will have an impact upon the majority-rule state that follows. Structural changes that have been introduced to this point include municipality status for all black townships in South Africa with the beginnings of multiracial metropolitan government in regional services councils; the creation of appointed multiracial executive committees, made up of whites, Indians, coloureds, and Africans, which govern the country's four provinces (and the abolition of the four all-white provincial councils); a regional planning system that includes, at least in theory, the country's ten homelands; and, at the national level, a proposal for negotiations over the future of the central government through the establishment of a "national council," which would include blacks from outside the homelands as well as representatives of homeland governments. This "national council" is designed to bring blacks into the racially based "tricameral" parliamentary system introduced in 1985, a system that provides representation for South African Indians and coloureds as well as whites but not for the black majority.

It was this 1983 constitution, with its built-in majority for the Nationalist Party in the tie-breaking president's council, that created an executive state presidency.[8] While the racial nature of the recent government proposals for reforms has led extra-parliamentary forces to reject the national council at this point, all groups, including the ANC, accept the principle of a negotiated settlement to South Africa's problems. This could lead, after the scheduled white, coloured, and Indian national elections in September 1989, to the release of Nelson Mandela, the removal of the state of emergency, and the unbanning of proscribed organizations. Particularly if it were accompanied by the abolition of the Group Areas Act, such a scenario could set the stage for meaningful negotiations in the early 1990s.

Related to the patterns of domestic reform and resistance has been the impact of international sanctions and the extent to which this has prevented new capital from flowing into South Africa. The current low level of new investment is likely to be heavily impacted by the 1988 Dellums Bill, which mandates an almost complete termination of all trade between the United States and South Africa. Even if the bill has not been passed in final form in 1989 or later, it has already had a major impact on policymakers and bureaucratic elites in South Africa. There is a growing realization among politically aware South Africans, both black and white, that there will be no economic upswing or new investment until there is a final political dispensation in South Africa that is widely accepted by large segments of both the domestic and international communities. Failure to move toward a negotiated settlement for majority rule will most certainly lead to a further deterioration of the South African economy.[9] More and more countries will likely increase their pressures for reform and, domestically, black South Africans will become more and more desperate and violent in their protests.

Regional and international developments remain somewhat ambiguous. In part pressured by the cost of its war in Angola (which is reputed to cost some 4 billion rand a year), there was in the summer of 1988 significant movement toward peace settlements in Namibia and Angola. If this trend holds up after the shaky start of UN administration of Namibia in April 1989, there could well be a settlement of the conflict in the near future. The settlement in Angola and the resulting independence for Namibia is likely to be combined with increasing tension between South Africa and its neighbors over the use of their territory by ANC and PAC guerrillas. A particular tension has developed between South Africa and Botswana over the infiltration of ANC operatives into South Africa through the northeast part of that country. According to South African intelligence, about half of the ANC incursions into South Africa now come through Botswana.[10]

Against the backdrop of these recent developments in South Africa, this book critically examines the dynamics of political change and conflict in South Africa in the domestic, regional, and international arenas. The assumption that guides this discussion is that in order to understand the process of change currently unfolding in South Africa and in the Southern African region, one must come to grips with the salient exogenous as well as endogenous factors contributing to the character of that change. Not only must we understand the dynamics of race, class, clientelism, and culture inside the country, we must also understand how factors external to South Africa contribute to the debates and struggles raging domestically.

The remainder of this book is divided into three parts. The first deals with theoretical perspectives on social change in South Africa; the second focuses on the political economy of change in the domestic arena; and the final part of the book addresses the interaction between domestic and international politics as they relate to both South Africa and the Southern African region.

In the first section of the book, three authors examine different theoretical perspectives on the process of social change in South Africa. In Chapter 2, Arend Lijphart focuses on the problem of constitution-making for a new political dispensation in South Africa. Lijphart argues that for the constitutional process to be successful, it is essential that problems of ethnicity be taken into account. For Lijphart, self-determination or voluntary identification is preferable to the predetermination of group membership by the state. He advocates both the use of proportional representation and "cultural councils" to provide representation and protect ethnic minorities from the power of the state.

Two major issues come out of the Lijphart chapter that will have to be addressed by scholars who advocate a "group" or ethnic approach to politics in South Africa. First, to what extent does an ethnic approach mirror the current image of the South African government's approach to constitutional dispensation (and mask racial fears with ethnic divisions), an approach that has been rejected by both the parliamentary opposition as well as the internal and external extra-parliamentary groups? Second, critics of the group approach argue that it is patterns of class division, reinforced by ethnic separation, that are the primary dividing lines in South African society.

In Chapter 3, Donald Rothchild focuses on incentive strategies, which can be introduced from the outside, to promote negotiation among the South African government and the extra-parliamentary forces. According to Rothchild, the South African system is not conducive to negotiations at this time. A polarization of positions, between supporters of the government's ethnically based reforms and the parliamentary and extra-parliamentary opposition, which advocates either a federal or a unitary system with one person–one vote, precludes significant negotiation. For Rothchild, the key to a least violent outcome is the development by influential foreign governments of a strategy of conflict management. This would require two components: first, direct international intervention in the event that there is actual or potential massive loss of life; and second, and more immediately, the use of economic leverage to force negotiations. Rothchild provides us with a theoretical framework within which the antisanctions movement in the United States and Western Europe operates.

For Rothchild, the question is not whether to use economic leverage, but the manner in which economic leverage is used. The "soft track" option, something like what some Republican Party specialists on Southern Africa advocate, is to use "best offices" communication, with both sides coupled by economic side payments in the event of significant progress. Rothchild's "hard track" option requires that strong positive and negative incentives be used to push toward negotiations. These include sanctions against the South African state combined with diplomatic support and economic aid to the Front Line States. This is the pattern of U.S. technical assistance that was introduced in the 1986 sanctions legislation. One question that might be raised is what role assistance to nongovernmental groups within South Africa dedicated to a nonracial society would play in the "hard track."

C. R. D Halisi, in Chapter 4, examines racial proletarianism and political culture in South Africa. To Halisi, the major fault lines in South African society are not racial divisions but the class divisions that are reinforced by racially exclusive legislation and administrative fiat. He argues that racial proletarianization as a process has meant an intersection of race, class, and power relations into a political culture that shapes both social conflict and cooperation. Furthermore, he asserts, the development of such a political culture reduces the likelihood of race-neutral democracy and could even set the stage for intrarace class collaboration. Halisi sees the emergence of a kind of *herrenvolk* logic designed to deny forever the black South Africans' birthright of first-class citizenship in their own land. In fact, such a logic assigns blacks to a permanent lower caste, with no citizenship rights.

The second section of the book examines the political economy of domestic change in South Africa. In Chapter 5, Tsehloane Keto examines what he calls a "zonal" analysis of black politics in South Africa. Rather than a single pattern of black politics, he sees four different patterns identified by four political zones. The Keto chapter provides an excellent, up-to-date summary of the current situation on the ground in South Africa. For Keto, the four zones of South African black politics are the Eastern Cape, where union and community action politics occur within the shadow of the two Khosa-speaking homelands of the Transkei and the Ciskei; the Western Cape, where the role of the "coloured" population is significant; Natal, where black politics is characterized by conflict between Gatsha Buthelezi's Inkatha movement and the UDF/ANC supporters; and the Transvaal/Northern Cape/Orange Free State heartland, where "peak" organizations of both the multiracial movements such as the UDF and the black nationalist groups such as the Azania People's Organization (AZAPO) and the National Forum had their headquarters before their effective banning in February 1988. Keto's chapter provides us with a forceful argument for a transethnic but regional approach to understanding South African politics.

The role that black labor plays in the politics of protest is the focus of Pearl-Alice Marsh's study in Chapter 6. Marsh describes the emergence of the black trade union movement over the past two decades in an effort to assess the political role the movement has assumed. She finds that, though black labor in South Africa has a great deal of political potential, it has not been able to realize that potential because it is consumed with enormous economistic types of issues in the workplace. Marsh strongly argues that "trade unions are not political organizations but are worker organizations and have that constituency, operating in the place of production, to protect." Nevertheless, Marsh suggests, black labor may not be able to avoid becoming politicized as the social and political crises inside South Africa deepen.

The role that business will play in the process of change in South Africa is the focus of Chapter 7, by Heribert Adam and Kogila Moodley. Adam and Moodley argue that the role of the 5 million whites in South Africa will be critical for change to occur. Within this context, the role of white business is a crucial component of any potential change in South Africa. The problem, according to Adam and Moodley, is that business pays only lip service to reform. Business, potentially, can play two roles: first, it can transform the workplace into a model, nonracial industrial "democracy" along Swedish, or perhaps Japanese, lines; second, business can facilitate negotiations between the ANC and other opposition groups and the South African government.

Given the shift to the right among South African white voters and the development of a militarized bureaucratic implementation process, however, Adam and Moodley conclude that the majority of whites do not yet perceive a crisis. It is this perception of crisis that may provide the vehicle for business representatives to play a role in negotiating the political restructuring of South Africa. The pending increase in the level of sanctions by Western Europe and the United States, along with the absence of new investment that results from sanctions pressures, may lead white South Africans to a perception of the impending economic and political crisis their country faces.

The third part of the book examines the role that South Africa plays in the international and, in particular, the Southern African regional context. In Chapter 8, Richard Weisfelder examines the role that the Southern African Development Coordination Conference (SADCC) plays in weakening the dependency links between the black-ruled states and South Africa. According to Weisfelder, the weakness of the SADCC states may be to their regional advantage, and he attempts to test the hypothesis that the SADCC states can gain greater capacity though their collective efforts. At issue for Weisfelder is the extent to which SADCC states can collectively bear the short-term costs that are necessary to extract concessional changes from South Africa. According to Weisfelder, the SADCC region is weaker in the 1980s than it was in the late 1970s. And yet, he argues that it is possible for the region as a collective to engender long-term gains. Pressure on SADCC from South Africa, for example, threatens the large trade surplus that South Africa enjoys with the region. South Africa will also lose extensive employment opportunities and crucial foreign exchange that its trade with SADCC generates if the international community comes in to fill the breach. Most critically, Weisfelder argues that in the event of increased conflict between South Africa and SADCC, both parties, not just SADCC, will lose.

In Chapter 9, James Scarritt provides us with a case study of the impact of South Africa upon one of the Front Line States—Zambia, which perhaps more than any other state has paid "the high price of principles"[11] for its support of the liberation struggles in Zimbabwe, Angola, Mozambique, and now in Namibia and South Africa. Scarritt focuses on the impact of the "South African Presence," actual and perceived, on Zambia. Although Zambia has been what Scarritt calls a "secondary target," South Africa has taken many destabilizing actions against the country. Of significance is the way South Africa has played upon dominant class needs in Zambia in order to mute the Zambian state's challenge to South Africa. Thus, according to

Scarritt, Zambian elites have moved to accommodate the South African state whenever possible.

John Sullivan, in Chapter 10, examines the nature of military conflict in Southern Africa and documents the increasing militarism that characterizes relationships among South Africa and its neighbors. Sullivan argues that the neighboring states, particularly those in the front line grouping, must play a balancing act between ANC pressures for refugee and transit rights and South African demands that the neighboring states stop the ANC use of their territory for guerrilla activities within South Africa. Given South Africa's overwhelming military capabilities, peace and stability in the Southern African region cannot be guaranteed without a solution to South Africa's military problems.

Finally, in Chapter 11, Louis A. Picard and Robert Groelsma examine the evolution of U.S. foreign policy toward Southern Africa. Historically, there has been a strong tendency toward disinterest in Southern Africa among U.S. foreign policy elites. When interest in the region has surfaced, U.S. political leaders have tended to see developments in Southern Africa within the context of East–West great power confrontation. It is the thesis of Chapter 11 that regional and domestic dynamics within and among the Southern African states, rather than great power politics, define the dynamics of political conflict in that troubled region. Furthermore, since 1984, and especially in the glasnost spirit of the late 1980s, public interest in Southern Africa has raised the question of the extent to which this East–West framework might be replaced by a North–South and a regional framework. To what extent does the politicization of the South Africa issue domestically within the United States suggest a greater use of U.S. economic pressure to promote domestic international political change within South Africa and the Southern African region?

Tom Lodge, a long-time and objective observer of South African politics, argues that South African politics can be understood in terms of a series of concentric circles. "Each circle," he states, "represents a different degree of access to political power and material privilege." In the inner circle are the government, with Parliament, the parliamentary political organizations, and the civil service. Traditionally, the first circle has embraced only whites, though since 1983,

> its parameter has been expanded to include Indians and Coloured people, though not in terms of full equality with whites. The first circle, then, exists primarily for the benefit of twenty-eight percent of the population or nearly eight million people, though the political machinery within it affects the lives of many millions more.[12]

Of the three outer circles, the first represents the apartheid political arrangements that exist for blacks in the towns (e.g., municipal councils), and the second represents legislatures and government structures in the ten homelands. For most black South Africans these arrangements provide little in the way of genuine participation. According to Lodge,

> The third circle represents the extra-constitutional politics of the townships and the factories. If it is a politics without a franchise it is not altogether a politics without power, for its constituents live and work their lives in the most strategic positions in the country's economy. Which brings us to the fourth circle which defines the boundary of the system. Here political life is fragmented and localised. The politics of the African rural poor often consists of a struggle for resources at the most basic level of existence. Here people usually have neither rights nor power.[13]

The authors of this book hope that their research and analysis will provide a basis for an understanding of the restructuring process South Africa's "concentric circles" are now undergoing. What the nature of the new arrangements will be is not yet clear. That a transformation is occurring, however, is without doubt. Gradually, internal and external pressures will push the government toward negotiation with what Lodge calls the "third circle" of South African politics. It is only at that point that a process can begin to address the needs of that forgotten group in South Africa, the unorganized rural poor.

NOTES

1. These figures come from Keith Gottschalk, "State Strategy and the Limits of Counter-Revolution," in Glenn Moss and Ingrid Obery, eds., *South African Review* 4 (Johannesburg: Ravan Press, 1987), pp. 503–506.

2. *Ibid*, p. 506.

3. Groups that are commited to unrestricted majority rule in Southern Africa and to resisting the unilateral and partial reforms introduced by the Botha administration; see Tom Lodge, "State Power and the Politics of Resistance," in *Work in Progress*, no. 50/51 (October–November 1987), pp. 3–6, for a discussion of this resistance.

4. An eighteenth, the End Conscription Campaign, was proscribed by the state on August 23, 1988. See David Braun, "Anti-Draft Group 'Banned' by Vlok," *Star* (Johannesburg), August 22, 1988.

5. See, for example, Ivor Sarakinsky, "The State of the State and the State of Resistance," in *Work in Progress*, no. 52 (March 1988), pp. 47–51, and Jacklyn Cock, "A High Price for Freedom: Militarisation and White South Africa," in *Work in Progress*, no. 53 (April–May 1988), pp. 19–23.

6. The best analysis of the conflict between South Africa and its neighbors is Joseph Hanlon, *Beggar Your Neighbours: Apartheid Power in Southern Africa* (Bloomington: Indiana University Press, 1986).

7. An analysis of this by an academic close to the Nationalist Party is G. C. Olivier, "The Prospects for Future Stability or Instability in South Africa" in Calvin A. Woodward, ed., *On Razor's Edge: Prospects for Political*

Stability in Southern Africa (Pretoria: Africa Institute of South Africa, 1986), pp. 121–133.

8. An up-to-date account of these changes and their impact upon South African politics is found in Philip H. Frankel, et al., eds., *State Resistance and Change in South Africa* (London: Croom Helm, 1988).

9. Newspaper accounts in South Africa reflect this concern. See, for example, Michael Chester, "Sitting on an Economic Time Bomb," *Star* (Johannesburg), July 14, 1988, p. 10; John Spira, "Why Alarm Bells Are Ringing for Sick Rand," *Star Review* (Johannesburg), July 31, 1988, p. 1; and "Growth Likely to Stay Sluggish," *The Citizen* (Johnannesburg), August 6, 1988, p. 17.

10. See David Braun, "Terror Trail to SA Leads Through Botswana-SAP," *Star*, August 24, 1988, p. 3.

11. Richard Hall, *The High Price of Principles* (London: Hodder and Stoughton, 1969).

12. For both quotes see Tom Lodge, "Introduction," in Shelagh Gastow, ed., *Who's Who in South African Politics* (Johannesburg: Ravan Press, 1985), p. 1.

13. *Ibid.*, pp. 1–2.

PART I
Theoretical Perspectives
on Social Change in South Africa

2

The Ethnic Factor and Democratic Constitution-Making in South Africa

AREND LIJPHART

In my first attempt to apply consociational theory to the case of South Africa, I asserted that "South Africa's basic problem is that it is a plural society with extremely deep cleavages dividing the different segments of its population."[1] I still believe that this is a correct statement of the problem, but now I also think I should clarify it by adding two crucial distinctions: (1) a distinction between different cleavages, racial and ethnic; and (2) a distinction between different "basic problems," the current political problem and the future problem of agreeing on a democratic constitution for the South African plural society. It is the second—the constitutional—problem that I address in this chapter, and it is the second type of cleavage—the ethnic—that forms the main challenge to the constitution-makers.

Moreover, in the South African case, the ethnic factor is unusually complicated because, in addition to the fact of ethnicity itself, the constitution-makers will have to deal with two further problems: (1) the difficulty of objectively identifying the ethnic groups—a problem caused by the government's unilateral imposition of group boundaries, which makes it impossible to judge whether the groups, thus defined, are natural or artificial ones; and (2) the fact that significant actors in South Africa deny the existence of ethnicity and/or its relevance for constitution-making. I am convinced that, from the point of view of social science, the denial of ethnicity is a myth, but it is a myth that is part of the South African political reality and that has to be constitutionally accommodated.

In order to avoid any possible misunderstanding or misinterpretation, I should like to repeat that I regard ethnic and racial divisions as completely different kinds of divisions, and I do *not* think that race and ethnicity can be equated in any way in South Africa. When I speak of ethnic groups in South Africa, I think of groups that are defined in terms of language and culture, not physical traits. Because of the difficulty of identifying the ethnic groups of

13

South Africa, I cannot give an exhaustive list of these groups, but the Zulus, Xhosas, and Afrikaners can serve as examples.

THE END-OF-ETHNICITY MYTH

There are good reasons for the opponents of the South African government both to dislike ethnicity and to think of race and ethnicity as equally objectionable concepts. Race and ethnicity have both been the tools of minority rule and the suppression of the majority. The official racial categorization was the rationale behind the tricameral Parliament established by the 1983 constitution: a strong white chamber, weak coloured and Asian chambers, and no representation at all for the African majority. Ethnic criteria were used to set up the so-called homelands for Zulus, Xhosas, Tswanas, and other African ethnic groups. Hence, it is easy to understand Archbishop Desmond M. Tutu's emotional statement: "We Blacks . . . execrate ethnicity with all our being."[2]

There are also good *political* reasons for those opposing the government to de-emphasize ethnicity. The National Party government mainly represents a single cohesive minority ethnic group—the Afrikaners—whereas the opposing majority is divided into a large number of ethnic groups. Since unity spells strength and division weakness, it is just as logical for the government to stress ethnicity as it is for the opposition to play it down. Inkatha appears to be an exception to this statement since it belongs to the opposition but is also a largely ethnically based organization. However, the fact that the Zulus are the largest ethnic group in South Africa, constituting about 20 percent of the total population, gives them a clear political advantage in exploiting their numerical strength.

Finally, there are two plausible—but, upon closer analysis, unconvincing—reasons to believe that ethnicity is in fact of minor importance in the future of South Africa. One of these is unique to the South African situation; the other rests on a general analysis of trends in ethnicity. What is unusual in South Africa is the extent to which ethnicity has become a tool of control and oppression. Hence, it is tempting to regard the ethnic divisions as the government's artificial creations and to assume that they will disappear once white minority control ends. In my view, this line of thinking turns things upside down. Ethnic differences are an unalterable fact, and what the government's widely despised policies have succeeded in doing is not to manufacture them artificially but to counteract and soften them artificially. Consequently, when minority rule ends, ethnicity, instead of quietly disappearing, is bound to reassert itself.

The history of decolonization in Africa and Asia reinforces this prediction. The colonial authorities, too, frequently manipulated ethnic differences, but these were nevertheless downgraded in the common struggle for independence; upon or shortly after independence, however, ethnicity almost invariably made a strong comeback. Michael Massing may well be correct when he says that Inkatha's "appeals to ethnicity run counter to the direction of contemporary South African politics,"[3] but it is quite wrong to assume that this trend can simply be extrapolated to the politics of postapartheid South Africa.

The second reason for assuming that ethnicity is a barely relevant factor in thinking about South Africa's future is the belief that the processes of modernization, industrialization, and urbanization have undermined ethnic divisions and differences. For instance, in contrast with my own view that South Africa is one of the "extreme cases of plural societies,"[4] Heribert Adam and Kogila Moodley raise the question of whether it is a plural or a common society and conclude that the latter answer is the more correct one: South Africa is not "genuinely plural" and "little cultural distance separates the urbanized population groups in South Africa."[5]

The view that ethnicity is an old-fashioned habit that people will outgrow as they modernize was universally accepted by social scientists in the 1950s. An instructive example occurs in *Political Community and the North Atlantic Area* by Karl W. Deutsch and a team of collaborators. The authors pose the question: "Are nationalistic conflicts increasing or decreasing in the mid-twentieth century within the North Atlantic area?" They see only a slight decline of nationalism at the state level but argue that "as far as minority groups *within* states are concerned, these appear not to be at all dangerous." Citing the examples of the Alsatians, Flemings, South Tyroleans, and French Canadians, they state that the political activities of ethnic minority groups are "of minor importance" and conclude that "most of the area seems to have settled down in this respect, and only at its fringes, in Algiers and Cyprus, do we meet exceptions."[6] With the advantage of hindsight, we now know how wrong this superficially plausible prediction was. In fact, the ethnic factor has become more salient instead of gradually fading away. Beyond the North Atlantic area, too, as Crawford Young puts it, "in the 1950s, all roads seemed to lead to national integration. . . . The doctrine of 'nation-building' reigned supreme." And here too, of course, the forecasts were radically wrong: "Rather than an inexorable trend, the eclipse of cultural pluralism was a momentary conjuncture."[7]

Likewise, the apparent decline of ethnicity in South Africa is a momentary conjuncture. Why do such sophisticated and well-informed observers as Adam and Moodley see it as an inexorable trend? One explanation is that they are still beguiled by the notion that modernization and industrialization are the enemies of ethnicity. They contrast the "binding economic interdependence" of South Africa with the situation of only "semi-industrialized Lebanon, Cyprus, Nigeria, Sudan, and Sri Lanka." Moreover, they misread the evidence of the industrialized world when they conclude: "The economic unification of Europe or the demise of Quebec nationalism

... shows how ethnic sentiment declines when it impedes economic advantages and symbolic needs are fulfilled differently."[8] Quebec nationalism may have lost some of its strength in recent years but is far from dead; and in Europe, national and ethnic sentiments are still so strong that economic unification has failed to bring about any true supranational political integration.

A different problem with Adam and Moodley's analysis is that they are not always clear about what ethnicity means. Most of the time they correctly equate ethnic with cultural divisions, but sometimes, unfortunately and misleadingly, they lump ethnicity with race. For instance, they mention the possibility of an "eventual *de-ethnicization* of the ruling National Party, by allowing non-Whites to become members."[9] The correct term here is obviously *de-racialization*. What is more, if what they have in mind is the possibility of Afrikaans-speaking members of the coloured community joining the NP, this would really mean the NP's *ethnicization* instead of de-ethnicization.

Many observers who predict the end of ethnicity in South Africa simply ignore the evidence of strong and persistent ethnicity elsewhere. Adam and Moodley do not make this mistake; they explicitly compare South Africa with other plural societies, but the contrast they depict remains unconvincing. Every plural society in the world, including South Africa, has its unique characteristics, but nobody has been able to present a compelling argument that ethnicity in South Africa is so unique that we must expect it to develop in a completely different direction from the ethnicity that we find in other parts of Africa, in Europe, and in Asia. Hence, it is much safer to operate on the assumption that South Africa is basically like other plural societies instead of an—unexplained—deviant case.

PREDETERMINED VERSUS SELF-DETERMINED ETHNICITY

One of the crucial choices that consociational engineers face is whether to make an explicit identification of the segments that constitute the plural society or to make provisions that allow the segments to define themselves. In my book, *Power-Sharing in South Africa* (1985), I have argued that because of the great difficulty—nay, impossibility—of determining those segments, including the ethnic segment, and because of the widespread hostility to the very idea of ethnicity in South Africa, the alternative of self-definition is optimal. Two devices can be used for this purpose: proportional representation (PR) and cultural councils. PR allows any group that wants to organize itself as a party to do so, to appeal for support among like-minded voters, and to be represented in proportion to its strength as proved by the electoral results. In a plural society, parties can thus become the representatives of self-determined segments. Executive power-sharing can also be achieved without predetermining the segments by specifying that the political parties elected to the legislature—which, in practice, will be segmental parties—be proportionally represented in the cabinet. Segmental autonomy in cultural and educational affairs can be provided by permitting and even encouraging any group that wishes to exercise such autonomy to organize itself as a cultural council, by delegating the necessary power to these councils, and by subsidizing them on a proportional basis.[10]

Although I strongly favor self-determination of ethnicity in the South African case, it is worth pointing out that explicit predetermination is not at all unusual. For instance, the 1970 Belgian constitution formally defines the Dutch speakers and French speakers as the main constituent segments; the 1960 constitution of Cyprus similarly defines the Greek and Turkish Cypriots; and Lebanon's 1943 National Pact is based on an explicit specification of Maronites, Sunnis, Shiites, and several other sects. Predetermination also has a number of advantages. It may increase the segments' feeling of security, and it makes it possible to provide overrepresentation for designated small minorities. The latter advantage should not be overstated, however. The minority veto is a much more potent weapon for defining minority rights than is inflating the minority's numerical strength. Moreover, minority overrepresentation is especially appropriate for plural societies in which a majority segment faces one or more minority segments. This is not the case in South Africa where all ethnic groups are minorities.

If the choice in South Africa were a dichotomous one between ethnic self-determination and predetermination, the decision would be very simple. The latter is not a realistic possibility at all; this leaves the former as the only option and as an excellent option. However, we must also consider the possibility and desirability of various combinations of self-determination and predetermination. Two such possibilities deserve a careful examination: (1) a constitution that mentions one or more segments by name but also allows other segments to define themselves by means of PR and the formation of cultural councils; and (2) the kind of compromise proposed by the 1986 Indaba for the KwaZulu-Natal area.

For the purpose of discussing the first of these compromises, let us assume that the Afrikaner ethnic group will insist on being explicitly recognized in the constitution and that the non-Afrikaners are willing to accommodate this wish. What kind of constitutional arrangements would have to be made? As far as voting and representation in the legislature are concerned, a separate Afrikaner voter register could be set up in addition to the general register, and a number of parliamentary seats could be reserved for the Afrikaners. In addition to a general provision for cultural councils, the constitution could specifically recognize the right of the Afrikaners to have an autonomous cultural council with responsibility for Afrikaans schools and cultural institutions. If, in the constitutional negotiations it became clear that the Afrikaners or any other group—I am simply using the Afrikaners as a hypothetical example—strongly favored such a predetermined status for themselves, it seems to me that a compromise should be possible, but that two further qualifications are necessary. First, membership in a predetermined group must be voluntary; that is, an individual Afrikaner must have the right not to affiliate with the Afrikaans cultural council and to register his or her name on the general instead of the Afrikaner voters' list. Second, the number of reserved parliamentary seats should be prorated according to the number of voters on the special voter register, and the resources given to the cultural council should be based on the number of members affiliating with it; for instance, if the Afrikaners constitute 10 percent of the total population but only four-fifths of them choose to register as Afrikaner voters, the percentage of reserved seats should be 8 instead of 10 percent.

The proposals of the KwaZulu-Natal Indaba, formulated after almost eight months of deliberations in 1986, illustrate a second type of compromise between the principles of predetermination and self-determination. A bicameral legislature is recommended in which the 100-member first chamber is elected by all voters on a common roll by means of PR, and the 50-member second chamber is also elected by PR but *within* predetermined groups. The relevant provision reads as follows:

> The second chamber will consist of 50 members composed of representatives of the following groups:
>
> • The African background group (10 members)
> • The Afrikaans background group (10 members)
> • The Asian background group (10 members)
> • The English background group (10 members)
> • The South African group (10 members).[11]

Judged in terms of the same criteria applied to the example of partial predetermination discussed above, a positive aspect of this proposal is that it does not force any individual into a specific group against his or her wishes. The "South African group" serves as a residual category for those who do not fit any of the four "background groups" and for those who prefer to opt out of one of these groups. On the other hand, the "background groups" do not have their representation prorated for such defections, and three of them—the Asian, Afrikaans, and English—are already overrepresented to a considerable extent given their shares of the total KwaZulu-Natal population. Another questionable aspect of the "background groups" is that they appear to be at least partly defined in terms of race instead of ethnicity; this is particularly true of the largest of the groups, which is labeled African rather than Zulu, though it is true that most Africans in KwaZulu-Natal are in fact Zulus.

Furthermore, while the Indaba's proposal does not force the *inclusion* of any individual in any particular "background group," it does entail the possible *exclusion* of an individual from a group to which he or she claims to belong: "Save in the case of the South African group, a voter in a second chamber election must belong to the group whose candidate he intends to vote for."[12] The provisions for handling this difficult matter are elaborate:

> The Electoral Law will contain criteria for the identification of voters. No criteria will be laid down for the General Interest Group [i.e., the South African group], as any voter may decide to fall into that category.

> The Electoral Law will provide for the resolution of disputes arising out of a voter's choice to fall into a given category (except the General Interest Group). An Electoral Commission and the electoral officers will play an important role in this regard.

> Voter identification takes place on election day:

> a. A voter reports at the relevant table and states the category of his choice for the second chamber election.
> b. If the official manning the table is in doubt about the voter's choice, or if any interested person or party objects against the voter's choice, the voter is immediately brought before the electoral officer who makes a ruling.
> c. If the voter accepts the ruling of the electoral officer, he receives his ballot paper and votes regularly.
> d. If the voter or the objector does not accept the ruling of the electoral officer, the voter still votes in the category of his choice, but his vote is sealed in a marked envelope. (Alternatively, the voter may vote in the General Interest category out of his own choice, in which case his vote will be counted like any other.)
> e. Marked votes are not counted with the regular votes, but when the result is announced, an announcement is also made as to the number of marked (challenged) votes.
> f. If the voter pursues the objection within the prescribed period to the Electoral Commission, and the objection is upheld, the vote becomes regular and is counted.
> g. If "regularised challenged votes" eventually make a difference to the election result, another candidate may be declared elected.[13]

Having chosen to recognize predetermined groups, the Indaba was necessarily forced into making such rules. They could have been worse; in particular, it should be noted that these rules avoid any *permanent registration* of individuals as members of groups. Nevertheless, I must admit that I find this kind of potentially invidious categorization of people on the basis of criteria that include physical characteristics quite distasteful. On the other hand, I must also admit that such procedures are not essentially different from those entailed by affirmative action programs in the United States. Special or preferential treatment of a certain group necessitates judgments on who belongs to the group and who does not.

It should also be pointed out that self-determination is not entirely free from the problem of the possible exclusion of individuals from organized groups either. Self-determination means that the state is not in the business of including or excluding anyone, and that individuals can vote, freely and without restrictions, for any political party. However, voluntary associations like political parties and groups seeking to set up cultural councils may want to protect their integrity by controlling the admission of individual members—which necessarily entails the possible denial of admission to some applicants.

This matter becomes even more difficult and sensitive if such associations define themselves not only in cultural and ethnic terms but also, explicitly or implicitly, in terms of race.[14] If, for instance, an Afrikaner or a black consciousness group wants to be racially exclusive, should it be allowed to organize in this way? I believe that racist exclusiveness will be a rare occurrence, and that it will be even rarer for racist groups to receive applications for membership from individuals whose skin color is lighter or darker than the group's norms. Since parties are vote maximizers, they are unlikely to be categorically exclusive. But for the few groups that may want to be narrow-minded and bigoted in defining themselves, the best policy is simply to let them be narrow-minded and bigoted—provided that this does not affect the political rights and economic opportunities of other citizens.

My reason for recommending such tolerance for racial bigotry is practical, not moral. It will be much less contentious for South Africa as a whole to permit a few organizations to be self-avowedly racist than to monitor every group for its nonracist character, especially because many cultural-ethnic associations—unintentionally but in actual fact—will not have a racially diverse membership. For instance, a Xhosa cultural association or ethnic party is most unlikely to have many nonblack members. Racist exclusiveness, as rare as it will probably be, remains offensive, but, instead of regarding it as an insult to the excluded, it should be seen primarily as the excluders' self-inflicted indignity.

OPTIMAL AND ACCEPTABLE COMPROMISES

It is clear from the above discussion that I consider self-determination of group membership vastly preferable to even a partial reliance on predetermination. In forging a democratic constitution for South Africa, however, the more important question concerns what is acceptable rather than what is optimal. For the purpose of addressing the question of acceptability, let us adopt the role of mediators and assume that the two parties that would be the hardest to persuade to accept a constitutional compromise are the African National Congress and the National Party. What kind of compromise on the question of ethnicity would we regard as fair and reasonable and would we present as such to the two parties?

To the ANC, which is reluctant to admit the relevance and legitimacy of the very concept of ethnicity, we would have to present three arguments in favor of a self-determined ethnicity. First, we would point out that their view of ethnicity in South Africa should not be distorted by their negative reaction to the government's abuse of ethnicity. After all, as Adam and Moodley state, even their own Freedom Charter, which is "the core blueprint of the apartheid opposition, flirts with group rights by stating in its second clause: 'All national groups shall have equal rights'," and upholds the "right of all people to 'develop their own folk culture and customs'."[15]

Our second argument would be that PR and cultural councils are completely evenhanded in their effect on all groups, ethnic or nonethnic. PR does not favor any particular majority or minority. If those who believe in a common society are right, they have the chance to be proved right by seeing nonethnic instead of ethnic parties emerge and by seeing no groups apply for cultural councils. PR does not artificially manufacture ethnicity in societies where no basic ethnic divisions exist. It has been used for many decades in Scandinavia and the Republic of Ireland without turning these countries into plural societies.

Third, it would be important to point out that, though the dominant political tradition in South Africa is majoritarian—a tradition inherited from the British colonial rulers—majoritarianism is clearly *not* the prevalent norm among the world's democracies. For instance, among the twenty-one countries that have enjoyed continuous democratic rule since the end of the Second World War, about two-thirds use PR and only four use the British plurality system.[16] Moreover, in three of the countries in the latter group— Canada, New Zealand, and Britain itself—plurality is no longer as widely accepted as it used to be, and a shift to PR is becoming more likely; the United States is the only exception. When we look at entire political systems, not just the electoral systems, similar evidence emerges. As Robert W. Jackman reads it, "majoritarianism is *not* the norm," and only two countries, Great Britain and New Zealand, "can unambiguously be classified as majoritarian."[17]

It is significant that Adam and Moodley do not advocate a majoritarian constitution for South Africa despite their assumption that South Africa is a common, not a plural, society. At one point they appear to endorse majoritarianism when they state that "the relatively weak South African cultural cleavages do not form the obstacle to democratic majoritarianism they do in genuinely plural societies." But their specific recommendations are decidedly unmajoritarian. They support PR for elections at all levels as well as the idea of autonomous cultural councils; in practical terms, they say, the latter would mean that "the state does not interfere with the educational preferences or language rights of any sizable group. It also means that the state should proportionally subsidize private religious or language education while maintaining a public school system of equal standards for all communities." Finally, they also endorse "the consociational prescriptions of veto rights for minorities in existential matters as well as required representation on all administrative bodies." Together these unmajoritarian rules based on self-determined ethnicity would lead to "an optimal and widely legitimate democratic system."[18]

The ANC will have to be persuaded to accept self-determined ethnicity instead of no ethnicity in any form. In contrast, the NP—assuming that it has accepted the premise of democracy and universal suffrage—will have to be convinced of the superiority of self-determined instead of partially predetermined ethnicity. Two arguments would be crucial. One is that in terms of objective rights and powers, a system of self-determination offers just as much autonomy, security, and a share of political power at all levels as a system that explicitly defines the Afrikaners (and perhaps one or a few other groups, such as the Zulus) as protected minorities. The benefit of the latter would be purely symbolic. The second consideration is that any system of predetermination, especially voting on the basis of predetermined groups, entails the troublesome question of assigning individuals to these groups—a question with which the KwaZulu-Natal Indaba struggled, as discussed earlier, and which should be avoided as much as possible.

Even if the symbolic significance of an explicit recognition of the Afrikaner community would weigh heavily for the NP, I argue that they should not make it into a breaking point. However, if they do insist on it, should the ANC absolutely refuse this concession? A reasonable compromise would be to accept a degree of predetermination but only on three conditions: (1) that it be clearly understood that only partial and not complete predetermination is to be considered; (2) that groups can claim predetermination only for themselves and not for other groups; and (3) that individual affiliation with predetermined groups be completely voluntary.

My own bottom line remains that complete self-determination of ethnicity is optimal, that a combination of self-determination and carefully defined predetermination is acceptable, and that complete predetermination is unworkable and unacceptable in South Africa. Together, the optimal and acceptable solutions offer a broad range of possibilities from which the contending parties and groups can choose a realistic compromise.

CONCLUSION: OPTIMISM
WITHOUT WISHFUL THINKING

Ethnicity and ethnic divisions are facts of life in South Africa. It is tempting to play down the ethnic factor both because it superficially appears to have been declining in importance during the last decades and because it would be much easier to find a democratic solution for South Africa if the country were a basically homogeneous or an only mildly divided society. Unfortunately— I, too, wish it were otherwise—the latter image does not stand up to sober comparative scrutiny. South Africa's ethnic divisions cannot be wished away.

But giving up wishful thinking does not mean giving up hope. I have demonstrated that there are several constructive methods to deal with the ethnic factor in a democratic power-sharing arrangement, even when—as in the South African case—it is extremely complex and contentious. The key is to rely mainly on the self-determination of ethnicity but to do so in a flexible and tolerant manner. This means that there is no contradiction between the proposition that South African society is deeply divided along ethnic lines and the proposition that a democratic solution is possible. We do not need to deny ethnicity in order to be realistic advocates of democracy.

NOTES

1. Arend Lijphart, "Federal, Confederal, and Consociational Options for the South African Plural Society," in Robert I. Rotberg and John Barratt, eds., *Conflict and Compromise in South Africa* (Lexington, Mass.: Lexington Books, 1980), p. 51.

2. Desmond Mpilo Tutu, *Hope and Suffering: Sermons and Speeches* (Grand Rapids, Mich.: Eerdmans, 1984), p. 51.

3. Michael Massing, "The Chief," *New York Review of Books* 34 (1987), p. 18.

4. Arend Lijphart, *Democracy in Plural Societies: A Comparative Exploration* (New Haven: Yale University Press, 1977), p. 236.

5. Heribert Adam and Kogila Moodley, *South Africa Without Apartheid: Dismantling Racial Domination* (Berkeley: University of California Press, 1986), p. 210 (emphasis omitted).

6. Karl W. Deutsch, et al., *Political Community and the North Atlantic Area: International Integration in the Light of Historical Experience* (Princeton: Princeton University Press, 1957), p. 159 (emphasis in the original).

7. Crawford Young, "The Temple of Ethnicity," *World Politics* 35 (1983), p. 655.

8. Adam and Moodley, *South Africa Without Apartheid*, p. 210.

9. *Ibid.*, p. 207 (emphasis added).

10. Arend Lijphart, *Power-Sharing in South Africa*, Policy Papers in International Affairs, no. 24 (Berkeley: Institute of International Studies, University of California, 1985), especially pp. 80–82.

11. KwaZulu-Natal Indaba, *Constitutional Proposals* (Durban, 1986), D.1.

12. *Ibid.*

13. *Ibid.*, E. 4.

14. I am grateful to Heribert Adam for challenging me to deal explicitly with this issue.

15. Adam and Moodley, *South Africa Without Apartheid*, pp. 213, 221.

16. Arend Lijphart, *Democracies: Patterns of Majoritarian and Consensus Government in Twenty-One Countries* (New Haven: Yale University Press, 1984), p. 160.

17. Robert W. Jackman, "Elections and the Democratic Class Struggle," *World Politics* 39 (1986), p. 134.

18. Adam and Moodley, *South Africa Without Apartheid*, pp. 210, 220–221, 225–226; see also David D. Laitin, "South Africa: Violence, Myths, and Democratic Reform," *World Politics* 39 (1987), pp. 273–275.

—————————————— 3 ——————————————

From Exhortation to
Incentive Strategies: Mediation Efforts
in South Africa in the Mid-1980s

DONALD ROTHCHILD

All South Africans need to be represented in negotiations to determine the system of government that will replace [apartheid]. Such negotiations are urgent. We cannot prescribe their outcome. But our policies and actions must be calculated to encourage the process of peaceful change.[1]

—Secretary George Shultz

We have tried talking to the [South African] government and it didn't work.[2]

—General Olusegun Obasanjo,
former Nigerian head of state and
cochair of the Commonwealth Eminent Persons Group

In such deeply divided societies as South Africa (as well as Northern Ireland, Cyprus, Lebanon, and Sri Lanka) some tacit and direct exchanges on specific issues of mutual interest can be identified, despite the deep cleavages among their elites and communal groups. Yet, where the rules of the game themselves are in contention, it is important to stress the hesitant and transitory process at hand. In the absence of shared values, "antagonistic negotiation" does not usually prove fruitful, especially in an age of electronic media and mass public participation.[3]

In the case of South Africa, an increasingly intense encounter between the Afrikaner-dominated state and the country's black-nationalist organizations makes the prospect of all-party negotiations, as sought in 1986 by Secretary Shultz, seem unlikely for the time being. In brief, there appears to be a lack of bargaining opportunities for the moment. Although the Commonwealth Eminent Persons Group (EPG) mission found that "no serious person we met was interested in a fight to the finish" and that "all favored negotiations and peaceful solutions," the facilitation of direct talks among rival domestic interests appears now to be beyond the reach of domestic and external third parties, especially in the aftermath of the spring

1987 elections in which the extreme right-wing parties received a surprisingly large percentage of the white vote.[4] Negotiations on black self-determination and the ending of white minority rule are clearly necessary if deterioration and a possible civil war are to be averted, but the will to bring such negotiations about is not sufficient under current circumstances. Therefore, if the nature of contemporary conflict in South Africa appears to stand in the way of a successful mediatory initiative, prudence requires a rethinking of this strategy, linking it to other, more compelling incentives for change. In South Africa, political problems require an altering of structures: hence, to be successful, a mediator must be prepared to intervene more actively than in other conflicts to ensure a positive, mutual gains outcome. The mediators must alter the conditions of conflict themselves.

The consequences of inaction are certainly apparent to many leaders, black and white. Averting the costs of internal violence and insecurity was clearly in the thoughts of jailed leader Nelson Mandela when, in the presence of the Commonwealth mission, he made an impassioned appeal to a South African cabinet minister, H. J. Coetsee, for direct talks between black leaders and the Botha regime to prevent a worsening of the situation in their country.[5] And, in fact, a number of current economic indicators do seem to point to increasingly difficult times over the long term. For example, gross fixed capital formation fell by 40 percent in 1985; the gross domestic product was down by 1 percent in the first quarter of 1986; voluntary disinvestment by multinational corporations was gaining momentum (the book value of U.S. investments in South Africa fell from $2.4 billion in 1982 to $1.3 billion in 1986, and the pace of disinvestment accelerated in the next year; a small net emigration took place in 1986 among whites (especially in the significant skilled manpower category) for the first time since 1977; the commercial rand declined precipitously, from $1.28 in 1980 to below 40 cents in 1986; a capital flight of $1 billion occurred between September 1985 and March 1986; and unemployment soared to 25 percent in the urban black community.[6] By the year 2000, according to one estimate, there will be 4.5 million unemployed persons in South Africa if present trends continue, and 9.8 million if meaningful sanctions are put into effect.[7] As summarized by a spokesperson at the Anglo-American Corporation, "We face declining morale, an aging capital stock, exodus of skills and increasing difficulties in labor relations."[8] To be sure, relatively high gold prices and the development of a siege economy will cushion some of these effects, but future economic prospects look anything but promising.

Political indicators, moreover, were equally unsatisfactory for the Afrikaner-led state. With the police and army losing control over the townships, and with administrative and educational systems in parts of the Eastern Cape degenerating, a situation of ungovernability, even "violent equilibrium," as characterized by Heribert Adam and Kogila Moodley, appeared to be emerging.[9] Whether and under what circumstances a future African-led state can reestablish governability remains unclear.

Under these circumstances negotiations between the government and black nationalists appear logical. They offer an opportunity for social learning and hold out the possibility of avoiding a spiral into mutual destruction, with its high costs in terms of increased social polarization, a widening repression, the development of a siege economy, and the economic and political dislocation of a broader subregion.[10] The analogies of Lebanon, Sri Lanka, and Northern Ireland come readily to mind. Unfortunately, however, intense conflicts over the rules of relationship do not easily lend themselves to rational processes of political compromise and peaceful change, especially where an entrenched racially or ethnically dominated state views structural transformation in deeply threatening terms.[11] Such state elites are less concerned with more equitable distributive outcomes than with their expectations about how rival leaders will structure intergroup relations in the future.[12] However, as perceptions of group conflict change, as the local balance of forces shifts, and as an appropriate mediator for this particular conflict emerges, the "ripe moment" for negotiations may appear.[13] Until that time, however, the scenario outlined by Secretary Shultz in 1986 would appear to be too straightforward and too culture-bound, and, to the extent that it diverts us from the struggle to alter political structures, not very helpful in promoting the process of change.

FALSE ANALOGIES TO PREINDEPENDENCE NEGOTIATIONS IN COLONIAL AFRICA

To gain an understanding of the process at hand, it is important to stress at the outset that the South African negotiating context is unique, making analogies to previous independence "bargains" largely false and misleading. To start with, the proportion of whites to nonwhites is considerably higher in South Africa than in the other countries of Africa (with the notable exception of French-ruled Algeria). Furthermore, not only is the white "community" more securely entrenched, but it has abundant resources and a closely bonded relationship with the state. South Africa is not only rich in natural resources, but it is an industrialized society with transportation links by road and rail with the north and by air and sea with the world at large. Its relatively large, white middle class is locked into an intimate relationship with the Afrikaner-run state, a relationship that affords it access, benefits, and protection. Any major concessions by the state are likely to be interpreted by sections within the white community as threatening to their collective interests, leading, in subsequent elections, to a right-wing drift. This tendency appeared in the 1987 elections and had a hardening effect on the government and on whites in general. Hence, until the costs of the status quo rise considerably (i.e., to the point where dominant elements within the ruling class perceive their interests to be threatened by isolation and effective sanctions), bargaining seems unlikely to alter the basic rules of relationship between groups, as it did in more vulnerable Zimbabwe, but only after a bitter and protracted civil war. To quote Heribert Adam:

> The costs of racial privilege maintenance are also increasing through heightened internal unrest, escalating guerrilla incursions and international ostracism. However, unlike the Zimbabwe situation, since blacks cannot force whites to negotiate their capitulation, the conflict remains an uneasy stalemate.[14]

But if the South African context is different from that of the states to the north during the decolonization phase, the processes of mediation and negotiation are likely to pose even more striking hurdles. Unlike Kenya and Zimbabwe, South Africa is not a classic example of external colonialism. It is a sovereign state, with membership in the United Nations. This gives the state, though not its government, legitimacy in the eyes of the international community. As such, the South African state is free to enter into negotiations with other states or sections within its own country as it chooses to do. Consequently, when state officials decide to break off contacts, as happened in May 1986 with the Commonwealth EPG mission, there is little that the world can do about it—at least until the context of relations is altered. Thus, whereas the British, in Kenya and Zimbabwe, were the colonial master and in a position to force political exchanges between rival parties from above as a price of stability and independence, there is no natural mediator for the South African domestic conflict credible in the eyes of both parties and able to maintain a momentum of ongoing negotiations. A variety of external mediators might be able to offer some incentives to the various parties to bring them to the bargaining table, as we will see in the following section, but it is a delicate process with a clear possibility of failure.

The reasons this process might fail are not hard to find: not only is trust in short supply and aims divergent but mutual interests (i.e., the avoidance of damage) may not be sufficiently compelling to bring the parties to a positive-sum outcome. Therefore, unlike mediation in Kenya and Zimbabwe, mediation in South Africa may prove unequal to the task of negotiating the terms under which minorities might remain in South Africa. Hence, a more deeply conflictive outcome (e.g., subjection, displacement, partition, intensified guerrilla warfare, or "violent equilibrium") may mark the scene in the years ahead. As Malcolm Fraser and Olusegun Obasanjo, the cochairs of the Commonwealth mission, noted: "Once a guerrilla struggle has commenced, it will be almost impossible to return to the negotiating table until one side becomes exhausted by long years of conflict."[15]

THE FAILURE OF PRIOR
MEDIATION EFFORTS IN SOUTH AFRICA

For all the apparent logic of a negotiated settlement, "honest brokers," as General Obasanjo described the Commonwealth EPG mission, have come away soured by their experience with attempted mediatory efforts in South Africa. Although the EPG mission described its role as "limited to the task of facilitating a process of dialogue for change," it actually went further and proposed a possible starting point for negotiations.[16] The mission's negotiating concept involved the following package of proposals: declaration of the government's intention to dismantle apartheid; release of all political prisoners; recognition by the state of the rights of freedom of speech and assembly; moratorium on government and opposition violence; and agreement between the government and the ANC on the need to "act simultaneously in fulfillment of their respective commitments."[17] The Botha government's response was equivocal. While raising questions regarding specific recommendations, it did nonetheless call for a continuation of the dialogue, proposing that a further exchange of views take place between the rival parties and the Commonwealth mission. For a brief time, some members of the cabinet, in particular Pik Botha, the foreign minister, seemed to be guardedly positive about the mission's mediatory initiative. Moreover, the ANC, under pressure from the United States, Britain, and West Germany, agreed to a "suspension" of the violence, giving the members of the mission some reason for hope about a positive outcome. Encouraged by the positive role it might play in this conflict, the Commonwealth mission labored on and sought to clarify the various perceptions that each party had as to the nature of the conflict and its possible solution.[18] Subsequently, however, as the Commonwealth mission came up against the hard reality of the government's nonnegotiable positions—the renunciation of violence, the preservation of group rights, the continuance of separate education and residential areas, and so forth—as well as the deliberate military raid by South African forces against three neighboring Commonwealth countries, it lost faith for the time being in a negotiated solution as a realizable objective. "The South African Government," it concluded, "is not yet ready to negotiate [a nonracial and democratic] future—except on its own terms."[19] Not only had President P. W. Botha concluded that the ANC would be unable to control future violence, but discussions with the Commonwealth mission had convinced his regime that concessions would not lead to reduced pressure but to new demands, backed up by the threat of sanctions.[20] Two other factors are also reported to have played a part in Botha's May 15 decision to terminate the discussions: the increasing signs of African unity on the issue of repudiating violence and the pressure from the State Security Council against negotiations. The upshot was as final as it was dramatic: the Commonwealth mission abandoned its mediatory effort and called upon the

Commonwealth countries and their allies to implement effective economic sanctions. In the current crisis, the Commonwealth effort at mediation was deemed inadequate to the task at hand; in the long term, however, it may have helped to set a framework for the protracted process of negotiations on the future of intergroup relations, which must follow.

After the breakdown of the Commonwealth EPG mission effort, a number of individuals rose briefly to the challenge of being peacemaker. Almost immediately, a European Community (EC) summit, under pressure from the British and West German governments, which sought to avoid the imposition of sanctions, endorsed a peace mission to South Africa by the British foreign secretary, Sir Geoffrey Howe. In endorsing Howe's trip in his capacity as the president of the Council of Ministers, the EC made very clear that if South African authorities did not respond positively to Howe's demands for a rescinding of the state of emergency, the release of political detainees, and a lifting of the prohibition on African parties, its member states would place a ban on the importation of coal, iron, steel, and gold coins. As anticipated by many before Howe's visit, the threat of EC sanctions was not sufficient in itself to push the Botha regime to the bargaining table. State President Botha resisted making any concessions to the European initiative, and the African nationalists and their Front Line States supporters, regarding the mission as a play for time on the part of the British, generally looked upon the Howe journey as a futile effort. In light of the Commonwealth mission's failure, the Howe effort was dismissed by Zimbabwe's prime minister, Robert Mugabe, as "a waste of time."[21] The Zimbabwean leader specifically rejected the notion that in this situation negotiations were preferable to economic sanctions. For Mugabe and other black leaders in and out of South Africa, Botha's rejection of Commonwealth mediation was a clear signal that the South Africans were not prepared to negotiate an end to apartheid, and this left the African leadership with little choice but to press for mandatory economic sanctions.[22] The gap between Botha and the African leaders was clearly too wide to be bridged by a lone intermediary, and, after a brief encounter with a number of the protagonists, Howe returned to Europe empty-handed.

Another example of failed facilitation occurred in September 1986 when Coretta Scott King, the wife of former civil rights leader Martin Luther King, Jr., canceled scheduled meetings with State President Botha and Chief Mangosuthu Gatsha Buthelezi. What began as an effort to start a dialogue ended soon after in embarrassment for the honest broker. Under pressure from the United Democratic Front, it became clear to King and others that this was not the appropriate time for "a dialogue" between the contending parties. As UDF leaders put it, King would have to choose whether she was "with the people or against the people."[23] Faced with these stark terms, King acted prudently and withdrew from the fray.

The depth of conflict over the basic rules of relationship in South Africa limits the middle ground and makes mediation among all the major parties a particularly difficult task under current circumstances. To use I. W. Zartman's expression, the mediator lacks "the informal power to make the parties decide."[24] For the mediator, involvement can also be deemed to entail a high price, particularly where the players perceive the conflict in zero-sum terms and where the need for third-party credibility can lead to embarrassing relationships, as happened in the case of Namibia where U.S. mediation caused the United States to become identified with South African purposes.[25] To be sure, a fine line must be drawn between reluctance to mediate and a self-fulfilling sense of low political efficacy. Nevertheless, where intergroup boundaries are pronounced and norms of reciprocity weak, as in South Africa, the scope for bargaining seems distinctly limited, and a third party might well have reason to draw back for a time from mediatory action on the grounds that the circumstances are not propitious.

At this juncture, then, the minimum consensus for meaningful negotiations in South Africa is not evident. For its part, the South African government gives every indication of not being prepared to compromise on the issue of "Grand Apartheid." This was quite apparent not only in the dialogues that it held with the Commonwealth mission and then with Howe, but also in its actions following the 1986 vote in the U.S. Congress on economic sanctions. A defiant Botha government insisted that its bargaining opposite, the ANC, is communist-dominated and that it must reject violence before the start of negotiations on the future of the country. "All this government has said," Foreign Minister Pik Botha declared in a television interview, "is that if the ANC, or any organization, or leader, stops violence, then they are obviously welcome to sit around the conference table with us."[26] But for the ANC to reject violence is to surrender its main bargaining chip in advance of serious talks, a demand that the cochair of the Commonwealth mission regarded as "unreasonable."[27] Moreover, the other nonnegotiable demands set forth by the Botha government—group rights, private enterprise, separate education, and so forth—appeared to the opposition to freeze the essentials of the status quo then in effect. The government, in brief, was willing to continue the process of "reform," but in such a way as to leave the structure of white dominance firmly in place.

By contrast, the African nationalist opposition sought an end to all manifestations of white hegemony and, most particularly, opposition leaders expressed serious doubts over the value of mediatory efforts under prevailing circumstances. A sample of the views of some of the more militant nationalist organizations on the utility of racial bargaining helps to underscore that point. The ANC, threatening a process of "ungovernability" leading to "people's power," envisaged little common ground between itself and the Botha-run state. Questioning the value of negotiations in the political environment of that time, ANC representatives noted that the Botha regime "relies for its survival on armed aggression within and outside South Africa. Massacres and assassinations are its means of livelihood. Our people have had to accept this reality and take the only course open to them."[28] Perceiving the struggle in totalist terms, the course seemed clear and unmistakable: to fight power with power. The effect was to leave little room for a negotiated settlement, at that time at least.

If anything, the exiled Pan-Africanist Congress of Azania (PAC) is even more militant in its views (unlike the ANC, for example, whites are excluded from its ranks); it insists on rejecting negotiations as a strategy of change in South Africa. Thus, the PAC speaks directly and bluntly on the issue:

> All suggestions of negotiations between the racists' regime and the oppressed Azanians fall flat on the crucial question of the basic purpose of such an exercise. . . . Our own rejection of dialogue or negotiations rests on the unacceptability of any peace talks that cannot center on the total abandonment of the present settler-colonial political system plus the full realisation of the inalienable right to self-determination by the indigenous African majority in our country.[29]

Similarly, the Black Consciousness Movement of Azania (BCM), which uses the Azanian People's Organization (AZAPO) as its main political voice, has become orthodox Marxist in its policy pronouncements in the last few years.[30] The BCM has been extremely hostile toward any proposal for a negotiated settlement. Declaring that "the Botha-Malan junta is not likely to negotiate with any genuine and credible freedom fighter," BCM went on to oppose "uncompromisingly" any guarantees for minority interests.[31] This ran directly counter to Botha's nonnegotiating principle calling for the provision of "visible and effective protection of minority groups and the rights against domination and for self-determination for such groups and communities."[32] Clearly the BCM objective of "destroy[ing] the racist settler-colonial state and build[ing] a democratic state where color, race, religion, sex or tribe shall not be a point of reference" was at cross purposes with the Botha regime's determination to preserve group rights and separate education systems.[33] Where Botha's policy sought to preserve continuity with the past, BCM would eliminate differences based on ethnic, religious, or gender-based identity.

In brief, the 1986 efforts to mediate the conflict were premature. The major antagonists diverge fundamentally for the time being in terms of the rules of relationships they view as acceptable, making negotiations extremely hazardous under these conditions.[34] As the *New York Times* commented in an editorial: "The antagonists in South Africa are not waiting for a broker to bring them to agreement."[35]

THE CONSTRAINTS ON NEGOTIATIONS

Thus far we have seen all-party negotiations to be necessary, but, because of competing preferences and principles, questions can be raised as to whether they can take place any time soon. In this, conditions in South Africa resemble the situation on the ground in Cyprus and Lebanon more than those that once prevailed in Kenya and Zimbabwe. To see the contrasts with the latter in more detail, it is essential to examine the various constraints on negotiations currently in evidence in South Africa. At that point it will be possible to look at some of the limited options open to the rivals, or more particularly for our purposes, to interested third parties.

The major constraints on South African negotiations at the present time are grouped under seven headings.

Threatening Intergroup Perceptions

To the extent that racial leaders and groups view their counterparts as determined to preserve or alter the basic rules of relationship among sectional interests to their decided advantage, all perceive their rivals in menacing terms. Their very survival—culturally, socially, politically, and even physically—is considered to be threatened to the core, and these elites and their constituents respond defensively. The ANC is not viewed by many of South Africa's whites as a liberation movement, but rather as a terrorist organization intent upon the destruction of the white-run state. Any compromise with militantly nationalist organizations such as the ANC is viewed as threatening the whites' position, for they assume that their opponent will view accommodations as a sign of weakness and respond by making new demands for concessions. Such "totalist" or "essentialist" perceptions feed on themselves, leading to a negative reciprocity expressed in terms of fearful and aggressive behavior.[36] In South Africa, the signs of such mindsets are increasingly apparent, and the effect is to make agreements difficult to conclude and to implement. Essentialist perceptions are particularly noticeable in certain sections of the white community. Viewing the African nationalist challenge as menacing to everything built by white enterprise over the years, State President Botha responded in aggressive terms: "We will not allow the spiritual and material inheritance of 300 years to fall into the hands of a revolutionary power clique without a fight."[37] A perceived threat was not deemed a matter for reasoned discussion and compromise, but one of high conflict. Similarly, external sanctions invoked by former global allies were not a cause for reflection and analysis as to the sources of conflict but were perceived as an attempt to break the Afrikaner will. After commenting in this vein, the Johannesburg newspaper *Business Day* went on to remark on the sanctions effort: "It won't work. Government, like its supporting constituency, perceives in black rule a moral threat—to language, to prosperity, to identity, and to physical security—and it is vain to think that such fears can be overcome by mere threats to property."[38] Such a broad-ranging perception of menace to group survival has a numbing and self-fulfilling quality irrespective of its fit with reality. Hence, emergency measures are put into effect as much for their psychological impact (i.e., as a display of state resoluteness in the face of various domestic and international challenges) as for their ability to deal with a specific peril or perils.

On the other side of the conflict, black nationalism has been more careful to attack the existence of white privilege but not the right of whites to live in the country where they were born. Nevertheless, the extent of state repression has led, at times, to a generalized picture of racial oppression that only the ending of white minority rule will eliminate. Expressing their anger toward the ordinary white worker as well as the dominant political elite, the South African Students Organization commented that "those who oppress us jointly and severally agree on the perpetuation of evils against us, from the 'simple white man' to the real destroyers of black lives in the 'House of Assembly', in the South African Defense Force and in commerce and industry. When the chips are down, they will all go to unbelievable lengths to protect their white interests."[39]

Certainly in all racial communities there are nonconforming members who are careful not to confuse threats and legitimate demands, but the point to reinforce is that totalist thinking and behavior is present and breeds its counterpart, reinforcing a negative spiral that predisposes political actors toward zero-sum expectations, not concessions and compromises. And those who are so incautious as to defy the prevailing hostility within their community run the distinct risk of ostracism, forced exile, and even the "necklace."

Divergence on Principles, Not Interests

What is perceived to be at stake in the South African conflict are not distributive interests (jobs, political and civil service positions, scholarships, budgetary allocations, and so forth), which are negotiable, but matters of principle. For the dominant whites, such issues as the maintenance of group rights, separate schools, and racially distinct residential areas, and the furtherance of private enterprise and capitalistic relations are matters of principle: they involve basic values on which whites will not compromise— at least until such a time that relations worsen noticeably. For the African nationalists, majority rule, the complete ending of white minority power and privilege, and individual (as opposed to group) rights are principles over which no accommodation seems possible. In the South African case, conflict management clearly involves a formula that reconciles the legitimacy of one person–one vote democracy with accepted protections for minorities and the rights of citizens to form political parties and compete for power. In brief, an agreement, to be meaningful under South African circumstances, must link security and power.[40] However, this is more easily said than achieved, especially given the perceptions of the main rivals. Until mutual concerns gain substantial acceptance in rival constituencies, as eventually happened in Zimbabwe after a long war and extensive third-party mediatory pressures and incentives, concessions are likely to be viewed as an indication of weakness and loss of face, not enlightened interest.[41]

A High Power Disparity in Favor of White Minority Interests

The control of the state apparatus, the industries, the educational system, and the communications and transportation infrastructure by people of European ancestry, even though a numerical minority, gives them a distinct edge in power relations in contemporary South Africa. Racial domination of the state and state agencies is particularly important in this regard, because the state plays a critical role in defining the relations between groups and in implementing its repressive rules.[42] By comparison with many states in other parts of the world, the South African state is greatly expanded in terms of its personnel and tasks. The result is to create a number of positions for Afrikaners, not only in civil service and administrative posts but also in state-run industries and the military-related complex. Whites employed in these positions act as a powerful interest group from within the state, pressing for the continuation of apartheid laws and an expansionist policy.[43] The result is a close-knit network of racial interests that pulls together behind the National Party leadership to manipulate the largely paralyzed and disunited majority. So long as racial relations reflect this striking power imbalance, the dominant minority will have little incentive for concessions, and the majority will be unable to organize to make effective claims upon the state. The result is to complicate greatly the process of managing conflict through a bargaining process between elite representatives at the top of the political system.

Perceptions of Victory

Although it is important not to take rhetoric at face value, certain key elites on each side, for the time being at least, regard their "victory" over rival sectional interests as a likely eventuality. The African nationalists, viewing negotiations with the South African regime as unproductive for the moment, are inclined to put their faith in the future, where they see themselves in a position to set rules of relationship that are egalitarian, nonracial, and in many cases, socialist. Many reject compromise on issues they currently regard as critical, for compromise offers little hope of altering the existing structure of relations in a fundamental manner. In such a situation, the remaining alternative, for all its apparent costs, is a protracted struggle, leading eventually to a transformed society.[44] Viewing history as on their side, Stanley Uys describes black morale as rising while that of the whites is falling. "Blacks know suddenly," he writes, "that they are going to win. They don't know how long it will take—at least five and possibly 15 years—but they are confident now that they are on the last lap of liberation."[45]

But while white morale is in a state of decline, it is not yet the case that this insulated community is fully aware of the impending changes that seem to lie ahead. Up to this time, the costs of maintaining the status quo have not seemed prohibitive to most whites, with the result that a policy of muddling along currently seems a not-unattractive course of action. Moreover, extreme right-wing pressures within the cabinet and in the country at large (in the May 1987 election, the Conservative Party won 26 percent of the vote and the Herstigte Nasionale Party another 3 percent) reinforce a tendency on the part of the dominant political elite to stay with the present policy. In analyzing why the Commonwealth mission failed to bring about negotiations, Malcolm Fraser, a former Australian prime minister and cochair of the EPG, wrote that "there are hard-line members of the cabinet who believe the government could either tough it out or shoot it out with the black population. At least one minister indicated that if enough young terrorists were shot, South Africa's kind of normalcy would be restored."[46] White politicians, fearing a loss of support should they adopt too conciliatory a tone, are quite explicit in drawing a connection between black militancy and the cause of reform.[47] Moreover, the warning to black nationalist organizations carries a message of strength and a firm determination to survive. "South Africa," declared P. W. Botha at the time his government launched raids against ANC bases in neighboring countries, "has the capacity and the will to break the ANC. I give fair warning that we fully intend doing it."[48] These are not the words or sentiments of a man prepared to preside over any fundamental change in the rules of relationship in his country. Rather than bargain in any significant way over the future of the society as he knows it, Botha and like-minded leaders are likely to make only limited reforms as they strive to preserve and strengthen white dominance. This rigidity reflects a view among the white elite that victory is possible, and that their view of future social relations can prevail if they are prepared to pay sufficient costs to that end. The effect of this mutual determination to bring about the vision of victory is to place roadblocks in the path of mutual gains formulas. As the middle ground recedes and residual commitments to negotiated solutions no longer seem realizable, increased state repression and collective violence may well come to the fore.

Fragmentation Within the Contending Groups

Meaningful bargaining at the top of the political system requires valid representatives who can speak for and, if necessary, exercise a degree of control over their constituents. Lack of legitimacy on the part of these representatives leads to a declining capacity for effective negotiations. The leader cannot be relied upon to uphold his or her end of the bargain, creating a sense of futility and uncertainty about the peacemaking process. Hence, conflicts of interest within the ranks of each bargaining group are not taken lightly by their opponents, for they are likely to understand that such differences complicate the process of arriving at decisions as well as implementing them. Moreover, the longer the process of intergroup negotiations is put off, the more likely fragmentation is to occur, resulting over time in an ever more complex negotiating context.

In fact, there are already clear signs of severe fragmentation taking place within the main South African groupings. Not only are the whites divided linguistically and ethnically among the Afrikaners, English, Portuguese, Jews, and others, but, perhaps more significantly in today's environment, between the pragmatists, the liberal left (university faculties and students, Frederick van Zyl Slabbert's Institute for a Democratic Alternative for South Africa, the Black Sash, the South African Council of Churches, etc.), and the radical right (most notably, the lower-middle-class Afrikaner elements making up the Conservative Party). The radical right represents a challenge that any government must take seriously, particularly in a country polarized along racial and class lines. Government leaders fear that any grave misstep in Namibia, or at home, that is perceived by the local white community as a sign of weakness will, in the short term at least, be reflected in a bandwagon effect favorable to the hard-line conservatives around Adries Treurnicht, the Conservative Party leader.[49] The effect is to weaken the regime's ability to act (if so inclined) in transforming the society in a more progressive direction at this juncture. Moreover, with respect to political negotiations with the genuine representatives of black opinion, government leaders find themselves limited in terms of their ability to make the kinds of broad-based accommodations necessary for a successful agreement.

On the African side, divisions between various interests are also apparent, not only among such moderates as the homeland leaders, the urban community councillors, and the Zulu-based Inkatha movement of Chief Mangosuthu Buthelezi, but among these groups and the various militant nationalists: the UDF (a broad-based movement of some 700 affiliated organizations), the ANC, PAC, and the BCM. As one analyst described the situation: "Black politics inside South Africa remain bedeviled by splits and suspicions."[50] BCM leaders have expressed resentment at the Commonwealth mission's focus upon Nelson Mandela as the main spokesman for black opinion in South Africa,[51] and divisions between the ANC and PAC were evident at the 1986 Non-Aligned Movement summit in Harare where both groups expressed an unwillingness to form a "patriotic front" in line with the precedent set earlier in Zimbabwe during the war and subsequent negotiations. Dismissing such an idea as unrealistic, ANC President Oliver Tambo described it as a "marriage of convenience."[52] At a minimum, such splits will have to be papered over (even negotiated) by leaders in both the white and black groupings if each side is to know with whom it is bargaining and is to be assured that its rival will be in a position to deliver on its promises. Alternatively, one major faction could strike a deal in the hope that other factions would eventually join with it, but it is a tactic normally fraught with peril, especially in a society deeply divided by racial suspicion.

The Mediators' Lack of Credibility and Incentives

As shown by the experiences with the Commonwealth mission and the individual efforts to facilitate a dialogue, external mediators are not, for the time being, in a strong position to influence outcomes on the South African scene. The general weakness of the mediators' position in this conflict stems from a number of factors. First, South Africa is not a colony in the sense normally used, ruling out external intervention of the sort seen in Kenya or Zimbabwe. The third-party intermediary lacks a legitimate basis for the kind of directed mediation (or arbitration, as one participant put it) that so marked the Lancaster House conferences in these two cases.[53] Second, there are few candidates left who have credibility with both sides in the current conflict situation. By their nature, highly polarized situations leave little middle ground, either for themselves or for their possible external mediators. As the external powers take a strong stand in favor of liberation or gradual reforms, they inevitably come to identify with one set of political actors or another, thereby forfeiting the high ground from which they might be able to facilitate no-fault negotiations.[54] Third, the weakened third-party intermediary, if one could be found, would have limited inducements of importance to offer the highly principled and deeply divided opponents that would be sufficient to alter the basis of choice. The Afrikaners, with their fear of *swartgevaar*—being overwhelmed by the black majority—are hardly likely to be influenced by incentives involving "payments"; the black leaders, who have already endured high costs in terms of psychological harassment and political and economic discrimination, are not likely to be attracted to the bargaining table by promises or grants of a distributive nature.[55] More is needed. In theory, mediators ought to be able to provide incentives involving "insurance," i.e., commitments by outsiders to be drawn into conflict to guarantee compliance with the terms of the agreement.[56] But few mediators would want to become so deeply involved in the highly polarized South African conflict to offer the kinds of insurance incentives that India committed itself to in Sri Lanka, and there is no certainty that even such an extensive involvement would be sufficient to bring about the desired end. In the future, as the rhythm of the encounter shifts, and the parties become more equal in their capacities, external third parties will be at a better vantage point to facilitate change, though even then there will be clear limits to what we can expect of external mediators.

A Widened Area of Conflict

Not only does protracted conflict whittle away at the middle ground within South Africa, but it tends to expand the arena of conflict. South Africa's long-standing destabilization policy combined with its determined effort to create subregional economic dependency upon its products and ports has already had the effect of widening the scope of the domestic conflict situation. Nevertheless, as collective polarization hardens and becomes a fixed feature of the Southern African scene as a whole, countries and leaders still lingering on the periphery are likely to become increasingly entwined in the dispute. There will no longer be a "free rider" option for states in the subregion. To ease the effects of this widening of the arena of conflict, Western states, given their orientation toward long-term stability, can be expected to proffer support for the creation of new opportunities in the front line countries: for example, they might give enhanced external assistance to the Southern African Development Coordination Conference (SADCC) and to the reconstruction and maintenance of the Beira corridor, thereby allowing for the transportation of an increased amount of goods between Zimbabwe and the ports of Mozambique. Such initiatives are likely to bring on defensive reactions from South Africa and its Mozambican allies, particularly the Mozambique National Resistance (RENAMO). The overall effect of this enlarging of the arena of conflict is likely to be an intensification and broadening of state and individual participation in the conflict and a raising of the stakes for all caught up in it. The effect of this seems predictable, for as the scope of conflict widens, mediation can be assumed to become an ever more complex task.

CONCLUSION: INCENTIVES FOR CHANGE

As this discussion has shown, merely exhorting political leaders to engage in direct bargaining, as Secretary Shultz and others did during the early years of the Reagan administration, does little to direct attention to the roots of the problem or to advance the process of political exchange. The reasons are apparent. Exhortation has limited, if any, impact where the leaders of government and social groups perceive their conflict in something approaching zero-sum terms. Moreover, those who engage in exhortation tend to assume they are dealing with political actors who will respond to their appeals as the exhorter would in his own domestic social situation. People in the United States, as former Secretary of State Henry Kissinger is quick to point out, are inclined to believe "in the efficacy of goodwill and the importance of compromise"—both admirable qualities, provided a bargaining culture prevails.[57] Unfortunately, South African political actors take a more menacing view of politics, requiring interested external facilitators to design a more complex package of incentives to move the bargaining process ahead. In brief, third-party intermediaries must develop a strategy of conflict management that mixes noncoercive and coercive pressures and incentives.

Clearly, the structure of state–societal relations makes this an unpropitious time for negotiations. The South African economy is stagnant, though it remains strong enough for the time being to absorb the costs of external sanctions. The African nationalist leaders are impatient for change but unable to make effective demands upon a state still sufficiently strong and determined to repress the outward manifestations of collective resistance. The consequence is a temporary bargaining void. An opportunity for dialogue and planned transformation is being squandered, in part because meaningful compromise, viewed as weakness, is unacceptable to the local actors for the time being, and in part because there are few if any external actors with sufficient interest and credibility to perform the role of mediator in this highly charged dispute.

So where does South Africa go from here? Contrary to the premises of "constructive engagement," time is of the essence if a long-term process of political and economic deterioration is to be avoided. How, then, might the various antagonists be encouraged "to change the game by starting to play a new one?"[58] Leaving out such internally determined outcomes as a successful revolution, partition, displacement, or "violent equilibrium" where there is little scope for third-party facilitation, a few points on external options in the face of this deteriorating situation deserve mention.

To start with, as Conor Cruise O'Brien points out, the world community cannot stand aside should a Nazi-style repression take place.[59] The states of the world, in Africa as well as the East and West, are deeply involved in the situation, and their domestic publics, combined with their competitive positions, would not allow for a posture of indifference in the face of extreme or even genocidal measures. Moreover, they must intercede, singly or collectively, should deterioration lead to a general threat to world peace. Whether this intervention would involve a U.S.-inspired operation, with international approval, to protect its own interests in the region (as O'Brien seems to foresee) or some other type of collaborative effort (such as Denis Healey's proposed Western naval blockade) remains unclear.[60] However, one thing appears evident: there are limits to how far the global powers can go in allowing a white-dominated state violently to repress the black opposition.

Keeping this military interventionist scenario in mind as a strategic possibility to prevent a state-inspired program of genocide, what other options remain open to the African, Western, and other world powers to promote a change of direction in South Africa? As both sides in South Africa become aware of a common interest in avoiding mutual damages, new alternatives are likely to emerge, opening the way again to external initiatives. In this event, what incentives might external actors use to facilitate peaceful change? To recognize the bleakness of the alternatives available to outside actors under current circumstances is not in itself a justification for inaction. For the moment, mutual perceptions on the scene are menacing and both sides insist upon their own terms, assuming a victory as not out of the question. But in the future, as the economy slides and the human costs of intransigence become apparent, an altered view of interests may emerge. At that point, the conflicting parties may be induced by an intermediary to give up one value in order to secure another. In light of this conceivable future opening for change, how might the world's powers design the broad lines of their strategy to prepare for new opportunities?

The need for strategy can never be far from the minds of practical statesmen. Foreign policy, as E. H. Carr observed, "never can, or never should, be divorced from strategy."[61] But strategy cannot be dealt with in the abstract; it must be considered in the context of the specific conflict at hand and must relate state purposes to domestic and international political constraints and military power. Seen in these terms, several elements in a realistic strategy for change in South Africa can be hypothesized. For one thing, it must be assumed that meaningful negotiations on the structure of intergroup relations are not likely to take place in response to the appeals of well-intentioned outsiders but in an effort to avoid rising economic, political, and strategic costs. Hence, external action must heighten a common awareness of increasing future costs if the incentives offered by third-party intermediaries are to prove significant. For another, the kinds of costs that will induce change cannot result from the actions of a single power but require collective measures of a determined sort. Earlier experiences with sanctions in Ethiopia and Rhodesia show how difficult it is to unite sovereign powers in a common purpose; even so, the moral outrage that exists over apartheid may prove unique in providing an adequate basis for an extensive (but probably less than universal) international cooperation.

The need to raise costs in order to promote the possibility for a necessary third-party mediation effort suggests, then, the basis for a two-track approach that might be relevant to extended conflict in this region. The first, or hard, track seeks to use a package of positive and negative incentives to increase the costs of inaction. It attempts to reward cooperation and to punish noncooperation by combining the inducements of purchase and insurance with diplomatic and economic sanctions and, thereby, to move the parties to a cooperative solution.[62] In this vein, Chester Crocker's statement in October 1987 that movement toward negotiations in South Africa requires "a mix of positive incentives and selective pressures" represents a cautious edging on his part toward the use of mixed incentives, and away from his earlier insistence on the use of unilateral incentives of a noncoercive type (i.e., "constructive engagement").[63]

What grounds exist for believing that a package of mixed incentives might induce the South African regime to rethink its intransigent stance some time in the future? Without trying to overstate U.S. or collective external leverage, the situation at this time is far from hopeless. Sanctions, clearly, must be seen by the target state as having an unutilized threat dimension, or they are unlikely to effect a change in behavior. The argument, as put forth by the Reagan administration, that the Comprehensive Anti-Apartheid Act of 1986 did not bring "significant progress leading to the end of apartheid and the establishment of a nonracial democracy in South Africa" is not a justification for inaction.[64] Further inaction would be interpreted by the South African regime as a diminution of threat capacity. Therefore, to preserve the threat intact, it seems necessary to give the screw another turn. Although arguing strongly against additional sanctions, Assistant Secretary of State for African Affairs Crocker nonetheless recognized the "important supportive role" of the 1986 sanctions in encouraging the forces of change in South Africa.[65] It could well be contended that an additional turning of the screw will reinforce this process.

But the hard track need not be limited to diplomatic and economic sanctions. It can be expanded to collective action on the part of African and Western states to extend military and economic aid to the hard-pressed Front Line States that currently suffer from various destabilization blows aimed at their ability to function smoothly—if not their very survival.[66] I will focus upon a possible expansion of the current Western initiative in the Beira Corridor Project, and its implications for raising the costs of internal deadlock within South Africa.

While being aware of the dimensions of South African fear and determination and of its economic and military strength, it is nonetheless evident that a hard track that isolates South Africa is potentially damaging to its industrial development and its dominance of the subregion. As Carol B. Thompson asserts, "In discussions of South African dominance and reprisals against its neighbors for forming SADCC, few analysts take into consideration that relations in the region are reciprocal."[67] Reciprocal in what respects? She stresses a number of significant examples in this regard: the difficulty of finding skilled miners to replace those from the Front Line States who are sent home; the possible costs of a SADCC trade embargo (estimated at 10 percent of the South African market); the possible loss of rail and port fees paid by the SADCC states (estimated at $400 million per year); the possible withholding of corporate dividends and individual pension payments (estimated at $70 million a year from Zimbabwe alone); and the possible denial of access to grain reserves in Zimbabwe (in 1986, Zimbabwe exported 250,000 tons of maize to South Africa).[68] Clearly, given the sums mentioned here, interdependence is asymmetrical but nonetheless two-directional; if SADCC looks to South Africa for important markets and transportation links, South Africa needs the SADCC countries' trade, transport earnings, and human and material resources. Also, the means are at hand to reduce greatly SADCC's dependence on South African transportation routes by rapidly improving and modernizing the Beira corridor transportation system. A modernized Beira corridor system, currently protected by some 14,000 Zimbabwean troops, would be in a position to meet most of Zimbabwe's transportation requirements in the very near future. Freight charges could be expected to decline, since the route from Harare to Beira is 350 miles, while the route from Harare to Durban is 1,250 miles. Moreover, an expanded military aid program for the Front Line States would further underline the extent of the external powers' opposition to Botha policies. Some military assistance initiatives have become evident in recent years. U.S. military aid has been extended to Botswana and Malawi for training and assistance, and $1 million in training and "nonlethal" equipment was proposed for Mozambique, only to be rejected by the Congress in 1985.[69] Although an extended military aid program by Western countries seems feasible and would send an unmistakable signal to officials in Pretoria, something more dramatic, such as a multilateral expeditionary force, seems unlikely in view of the cautious response that can be anticipated on the part of Western governments and their publics. In brief, the hard track would transform existing relations within the Southern African subsystem significantly, enabling the Western countries and the Front Line States to press South Africa to change its approach on the issue of negotiations. The alternative would likely damage South Africa's interests adversely. If it remained intransigent, it might no longer find itself able to act as a dominant subregional power; rather it would become a relatively peripheral and declining state with limited growth options. In psychological as well as economic terms the costs of muddling through would rise considerably.

The second, or soft, track would open the way to new options and respectability through external mediation. This would be a creative process of facilitation based on using various kinds of side payments to encourage common problem-solving approaches and, ultimately, agreements.[70] By initiating the dialogue, communicating among the possible bargaining parties, clarifying the issues, and proposing agendas, the third-party actor seeks to enlarge the pie, hoping to transform the situation into a positive-sum game. "The prenegotiatory period," as I. William Zartman and Maureen R. Berman observe, "is a time to probe and explore, and to show the other side examples of possibilities, but not a time to make specific promises."[71] The initial effort to set out a very general framework in which South African negotiations could take place found an early articulation with the Commonwealth EPG mission in 1986. Then, in September and October 1987, both Secretary of State Shultz and Assistant Secretary Crocker made further efforts to set out principles for possible negotiations on a constitutional solution that would link majority rule with security for minority groups. Crocker's "democratic precepts" were:

- A constitutional order establishing equal political, economic, and social rights for all South Africans

- A democratic electoral system with multiparty participation and universal adult franchise
- Effective constitutional guarantees of basic human rights for all South Africans as provided for in the Universal Declaration of Human Rights
- The rule of law, safeguarded by an independent judiciary with the power to enforce rights guaranteed by the constitution to all South Africans
- A constitutional allocation of powers between the national government and its constituent regional and local jurisdictions
- An economic system that guarantees economic freedom, allocates government social and economic services fairly, and enables all South Africans to realize the fruits of their labor, acquire and own property, and attain a decent standard of living[72]

Finally, the Reagan administration began to go beyond exhortation. Not only was the Reagan team accepting of the supportive role of past sanctions in late 1987, but it laid out some of the principles upon which future negotiations might be based. This mixed incentive approach was obviously only a beginning, but it did represent a cautious (too cautious!) movement to combine diplomatic and economic sanctions with insurance incentives on minority safeguards.

The Bush administration is not likely to change Reagan administration negotiating principles. As shown by the Rhodesian experience, this process of setting out guidelines for negotiations cannot be allowed to stop at this point but will have to be repeated and refined over time. The process of repetition itself contributes to the credibility of the final agreement, as shown by the case of Rhodesia where the terms of settlement did not vary substantially over time. Moreover, if the third-party mediator could succeed in separating political power from individual and group security, that individual or collectivity could contribute to the ongoing deliberations in a substantial manner.

In the South African context, a double process of facilitation seems most likely to encourage the major adversaries to begin a serious dialogue; that is, Western pressure on the South African government and front line pressure on the black nationalists within South Africa. Clearly, a coordinated third-party effort will be required to overcome the current impasse. If such an effort is to gain credibility, a sustained Western involvement in the affairs of Southern Africa is essential; moreover, any mediator emerging from this encounter must be seen as sufficiently impartial to be able to perform the difficult tasks of shaping the agenda and keeping the process in motion. As the Zimbabwe independence negotiations at Lancaster House showed, a mediator can have interests but be trusted (minimally) by the bargaining parties. Hence, the problem is to find an intermediary sufficiently concerned with the outcome to be willing to play the difficult role of broker, and who is acceptable simultaneously to all sides. This is a difficult, but by no means impossible, task under South African circumstances. There is considerable evidence at this time that the South Africans view the United Nations—and perhaps even the United States, following the passage of the sanctions law—as biased against them. But possibly the Contract Group or the Commonwealth EPG mission could be reconstructed, or a smaller power (for example, Britain or West Germany) could be acceptable to the contending parties. Provided that the intermediary has a minimum of legitimacy, that actor might, at a more appropriate time when the costs of inaction are less bearable, be able to build upon some version of this two-track approach to push the conflicting parties toward the bargaining table. The task is obviously complex and hazardous, but the challenge creates an opportunity not beyond reach.

NOTES

I wish to express my appreciation to I. William Zartman, Thomas M. Callaghy, Bruce Jentleson, Richard Sklar, Robert Price, Edmond Keller, Naomi Chazan, Arend Lijphart, Jeanne Penvenne, and John Ravenhill for their helpful comments. I alone am responsible for the views presented here.

1. George P. Shultz, *The U.S. Approach to South Africa*, July 23, 1986 (Washington, D.C.: Department of State, Bureau of Public Affairs, 1986), Current Policy No. 854, p. 6.

2. Olusegun Obasanjo, "Interview," *Africa Report* 31, no. 5 (1986), p. 5.

3. Anselm Strauss, *Negotiations: Varieties, Contexts, Processes, and Social Order* (San Francisco: Jossey-Bass, 1978), p. 208.

4. Commonwealth Group of Eminent Persons, *Mission to South Africa: The Commonwealth Report* (Harmondsworth, England: Penguin Books, 1986), p. 101.

5. *New York Times*, July 12, 1986, p. 3.

6. George P. Shultz, *The U.S. Approach to South Africa*, p. 2; Ronald Reagan, "Report to the Congress Pursuant to Section 501 of the Comprehensive Anti-Apartheid Act of 1986, *Weekly Compilation of Presidential Documents* 23, no. 39 (October 5, 1987), pp. 1110–1116.

7. John D. Battersby, "Sanctions: A War of Attrition," *Africa Report* 32, no. 1 (1987), p. 6.

8. *Wall Street Journal*, October 7, 1987, p. 39.

9. Heribert Adam and Kogila Moodley, *South Africa Without Apartheid: Dismantling Racial Domination* (Berkeley: University of California Press, 1986), p. 203.

10. Donald Rothchild, *Racial Bargaining in Independent Kenya: A Study of Minorities and Decolonization* (London: Oxford University Press, 1973), p. 145.

11. Noel Kaplowitz, "Psychopolitical Dimensions of International Relations: The Reciprocal Effects of Conflict Strategies," *International Studies Quarterly* 28 (1984), pp. 377–379; Donald Rothchild, "Hegemonial Exchange: An Alternative Model for Managing Conflict in Middle Africa," in Dennis L

Thompson and Dov Ronen, eds., *Ethnicity, Politics, and Development* (Boulder, Colo.: Lynne Rienner Publishers, 1986), pp. 87–93.

12. Robert Jervis, *Perception and Misperception in International Politics* (Princeton: Princeton University Press, 1976), p. 103.

13. I. William Zartman, *Ripe for Resolution: Conflict and Intervention in Africa* (New York: Oxford University Press, 1985), p. 9.

14. Heribert Adam, "The Manipulation of Ethnicity: South Africa in Comparative Perspective," in Donald Rothchild and Victor A. Olorunsola, eds., *State Versus Ethnic Claims: African Policy Dilemmas* (Boulder, Colo.: Westview Press, 1983), pp. 132–133; Heribert Adam and Hermann Giliomee, *Ethnic Power Mobilized: Can South Africa Change?* (New Haven: Yale University Press, 1979), p. 15.

15. Malcolm Fraser and Olusegun Obasanjo, "What To Do About South Africa," *Foreign Affairs* 65, no. 1 (1986), pp. 161-162.

16. Commonwealth Group, *Mission*, p. 20.

17. *Ibid.*, p. 103.

18. Foreign Broadcast Information Service, *FBIS Daily Reports—Middle East and Africa* 5, no. 84 (May 1, 1986), p. U4.

19. Commonwealth Group, *Mission*, p. 131. Also see *Manchester Guardian Weekly* 135, no. 4 (August 24, 1986), p. 7.

20. *Ibid.*, p. 16.

21. *Herald* (Harare), July 11, 1986, p. 1.

22. *Herald*, July 12, 1986, p. 2; *Manchester Guardian Weekly* 135, no. 1 (July 6, 1986), p. 1.

23. *Los Angeles Times*, September 10, 1986, p. 8.

24. Zartman, *Ripe for Resolution*, p. 9.

25. Donald Rothchild and John Ravenhill, "Subordinating African Issues to Global Logic: Reagan Confronts Political Complexity," in Kenneth Oye, Robert Lieber, and Donald Rothchild, eds., *Eagle Resurgent? The Reagan Era in American Foreign Policy* (Boston: Little, Brown, 1987), pp. 412–416.

26. Foreign Broadcast Information Service, *FBIS Daily Reports—Middle East and Africa* 5, no. 84 (May 1, 1986), p. U6. However, the U.S. Congress did regard this position as a reasonable one. Thus, the Comprehensive Anti-Apartheid Act of 1986 asserted that "it is the sense of the Congress that a suspension of violence is an essential precondition for the holding of negotiations." *Comprehensive Anti-Apartheid Act of 1986*, Public Law 99–440, 99th Congress (October 2, 1986), p. 1092.

27. Fraser and Obasanjo, "What To Do," p. 156.

28. African National Congress, *ANC Call to the People: From Ungovernability to People's Power* (Lusaka: African National Congress, 1986), p. 1; *Africa Research Bulletin* (Political Series) 22, no. 6 (July 15, 1985), p. 7687.

29. Azania People's Liberation Army, *Azania Combat* 1 (1986), p. 4.

30. See Colin Legum, ed., *Africa Contemporary Record 1983–1984* (New York: Africana Publishing, 1984), p. 743.

31. Black Consciousness Movement of Azania, "Comment: The Deception of the Botha–Malan Junta," *Solidarity* (February 1986), pp. 2–3.

32. Commonwealth Group, *Mission*, p. 175.

33. Black Consciousness Movement of Azania, "Comment," p. 3.

34. John de St. Jorre, "South Africa: A Reporter's Notebook," *CSIS Africa Notes* 60 (July 15, 1986), p. 4.

35. *New York Times*, July 17, 1986, p. 22.

36. See Leo Kuper, *The Pity of It All* (Minneapolis: University of Minnesota Press, 1977).

37. Foreign Broadcast Information Service, *FBIS Daily Reports—Middle East and Africa* 5, no. 95 (May 16, 1986), p. U4.

38. *New York Times*, July 14, 1986, p. 6.

39. Azanian People's Organization, Editorial, *Frank Talk* 1, no. 4 (September–October 1985), p. 3.

40. Stephen Low, "The Zimbabwe Settlement, 1976–1979," in Saadia Touval and I. William Zartman, eds., *International Mediation in Theory and Practice* (Boulder, Colo.: Westview Press, 1985), p. 104.

41. On the importance of providing face-saving concessions, see Russell J. Leng and Hugh G. Wheeler, "Influence Strategies, Success, and War," *Journal of Conflict Resolution* 23, no. 4 (December 1979), p. 681.

42. See Henry Bienen, "The State and Ethnicity: Integrative Formulas in Africa," in Rothchild and Olorunsola, *State Versus Ethnic Claims*, pp. 105–107.

43. Gavin Relly, "The Costs of Disinvestment," *Foreign Policy* 63 (Summer 1986), p. 135.

44. African National Congress, *Attack, Advance, Give the Enemy No Quarter!* (Lusaka: African National Congress, 1986), pp. 2–3.

45. Stanley Uys, "Blacks Now Know They Are Going to Win," *Manchester Guardian Weekly* 134, no. 22 (June 1, 1986), p. 7. Also see *African Research Bulletin* (Political Series) 22, no. 6 (July 15, 1985), p. 7687.

46. *International Herald Tribune*, July 14, 1986, p. 4.

47. *South African Digest*, January 17, 1986, p. 41.

48. *South African Digest*, May 30, 1986, p. 467.

49. Robert I. Rotberg, "Namibia's Independence: A Political and Diplomatic Impasse?" *CSIS Africa Notes* 13 (May 5, 1983), p. 5.

50. Correspondent, "South Africa, Black Nationalists at Odds," *Africa Analysis* 6 (September 19, 1986), p. 2.

51. Interview, Nairobi, August 2, 1986.

52. *Africa News* 27 (September 15, 1986), p. 8.

53. Interview, London, July 4, 1986. Also see Jeffrey Davidow, *A Peace in Southern Africa* (Boulder, Colo.: Westview Press, 1984), pp. 115–121.

54. John W. Burton, "The Procedures of Conflict Resolution," in Edward E. Azar and John W. Burton, eds., *International Conflict Resolution: Theory and Practice* (Boulder, Colo.: Lynne Rienner Publishers, 1986), p. 105.

55. Robert Jaster, "South Africa's Narrowing Security Options," in Robert Jaster, ed., *Southern Africa: Regional Security Problems and Prospects* (New York: St. Martin's Press, 1985), p. 37.

56. Howard Raiffa, *The Art and Science of Negotiation* (Cambridge: Harvard University Press, 1982).

57. Henry Kissinger, *White House Years* (Boston: Little, Brown, 1979), p. 259.

58. Roger Fisher and William Ury, *Getting to Yes: Negotiating Agreement Without Giving In* (Boston: Houghton Mifflin, 1981), p. 122.

59. Conor Cruise O'Brien, "What Can Become of South Africa?" *Atlantic Monthly* 257, no. 3 (1986), p. 66.

60. Battersby, "Sanctions: A War of Attrition," p. 8.

61. Edward Hallett Carr, *The Twenty Years' Crisis, 1919–1939* (New York: Harper and Row, 1964), p. 110.

62. Morton Deutsch, Yakov Epstein, Donnah Canavan, and Peter Gumpert, "Strategies of Inducing Cooperation: An Experimental Study," *Journal of Conflict Resolution* 11, no. 3 (1967), p. 345.

63. Chester A. Crocker, "South Africa in Transition," address to CUNY Conference, October 1, 1987, p. 6. Mimeo.

64. Reagan, "Report to Congress," p. 1111.

65. Crocker, "South Africa in Transition," p. 4.

66. John S. Saul, "Development and Counterdevelopment Strategies in Mozambique," in Edmond J. Keller and Donald Rothchild, eds., *Afro-Marxist Regimes: Ideology and Public Policy* (Boulder, Colo.: Lynne Rienner Publishers, 1987), pp. 122–125.

67. Carol B. Thompson, "Beyond Flag Independence: The Quest for Economic Liberation in Southern Africa," paper presented at the African Studies Association, Madison, Wisconsin, 1986, p. 18.

68. *Ibid.*, pp. 19–20; see also *Africa News* 27 (August 18, 1986), p. 9.

69. Herbert Howe and Marina Ottaway, "State Power Consolidation in Mozambique," in Keller and Rothchild, eds., *Afro-Marxist Regimes*, p. 56.

70. Saadia Touval, *The Peace Brokers* (Princeton: Princeton University Press, 1982), p. 327.

71. I. William Zartman and Maureen R. Berman, *The Practical Negotiator* (New Haven: Yale University Press, 1982), p. 71.

72. Crocker, "South Africa in Transition," p. 2. These "democratic precepts" were based upon the secretary of state's formulation two days earlier. On this, see George P. Shultz, "The Democratic Future of South Africa," address to the Business Council for International Understanding, New York, September 29, 1987. Mimeo.

4

Racial Proletarianization and Political Culture in South Africa

C. R. D. HALISI

With reference to Europe, early in the twentieth century, Hannah Arendt commented on a "gigantic competition between race-thinking and class-thinking for dominion over the minds of modern men."[1] The echo of that pronouncement reverberates in South Africa today. The tension between race-thinking and class-thinking permeates every shade of political thought, particularly the predominant political ideologies of this era—liberalism, socialism, and populism.

RACIAL PROLETARIANIZATION
IN SOUTH AFRICAN STUDIES

George M. Fredrickson devoted his masterful comparison of South Africa and the United States to the exploration of what is often taken for granted—how the mere existence of races contributed to the formation of racial ideologies.[2] Fredrickson explores the impact of the racial organization of power on industrialization and therefore class relations in these two racially divided states. Comparative historical studies of South Africa and the southern United States have tended to argue that the study of race relations is best understood within the context of industrialization and is therefore relevant to the multidisciplinary concern with development studies. However, the very term *industrialization* is often a euphemism for a more fundamental process. As Charles Tilly observes, "in terms of impact on everyday life proletarianization is—and was—the most powerful process in the complex of changes that we vaguely and variously call industrialization, economic development, or the growth of capitalism."[3]

With similar insights, Stanley Trapido has skillfully employed Barrington Moore's notion of the labor-repressive economy to compare South Africa's pathway to industrialization with that of tsarist Russia and imperial Germany. His comparison accounts for the peculiar distortions of South African development. South Africa's primary peculiarity has been "the perpetuation of social dislocation among the African working population, both urban and rural, in a situation of industrial maturity."[4] Of all capitalist countries, South Africa alone has not incorporated the larger part of its working class into its modern social institutions; it alone has rejected the basic features of liberal democracy, such as free association, a common educational system, a unitary legal system, and universal suffrage. Clearly, the political dependency of labor repression on racial domination transcends all four phases of South Africa's economic development typologized by Trapido as: (1) commercial agriculture; (2) diamond and gold mining; (3) manufacturing industry; and (4) Afrikaner financial and industrial capital.[5]

In South Africa, proletarianization under the conditions of racial domination created a black working class; indeed it was a major factor in the formation of a modern black people or ethnic consciousness. As Immanuel Wallerstein reminds us, "people-formation is an integral part of class-formation."[6] Racial proletarianization has not only been a process of class formation but has also accelerated the formation of "black people" consciousness. In this respect, Oliver Cox's assertion that racial exploitation is merely one aspect of the problem of the proletarianization of labor has a degree of relevance to the South African case.[7]

In racially divided societies, the extension of democratic rights on a *herrenvolk* basis was a racial response to the general demand for democratization, as it created a proletariat divided not only by race but by the allocation of democratic rights. The exclusion of workers from democratic participation on a racial basis differentiated the relationships of black and white workers with the bourgeoisie. Cox captured the reality thus:

> While race relations and the struggle of the white proletariat with the bourgeoisie are parts of a single phenomenon, race relations involve a significant variation. In the case of race relations, the tendency of the bourgeoisie is to proletarianize a whole people—that is to say, the whole people is looked upon as a class—whereas white proletarianization involves only a section of the white people. The concept of "bourgeoisie" and "white people" sometimes seems to mean the same thing for, with respect to the coloured people of the world, it is almost always through a white bourgeoisie that capitalism has been introduced.[8]

The term *proletarianization* can be employed in several different senses. Giovanni Arrighi contends that masses are proletarianized when their participation in the money economy is no longer discretionary but necessary to meet their basic or subsistence requirements.[9]

Sound as this conception may be, its political dimension is too often minimized, and this can limit our ability to relate class oppression to racial domination. William Appleman Williams has more fully explained the political implications of proletarianization:

Marx meant a good deal more by proletarianization than simply working for wages on the assembly line in an urban manufacturing plant. . . . He meant the loss of any participating role in the principal decisions of the capitalist marketplace due to loss of any private property which played a part in the productive activities of the system. The overt sign of this loss of full citizenship was of course the change from entrepreneurial standing to the condition of wage labor.[10]

Tilly insists that the word *proletarianization* has three concentric circles of meaning. In the narrowest sense proletarians are people who receive wages from capitalists for relatively unskilled work performed in large establishments under intense discipline and are in this sense creatures of the last century or so of capitalist industrialization. The term *proletarian* can, however, be placed in a wider historical context. Marx's analysis of the English proletariat stresses agricultural labor and the influence of enclosing landlords rather than factory owners. Therefore, proletarianization has two components: (1) workers' increasing dependence for survival on the sale of their labor power; and (2) capitalists' increasing control over the means of production. As long as *capitalist* and *control* are used fairly generously, the origins of proletarianization go back to the beginnings of capitalism. In its third and broadest meaning, the term *proletarian* includes anyone who sells labor power irrespective of modalities of the sale. In this sense, says Tilly, the terms *socialist proletarian* or *proletarian Ph.D.* imply no contradiction.[11]

While white settlement in South Africa was linked to early forms of international capitalism, racial domination produced its class counterpart—racial proletarianization. Therefore, theorizing about the nature of South African society forces both the activist and the academic to gaze upon the two faces of Janus—race and class. The difficulties of this task have been reflected in both historiographical and sociological literatures. The early debate between nascent academic Marxism and pluralism was often over the relationship of class and race as distinct stratification systems. Upon closer examination, however, rigid distinctions between race- and class-based analyses of non-European peoples can prove misleading. Cox reexamines the arguments of John S. Furnival and Julius H. Boeke, two pioneer pluralist thinkers, and finds that they, unlike some of their successors, did not ignore the more universal aspects of capitalist transformation. Furnival and Boeke view pluralist analysis as an approach directed toward understanding the impact of capitalism on the native cultures of the world.[12] Cox finds that the problem of capitalist transformation underlies the disagreements between pluralist and Marxist thinkers.

With respect to the academic study of South Africa, the pioneering work by H. J. and R. E. Simons, which attempts to confront both class and color from a Marxist point of view, did much to stimulate a reconsideration of race-class analysis.[13] Leo Kuper, who reviewed the Simons and Simons book, thinks highly of the honesty with which the authors confront the issues of race and class; ultimately, however, he finds that the validity of class struggle has not been upheld. "I am not sure," Kuper says, "but I think that the authors are telling us that, in South African society, race and nation and constitutional rights are major determinants of political qualifications."[14]

The ability or inability of capitalism to assimilate and transcend older economic and political arrangements based on race or to coexist with strict racial segregation has led to a lively controversy over the nature of capitalist industrialization and its relation to the state and the economy. These early debates have contributed to the growth of a sometimes insightful revisionist movement in South African scholarship.

In the South African context, academic analyses have been examined in light of their implications for strategies of social change and related to ideological trends within the political arena. For example, Harold Wolpe, like many other scholars, equates pluralism with liberalism and considers pluralist analysis to assume that economic pressures will eventually reform the racist character of the state. Radical scholars, on the other hand, are those who insist that only the political action of the nonwhite masses will transform the racial order.[15] This dichotomy may oversimplify the issue inasmuch as other questions must also be addressed: for example, what combinations of political action will be needed on the continuum from reform to revolution; and what combination of class forces might sustain decisive political action?

Sam Nolutshungu's thoughtful work on political change in South Africa was published several years after Wolpe's. He agrees that radical and reformist positions can be distinguished by their respective views on these matters: whether the termination of racial domination is possible under capitalist conditions; whether an economic determination for racism is posited.[16] Likewise, Wallerstein draws a distinction between Marxist and cultural nationalist analyses of race on the ground that Marxists analyze race in class terms.[17] Daiva Stasiulis, in a reassessment of pluralist and Marxist analyses of racial discrimination in South Africa, proffers a Marxist analysis that can explain racial discrimination as an integral part of the growth of capitalism. In contrast to the mainstream of Marxist arguments, she concludes that "one can grant pluralists their contention that capitalist development and racial discrimination are contradictory to one another, recognizing that their hypothesis is reached from a fundamentally incorrect analysis."[18]

Recent reassessments of race relations have increasingly insisted on the centrality of black politics in the transformation of the apartheid system. Michael Burawoy believes that a weakness of Stanley Greenberg's otherwise excellent study, *Race and State in Capitalist Development*, is the omission of black classes as a focus of analysis, which makes it impossible for Greenberg to unravel the forces that will shape the South African future and have shaped its history.[19] In short, it has never been easy for theorists to untangle the dynamics of class formation from those of race formation; too often it is assumed that race consciousness is static and does not need explanation.[20]

To the contrary, race consciousness is political in nature and may be developed into a progressive or conservative perspective. Thus, an awareness of racial oppression distinguishes the political thought of black social classes from that of their closest European counterparts; racial militancy often transcends class distinctions. C. L. R. James, in one of his characteristically perceptive comments, declares that "racial consciousness which has been so mercilessly injected into the Negro is today a source of action and at the same time of discipline."[21]

Some sociologists have been inclined to embark upon historical analyses attempting to locate the factors that have given rise to various stratified orders; several of them would agree that "stratification is always and everywhere the result of conquest."[22] Usually, conquest, migration, or slavery have established foundations for racial proletarianization.[23] For blacks in the southern United States, slavery and proletarianization were closely linked, whereas in South Africa conquest replaces slavery in the case of the African majority; however, a significant number of coloureds also have an experience of slavery in their past.

Where oppression has been multifaceted, various forms of radical consciousness usually coexist. The conquest of Africans by Europeans, or blacks by whites, also represents a conflict between societies at various stages of development and organized in different modes of production. Political developments indigenous to South Africa, though distinct, were never isolated from international developments. The growth of international capitalism characterized by the global proletarianization of labor, the accumulation and monopoly of capital, and the formation of advanced industrial economies related to one another and the less developed world by an intricate market, created connections between political and social conflict in South Africa and the powerful centers of Western capitalism. As Cox hastens to point out "assimilation . . . is peculiarly an attribute of the capitalist system."[24]

Revisionist academic analyses of South Africa (referred to by some authors as the New School) have made important historiographical and theoretical advances but cannot claim, any more than can their predecessors, to have transcended the necessity of living within the conceptual purgatory of race and class interpretations of politics. Neville Alexander is disappointed by the fact that while the New School "torpedoed the race-relations framework within which all previously liberal and avowedly Marxist analyses had examined the South African formation . . . the concept of race was left standing as though it could not be shaken."[25] Alexander views "race" as an ideological construct that must be abandoned and replaced by a "raceless" revolutionary analysis. In fact, the rapidly developing historical literature on South Africa *can* be read as a social theoretical commentary on race–class dynamics within the development of South African capitalism.

Progressive historians and other scholars have sought to refute or revise the considerable factual and interpretive foundations of earlier historical, anthropological, and sociological writings, as well as to confront the dominance of the liberal paradigm. Indeed, the polarization between the Marxist and liberal interpretations of South African politics—while by no means reconciled—has fostered a common recognition of the importance of scholarly sensitivity to both race and class as interdependent variables. Scholarly consideration of race and class factors abound with internal theoretical implications for both schools of thought.

Some Marxist historians are sensitive to the tension between Africanist and materialist historiography. William Freund conceives the relationship as a war between two opposing camps. Peter Delius, on the other hand, acknowledges that a fusion of Africanist and materialist concerns took place during the 1970s.[26] The New School's historical research agenda revolved around the fairly coordinated attempt to revise South African historiography, and therefore the analysis of racial conflict and consciousness, within a Marxist framework.

An undeniable contribution of contemporary historical and sociological scholarship to the study of political movements has been the exploration of racial proletarianization and the articulation of three distinct forms of class action—class formation, conflict, and collaboration—within the framework of racial oppression. In South African studies, the attempt to unravel class and race dynamics has had a particular impact on scholarly awareness of the social character of black peasant and worker movements and the distinctive nature of their participation within the larger struggle for black liberation.

Shula Marks and Richard Rathbone, in an introduction to a collection of articles that focus on industrialization, social change, and African consciousness in South Africa, carefully enumerate the shortcomings of much of the neo-Marxist history on the questions of class formation, culture, and consciousness, but they argue for the validity of the core insights into the dynamics of class and race advanced by neo-Marxist scholarship.[27] Some versions of "materialist history" have proved better able to accommodate distinct forms of consciousness and resistance. E. P. Thompson, in his classic study of English workers, is convinced that "we cannot understand class unless we see it as a social and cultural formation, arising from processes which can only be studied as they work themselves out over a considerable historical period."[28]

Structuralist-oriented Marxist historians criticize the degree to which Thompson deviates from an orthodox Marxist interpretation of class in favor of a cultural analysis of worker *experience*, but they concede that the strength of his approach lies in its contribution to an understanding of the consciousness and the culture of working classes. Marks and Rathbone warn their readers that "for all the emphasis in these essays on consciousness and culture and our quite explicit debt to Edward Thompson we return . . . to the assertion that a person's class is established by nothing but his objective place in the network of ownership relations."[29] Thompson's view of class can be said to contain three important insights: (1) class formation should not be viewed as a process that affects passive groups of workers; (2) class is neither a structure nor a category but rather a pattern that emerges in human relationships; and (3) class is as much a cultural as an economic formation.[30]

These insights are equally valid for the contour of race formation. Either race or class consciousness can be the unifying concept for a large number of otherwise disparate historical events. Not unlike Thompson's observations about class and class consciousness, race formation can be viewed as a process; racism is a pattern that emerges in human relations while racial domination and forms of resistance are both cultural and economic. Maurice Duverger has correctly argued that "biologically race has no political significance, but because of the collective images it provokes it is sociologically of political significance."[31] The coexistence of class and race processes within the South African social formation has provided the central intellectual problem for much of the scholarly study and debate; it also has profound consequences for courses of political action.

For example, Black Consciousness interpretations of South Africa stress the history of black people as a conflict with "The White Man"—a designation that carries distinct emotional significance in black communities having experienced the full weight of racism. With respect to blacks in the United States, the tradition of "Black History" constitutes not only an academic but an ideological response to racist historical falsification. Those interpretations of South African history that place emphasis on the conflict of the African people with encroaching Europeans remain a powerful source of political legitimation for proponents of Black Consciousness thought. Even the progressive stance of nonracialism, meant to refute apartheid ideology, has elicited competing definitions from advocates of Black Consciousness and multiracialism.

The best of the historical writings on South Africa over the last decade or more have sought both to reconstruct the preindustrial authenticity of African people and to explore the role that culture and consciousness have played in the transformation of Africans (and all blacks) into an exploited working class. Such writings seek to capture the complexity of black resistance within the context of capitalist development. Thus, Simons and Simons suggest the transformative potential of black nationalism with the phrase "national in form, socialist in content."[32] They relate how the meaning of this phrase eluded the expert Marxist I. I. Potekhin, renowned as the father of African studies in the Soviet Union. According to Potekhin, the early African National Congress was an organization of compradore chiefs. Simons and Simons contend that Potekhin "did not adequately examine the process of amalgamating scores of formerly independent and often antagonistic societies into a single nation."[33] His failure to recognize this occurrence, they conclude, made it impossible for him to understand that the opposition of chiefs at times played a progressive role and bequeathed something essential to African nationalism.[34]

In South Africa, as in the United States, the impact of slavery and segregation on capitalist development is crucially relevant to the study of both class conflict and race relations. Neo-Marxist historiography in South Africa received its impetus from an expanding expatriate intellectual community that drew on a variety of intellectual movements for its inspiration: the *Annales* school; British social and socialist history; U.S. writings on slavery and race; French Marxist traditions; and the Latin American underdevelopment debate.[35] Marxist writings have not ignored the realities of black exploitation in South Africa. Martin Legassick remarks that "the entrenchment of racialism in the institutions of society meant the correlation of development with whiteness, and underdevelopment with blackness. The correlation was not and is not complete, but is cruelly strong."[36] Similarly, Ben Turok argues that "black deprivation is uppermost. . . . They are first black and then proletarian."[37]

Nolutshungu cogently summarizes the race–class dimension of South African politics:

> The ideological category of "race" has been the primary line of political differentiation: indicating whose consent or acquiescence is to be sought and who is to be primarily coerced. Race performed a double function—legitimation, and of providing a practical principle of political organization. . . . The first and most evident effect of racialising politics has been to create a winning combination of coercion and consent, a distinctive technology of domination suited to the heritage of colonialism and its continuing economic processes (i.e., forcible proletarianization and territorial dispossession, and the collective anxieties and hostilities integral to conquest).[38]

However, several neo-Marxist scholars do choose to stress the universal (class) dimension of economic exploitation. The exploitation of black men and women, it is maintained, is the exploitation of men and women in general. Marx himself once remarked: "What is a Negro? A man of the black race. One explanation is as good as the other. He becomes a slave in certain relationships."[39] In this spirit, Wolpe argues that "poverty is not a function of race or colour, it is the outcome of the actions of men pursuing economic ends in specific social structures."[40]

Sensitive class analysis of racially conscious politics largely depends on the manner in which class is conceptualized. The attempt to conceptualize other forms of consciousness within a class framework poses fundamental questions concerning class determination.[41] Economistic interpretations of black oppression are often rejected by race-conscious blacks. Steven Biko and other Black Consciousness radicals felt that racism had assumed a dimension that could not be reduced to solely economic relationships. Furthermore, the demand for racial equality and black self-determination has proved more fundamental than debates over the virtues of capitalism or socialism.

The political-economic dimension of racial domination and exploitation is unavoidably accompanied by a social-psychological dimension. Eugene Victor Wolfenstein contends that racism is a form of false consciousness and that Marxist theory must be psychoanalytically mediated if it is to explain racism. He remarks: (1) that racial consciousness is not reducible to class interests; and (2) that not all forms of race consciousness are equal or equally rational. On a number of bases, racism is radically different from race consciousness. These two forms of consciousness generate contrasting social movements. Wolfenstein observes:

> Racial movements must be judged to be historically progressive while racist movements must be judged regressive, from the perspective of proletarian interest. . . . Racial liberation must be worked through before there can be meaningful interracial solidarity.[42]

Marxist or liberal histories that depict blacks as victims of economic forces are suspect in the eyes of many black intellectuals. Both liberal and Marxist interpretations, according to Wilmot James, "share a basic claim about the transformative effects of capitalist development on racial and gender differences within the working class."[43] The persistence of racially stratified worker groupings undermines the "commodification thesis"—the view that capitalism transforms all qualitative social distinctions into market distinction and aggregates labor into an undifferentiated commodity of labor power.[44]

Academic and ideological analyses share as their object the problem of political change, and this demands an assessment of the agents of change and the form of consciousness that motivates and inspires collective action. Peter Ekeh's definition of ideologies as "interest begotten theories"[45] can be applied to academic as well as ideological discourse, and the two frequently converge. Academic controversies regarding the primacy of race or class broach the two enduring and recurring ideological tendencies in liberation ideology. Questions related to a sociology of knowledge perspective are therefore bound to surface as an aspect of African history that, according to Alessandro Triulzi, exhibits more theoretical vitality than does European history. Triulzi acknowledges that ethnocentric conceptual and classificatory schemes are the first targets of the historiographical decolonization of Africa.[46]

South African history exhibits a similar, if not superior, theoretical vitality. South Africa is exceptional in the sense that decolonization of not just history, but social science analysis in general, also implies deracialization. In the academic arena, deracialization will undoubtedly mean a closer scrutiny of the way class and race are interrelated. Liberal and Marxist ideologies alike have been questioned from a sociology of knowledge perspective. For example, Selim Gool believes that the tendency of the New School's discourse to lean toward obsession with an exclusive theoretical language—what sociologist Alvin Gouldner refers to as a "sociolect"—is partially due to the South African expatriate character of the scholars responsible for evolving the paradigm.[47]

While the historical advancements of the New School are far too valuable to be dismissed as "White History," a rethinking of the implicit intellectual politics will escalate as black intellectuals are inducted into the scholarly ranks. This new historiography will not merely be criticized by autarkists insisting that only racial insiders can write black history—a position that has been articulated by scholars from independent African countries.[48] The insider–outsider argument that contends that only blacks can write authentic history will be the least damaging assault upon the more sophisticated historical scholarship written from any perspective. Sophisticated scholarship will demand sophisticated criticism. Nonetheless, black scholars have tended to be strongly concerned about the treatment of racial consciousness, resistance, and domination. Wilmot James argues that "both Marxist and non-Marxist . . . tend to view blacks as passive recipients of racial oppression. . . . We simply cannot account for the transformation to apartheid without incorporating black struggles into our analytical framework."[49]

However, the insights of revisionist research regarding black politics constitute its most politically controversial contribution. Revisionist historians reconstructing the development of the black proletariat have surmised that the demands of black workers have often been subsumed—to their disadvantage—by the broader demand of the urban-based African bourgeoisie. Some historians contend that black nationalist ideology that tends to collapse the class identity of black workers into that of all black people constitutes a form of populism. A further theoretical assertion is that there is no contradiction between race and class consciousness within genuine working-class movements. Reproducing the lyrics of a Zulu work song that spoke of the black man as poor and the white man as bad, Marks and Rathbone conclude that in the consciousness of African workers racial and class domination were identical.[50] A black garment worker, while exhibiting her pay stub, eloquently explained the nature of her exploitation both as a worker and as a black:

I produce sweaters for these whites, about 250 of them a week. I have seen these same sweaters in the store; they cost thirty-two Rand each. But when they take out of my pay check, I am left with twenty-seven Rand, less than the cost of one sweater.[51]

The manner in which the working class has been formed is a crucial consideration in racially heterogenous societies; when it is ignored, mass political culture can hardly be understood. For the South African black majority, proletarianization has not simply meant the transformation of gatherers, hunters, herders, agriculturalists, and the once homogeneous societies based upon these economies, into propertyless and rightless captives of a capitalist economy and a racialist state. Blacks have experienced the tragedy that is South Africa's both as individuals and collectively as a people. Ernesto Laclau has argued that worker consciousness will depend on the social formation in question and that workers will respond to popular democratic struggles.[52] On this point he is emphatic: "[W]hile classes may be in struggle 'class struggle' devoid of all other determinations is an abstraction."[53] In a highly developed capitalist society, such as South Africa, "racial struggle" devoid of class determinations is no less an abstraction. In South Africa, events constantly send scholars, reformers, and revolutionaries alike back to the fact that neither race nor class can be subsumed one into the other.

The very process that led to the formation of a black working class forged a black people and a common resistance to labor and racial exploitation. Clearly, the concepts *black* and *proletariat* interact and, at times, compete as core ideas in black political thought and action. This interaction can take diverse forms and is ever changing. During the latter part of the 1960s, Black Consciousness intellectuals extended the term *black* to all nonwhite South Africans.

South Africa—the first industrial society on the African continent and the golden womb of the world economy—witnesses a political dynamic that combines the social categories of settler colonialism with a political content that approximates that of Western capitalist states. Naturally, political consciousness has emerged in many forms in the black population, i.e., as ethnic-based resistance to conquest, as worker militancy opposed to economic exploitation, as African nationalism demanding true political power, and as Black Consciousness calling for an end to cultural hegemony and self-degradation. Political consciousness and the vernacular of black resistance are almost synonymous in the minds of the vast majority of South Africans.

RACIAL PROLETARIANIZATION AS POLITICAL CULTURE

The African peoples of the Southern African region display a high degree of cultural similarity. Monica Wilson observes that the political, social, and particularly the intellectual systems of Southern African peoples are closely related.[54] This observation can be extended to include the Khoisan who were not as culturally distinct or isolated as is often claimed. African ethnicity—Zulu, Xhosa, etc.—is older than the concept of a racial order. However, ethnic identity and consciousness, while never static, infuse but do not subsume racial thought and identity.

Furthermore, the mining and industrial economies in South Africa attract migrant laborers from the surrounding African countries. In a given year it is not uncommon for South African employment to account for as much as one-third of the wage employment of workers in neighboring countries. The prevalence of migrant labor for over 100 years has regionalized the effects of proletarianization. As the major social process in the development of contemporary black political culture, racial proletarianization has circumscribed ethnicity and forged an overriding cultural homogeneity expressed in the emergence of an urban black culture. This is not to suggest that proletarianization, or for that matter even racial proletarianization, of South Africa's diverse peoples was a uniform process. A growing number of historical studies relate the distinct experiences of various African peoples with migrancy as an initial form of proletarianization. African communities sought to integrate wage labor into their own cultural systems but this was possible only so long as access to alternative means of subsistence existed. Peter Delius, in his study of the Pedi people of the Transvaal, warns that the character of proletarianization was not static; specifically, he contends that nineteenth- and twentieth-century patterns were quite distinct.[55]

Racial proletarianization, we have argued, resulted from the appropriation of African land. Neo-Marxist historians in particular have reiterated that racial domination became an institutionalized part of class relations and the labor process in the mining industry. The mining revolution, which sparked South Africa's overall industrial revolution, accelerated the assault on African land-holding. "In fact," says Belinda Bozzoli, "the motive force of the new mode of production lay in its primary opposition . . . to black societies whose destruction would produce a proletariat."[56] More recently, Wilmot James has neatly shown that the equation of land and race was central to the transition from segregation to apartheid as distinguishable modes of development and to the concomitant transformation of black men from peasants to miners.[57]

C. M. Tatz distinguishes two coexisting regional political cultures in South Africa. At the heart of the so-called Southern view, or the Cape liberal tradition, lies the proletarianization of the Khoisan and, to some extent, the Xhosa. The more racialist Northern view reflects the extension of racial proletarianization to Africans of Natal, the Transvaal, and the Orange Free State.[58] In each province a distinct black political culture developed. Leo Kuper has painstakingly outlined some of the contributions of regional political cultures to the larger body of black nationalist philosophy and practice.[59] Tom Lodge, in his more recent study of black politics, is sensitive to the impact of distinctive regional political patterns on ideological preference, party affiliation, and traditions of resistance.[60] Everywhere, the political exclusion of Africans was shaped by the exigencies of racial proletarianization.

Bantu-speaking and Khoisan Africans, despite divergent experiences and the different periods of proletarianization, have independently and simultaneously opposed the implementation of both political and labor repression in South Africa.[61] Furthermore, the loss of land and other means of independent subsistence for the Khoisan and other Africans has conditioned both their transformation into a working class, and their sense of racial consciousness. Bernard Magubane has insisted that in the case of South Africa, conquest, capital accumulation, and cultural dislocation were inseparable.[62]

Racial proletarianization as a process has meant an intersection of race, class, and power relations into a political culture that shapes both social conflict and collaboration. The development of such a political culture limits the potential for nonracial democracy and can provide the impetus for experimentation with forms of *herrenvolk* democracy—democracy based upon intrarace class collaboration. The "logic" of a *herrenvolk* state, says George Fredrickson, is to organize a society in which "people of color, however numerous or acculturated they may be, are treated as permanent aliens or outsiders."[63] As in contemporary South Africa, studies of the implementation of the Cape Ordinances 49 and 50 of 1828 suggest that before the mid-nineteenth century racial reforms unavoidably impinged on class reforms, and vice versa.[64]

In this chapter, through a discussion of some of the important historical and sociological writings, I have sought to highlight the central problems that confront analysts concerned with social change in contemporary South Africa. Racial proletarianization, I have argued, captures an important facet of South African political development. Class formation was very often accomplished within the framework of racial domination. Therefore, the academic literature, even when concerned with class dynamics, cannot avoid the impact of racial domination on class action. Conversely, the better scholarship on race relations, even when cast in a liberal mold, cannot completely ignore the dynamics of proletarianization and industrialization. The liberal contention that capitalism will gradually erode apartheid constitutes recognition of a race–class conjuncture. And since this conjuncture is central, analyses of South African politics must come to terms with both race and class whether the arguments are correct or incorrect, honest or dishonest, conscious or unconscious. The complex process of racial proletarianization can be elucidated from liberal, socialist, or populist perspectives, but the reconciliation of race and class remains an unavoidable intellectual issue in South African social theory. Indeed, debates between earlier pluralist and Marxist scholars, as well as the more contemporary exchanges over the validity of liberal as opposed to neo-Marxist paradigms, are best understood within the conceptual rubric of racial proletarianization.

NOTES

1. Hannah Arendt, *The Origins of Totalitarianism* (Cleveland, Ohio: World Publishing Company, 1958), p. 161.

2. George M. Fredrickson, *White Supremacy: A Comparative Study in American and South African History* (Oxford: Oxford University Press, 1981). For a discussion of the historiography of comparative segregation see John W. Cell, *The Highest Stage of White Supremacy: The Origins of Segregation in South Africa and the American South* (London: Cambridge University Press, 1982).

3. Charles Tilly, *As Sociology Meets History* (New York: Academic Press, 1981), p. 181.

4. Stanley Trapido, "South Africa in a Comparative Study of Industrialization," *Journal of Development Studies* 7, no. 3 (April 1971), p. 314.

5. *Ibid.*, pp. 313–314.

6. Immanuel Wallerstein, "Race Is Class?" *Monthly Review* 32, no. 10 (March 1981), p. 50. In this article, Wallerstein defended a South African scholar who focused on the political economy of race and in doing so drew criticism from Marxist scholars. See Barnard Magubane, *The Political Economy of Race and Class in South Africa* (New York: Monthly Review Press, 1979).

7. Oliver Cox, *Caste, Class and Race: A Study in Social Dynamics* (New York: Modern Reader Paperbacks, 1970), p. 333.

8. *Ibid.*, p. 344.

9. Giovanni Arrighi, "Labour Supplies in Historical Perspective: A Study of the Proletarianization of the African Peasantry in Rhodesia," in Giovanni Arrighi and John S. Saul, eds., *Essays on the Political Economy of Africa* (New York: Monthly Review Press, 1973), p. 193.

10. William Appleman Williams, *The Great Evasion* (New York: New Viewpoints, 1974), p. 114.

11. Tilly, *As Sociology Meets History*, pp. 180–181.

12. Oliver C. Cox, "On the Question of Pluralism," *Race* 12, no. 4 (April 1971), p. 388. See also Julius Boeke, *Economics and Economic Policies as Exemplified by Indonesia* (New York: Institute of Pacific Relations, 1953) and J. S. Furnival, *Colonial Policy and Practice: A Comparative Study of Burma and Neterlands India* (New York: New York University Press, 1956).

13. H. J. and R. E. Simons, *Class and Colour in South Africa, 1850–1950* (Baltimore: Penguin Books, 1969).

14. Leo Kuper, *Race, Class and Power* (Chicago: Aldine Press, 1975), p. 283.

15. Harold Wolpe, "Industrialisation and Race in South Africa," in Sami Zubaida, ed., *Race and Racialism* (London: Tavistock Publications, 1970), p. 164.

16. Sam Nolutshungu, *Changing South Africa* (New York: Africana Publishing, 1982), pp. 1–7.

17. Wallerstein, "Race Is Class?" p. 51.

18. Daiva Stasiulis, "Pluralist and Marxist Perspectives on Racial Discrimination in South Africa," *British Journal of Sociology* 31, no. 4 (December 1981), p. 484.

19. Michael Burawoy, "Revolution in South Africa: Reflections on the Comparative Perspectives of Greenberg and Skocpol," *Kapitalistate* 9 (1981), p. 99.

20. Michael Omi and Howard Winant, in *Racial Formation in the United States From the 1960s to the 1980s* (New York: Routledge and Kegan Paul, 1986), have recently attempted to analyze racial formation in the context of the United States and to examine the U.S. state as a "racial state"—a state that has been in part organized around the reproduction of race consciousness in its white majority.

21. C. L. R. James, *Nkrumah and the Ghana Revolution* (London: Alison and Busby, 1977), p. 58.

22. John Rex, "The Concept of Race in Sociological Theory," in Zubaida, *Race and Racialism*, p. 47. Bernard Magubane has been another consistent proponent of the centrality of conquest in the development of African consciousness. See his "A Critical Look at the Indices Used in the Study of Social Change in Colonial Africa," *Current Anthropology* (1971), p. 422.

23. Marvin Harris, *Culture, People, Nature* (New York: Thomas Crowell, 1975), pp. 440–441.

24. Oliver C. Cox, *Race Relations* (Detroit: Wayne State University Press, 1976), p. 39.

25. Neville Alexander, "Race, Ethnicity and Nationalism in Social Science in Southern Africa," paper presented at the Fifteenth Annual Congress of the Association for Sociology in Southern Africa, University of the Witwatersrand, Johannesburg, July 3, 1984, p. 5.

26. See William Mark Freund, *The Making of Contemporary Africa: The Development of African Society Since 1800* (Bloomington: Indiana University Press, 1984), p. 14; and the introduction to Peter Delius, *The Land Belongs to Us* (Berkeley: University of California Press, 1984), p. 5.

27. Shula Marks and Richard Rathbone, eds., *Industrialisation and Social Change in South Africa: African Class Formation, Culture and Consciousness, 1870-1930* (New York: Longman, 1982).

28. E. P. Thompson, *The Making of the English Working Class* (New York: Vintage Books, 1963), p. 11.

29. Marks and Rathbone, *Industrialisation*, p. 8.

30. This concise summation of Thompson's position is provided in R. M. Godsell, "The Regulation of Labour," in Robert Schrire, ed., *South Africa: Public Policy Perspectives* (Cape Town: Juta, 1982), p. 204.

31. Maurice Duverger, *The Idea of Politics* (Chicago: Gateway Edition, 1966), p. 12.

32. H. J. and R. E. Simons, *Class and Colour*, p. 235.

33. *Ibid.*, p. 134.

34. *Ibid.* Richard Sklar, in "The Contribution of Tribalism to Nationalism in Western Nigeria," *Journal of Human Relations* 8 (Spring–Summer 1960), pp. 407–418, makes a similar observation with respect to nationalism in Nigeria.

35. Shula Marks, "Toward a People's History of South Africa? Recent Developments in the Historiography of South Africa," in Raphael Samuel, ed., *People's History and Socialist Theory* (London: Routledge and Kegan Paul, 1981), p. 301.

36. Martin Legassick, "Gold, Agriculture, and Secondary Industry in South Africa, 1885–1970: From Periphery to Sub-Metropole as a Forced Labour System," in Robin Palmer and Neil Parsons, eds., *The Roots of Rural Poverty in Central and Southern Africa* (Berkeley: University of California Press, 1977), p. 175.

37. Ben Turok, "South Africa: The Search for a Strategy," in Ralph Miliband and John Saville, eds., *The Socialist Register* (London: Merlin Press, 1973), p. 343.

38. Nolutshungu, *Changing South Africa*, pp. 60–61.

39. Karl Marx, *Wage Labour and Capital* (Moscow: Progress Publishers, 1947), p. 28.

40. Wolpe, "Industrialisation and Race," p. 164.

41. For a persuasive argument in favor of the primacy of political rather than economic factors in the determination of classes, see Richard L. Sklar, "The Concept of Power in Political Economy," in Dalmas H. Nelson and Richard L. Sklar, eds., *Toward a Humanistic Science of Politics: Essays in Honor of Francis Dunham Wormuth* (Lanham, Maryland: University Press of America, 1983), pp. 179–208.

42. Eugene Victor Wolfenstein, "Race, Racism, and Racial Liberation," *Western Political Quarterly* 30, no. 1 (March 1977), p. 181.

43. Wilmot James, "The Life Trajectories of a Working Class: South Africa 1969–1981," paper presented to the Africa Seminar, Centre for African Studies, University of Cape Town, Cape Town, May 9, 1984, p. 4.

44. *Ibid.*

45. Peter Ekeh, "Colonialism and the Two Publics: A Theoretical Statement," *Comparative Studies in Society and History* 17, no. 1 (January 1975), p. 94.

46. Alessandro Triulzi, "Decolonising African History," in Samuel, *People's History*, pp. 286–297.

47. Selim Gool, *Mining Capitalism and Black Labour in the Early Industrial Period in South Africa: A Critique of the New Historiography* (Lund: Skrifter Utgivna av Ekononmisk-Historiska Foreningen, 1983), p. 10.

48. James Coleman and C. R. D. Halisi, "American Political Science and Tropical Africa: Universalism vs. Relativism," *African Studies Review* 26, no. 3/4 (September–December 1983), p. 50.

49. Wilmot Godfrey James, "From Segregation to Apartheid: Miners and Peasants in the Making of a Racial Order, South Africa, 1930–1952" (Ph.D. dissertation, University of Wisconsin-Madison, 1982), pp. 5–6.

50. Marks and Rathbone, *Industrialisation*, p. 27.

51. This was related to me by a woman to whom I gave a ride from Soweto to her place of employment in Johannesburg in December 1976.

52. Ernesto Laclau, *Politics and Ideology in Marxist Theory: Capitalism, Fascism, Populism* (London: New Left Books, 1977), p. 109.

53. *Ibid.*, p. 105.

54. Monica Wilson, "The Sotho, Venda and Tsonga," in Monica Wilson and Leonard Thompson, eds., *Oxford History of South Africa*, vol. 1 (Oxford University Press, 1969), p. 182.

55. Delius, *Land Belongs to Us*, p. 62. See also Charles van Onselen, *Chibaro, African Mine Labor in Southern Rhodesia, 1900–1933* (London: Pluto Press, 1976); and William Beinart, *The Political Economy of Pondoland, 1860–1930* (New York: Cambridge University Press, 1982).

56. Belinda Bozzoli, *The Political Nature of a Ruling Class, Capital and Ideology in South Africa 1890–1933* (London: Routledge and Kegan Paul, 1981), p. 51.

57. See Wilmot G. James, "From Segregation to Apartheid." "Modes of development" is used here, as it has been used by Richard Sklar, to "refer to the form of both economic and political organization in a given nation as well as the strategy of change adopted by national leaders."

58. C. M. Tatz, *Shadow and Substance in South Africa* (Pietermaritzburg: University of Natal Press, 1962), p. 1.

59. See Leo Kuper, "African Nationalism in South Africa, 1910–1964," in Wilson and Thompson, *Oxford History*, vol. 2.

60. Tom Lodge, *Black Politics in South Africa since 1945* (London: Longman, 1983).

61. For a discussion of Khoisan resistance that is mindful of its parallels with later centuries of African resistance against the exigencies of racial proletarianization see Shula Marks, "Khoisan Resistance to the Dutch in the Seventeenth and Eighteenth Centuries," *Journal of African Studies* 13, no. 1 (1972), pp. 55–80.

62. Bernard Makhosezwe Magubane, *The Political Economy of Race and Class in South Africa* (New York: Monthly Review Press, 1979); see in particular the chapter, "Conquest and Cultural Domination."

63. Fredrickson, *White Supremacy*, p. xii.

64. Leslie Clement Duly, "A Revisit with the Cape's Hottentot Ordinance of 1828," in Marcelle Kooy, ed., *Studies in Economics and Economic History, Essays in Honour of Professor H. M. Robertson* (Durham: Duke University Press, 1972), pp. 26–56; Susan Newton-King, "The Labor Market of the Cape Colony, 1807–28," in Shula Marks and Anthony Atmore, eds., *Economy and Society in Pre-Industrial South Africa* (London: Longman, 1980), p. 172.

PART II
The Political Economy
of Domestic Change in South Africa

5

Tsa Batho: Zonal Dynamics of Black Politics in South Africa

C. TSEHLOANE KETO

Black politics in the South Africa of the late 1980s fall into two broad categories: (1) protest and liberation politics; and (2) "co-optation" politics. Protest and liberation politics operate outside the structures of the South African apartheid state, while co-optation politics work "within the system," through the politics of the "homelands," urban councils, the coloured and Indian branches of South Africa's tricameral legislature, and local and secondary structures of decisionmaking created for blacks by officials of the white-controlled South African state. Both streams of black politics interact and impinge on the lives, hopes, and aspirations of the country's black majority, as well as its current ruling white minority.

Viewed through the prism of history, Africans have actively participated in politics since the early days of clan polities, hundreds of years before people from Europe and Asia set foot on South African soil. Emerging and militarily aggressive European settler communities from the seventeenth century onward deprived Africans of political independence and consequently removed the indigenous people from their primary role in the politics of South Africa. By the second decade of the twentieth century, white South Africans, the descendants of the settler Europeans, had assumed political primacy and taken over control of resources in areas previously controlled by Africans. The former owners of the land, the Africans, became secondary economic players as laborers, squatters, and reserve dwellers. In addition, they assumed the role of peripheral political actors who resorted to protest politics after the military struggle to retain African independence was transformed into the black struggle to acquire equality of status with whites in white-dominated polities. Liberation politics is the stage in this struggle when affirmation of black access to political power and economic resources supplants the focus on equal opportunities and "fair" treatment for blacks in white-controlled polities. Co-optation politics emerged when functionaries of the white minority government created special political dispensations for blacks, dispensations consistent with the survival of historical white supremacy.[1]

The black experience in a secondary role in politics varied among the white-controlled polities of nineteenth-century South Africa. Out of the four British colonies that eventually came together to form the Union of South Africa in 1910, only one, the Cape Colony, had offered blacks (Africans and so-called coloureds—people of mixed race) a token participatory role through a selective franchise during the nineteenth century. By 1963, even this minor peripheral role for blacks in the politics of the Cape Province had legally vanished, and the two streams of black politics—"co-optation" and "protest–liberation" politics—assumed center stage.[2]

In the past quarter-century, protest–liberation politics have utilized two strategies—a nonviolent strategy and a strategy that incorporated armed struggle. Both protest and liberation politics have attracted the attention of theorists, ranging from neoliberal descriptive analysts to neo-Marxist theorists, as well as the so-called futurists. Often these "students of South African developments" and futurology become embroiled in irreconcilable "conceptual wars" regarding the interpretation of local and national black politics in South Africa, without examining the premise on which they base their arguments. The theoretical contribution of this study is a modest one. It posits a *zonal* framework that may yield better insight into and understanding of the dynamics of black politics in South Africa, as blacks become increasingly central to future political developments.

A zonal framework of analysis, informed by an Africa-centered history, focuses attention on the increasing role of South Africa's black majority. A zonal framework approaches political dynamics through the prism of four distinct but interactive regions that will be elaborated later in this chapter. This framework replaces the "ethnic" and "tribal" interpretation of political diversity with a schema of zones that tie contemporary dynamics to historical and social factors that have created an uneven national terrain for the milieu of black politics.[3]

THE CONTEXT OF BLACK POLITICS

South Africa is inhabited by people many of whom are African and black. For the purpose of this study, the term *black* will be used to include those South Africans who are usually classified as Africans, Indians, and coloureds. Blacks currently constitute four-fifths of the population, according to the 1986 estimates for all of South Africa. Demographic specialists project that by the year 2020, 90 percent of the people of South Africa will be black. Africans made up over 90 percent of the black population in the 1980 census and most of those blacks are relatively young. This young black population constitutes a constant "restive" element for the apartheid state.[4]

The dynamics of black politics that we will discuss here will be restricted to the period following the implementation of the so-called Reform Constitution of 1983, which left the black majority in South Africa still lacking a commensurate role in the country's central policymaking process. It is this contemporary black struggle for equality that is usually called "black politics" in most of the scholarly literature. Since 1910, much of the relevant black political activity in South Africa has operated outside the political institutions of the country's official decisionmaking bodies. After 1945, South Africa's white minority-controlled political system adopted a rigorous brand of white supremacist policy called apartheid, used the device of "homeland administration," and, in 1983, created a "multicameral legislature" in order to peripheralize black political activity permanently, even for those who "worked within the system."[5]

An important contrast has emerged to distinguish the main objective of white politics from the main objective of black politics. The dominant objective of white minority politics in South Africa has been and continues to be the retention of privilege and power for whites, through the manipulation of policy to create divisions among blacks and unity among whites, in order to maintain the status quo.

The distinctly rightward shift among white voters in the elections of May 1987, the banning of seventeen antiapartheid organizations in February 1988, and the municipal elections of October 1988 demonstrated once more that white politics are still heavily influenced by the objective of white supremacy and dominated by leaders who wish to exclude the country's black and African majority from meaningful democratic rights. There is now a significant segment of white "opposition" politics that is driven by the desire to exclude blacks even further. In vivid contrast, the dominant objective in the politics of the excluded and dominated black majority, as it is expressed and articulated by its major leaders and organizations, including those that are banned and those that have operated in exile in the last quarter century, has been the bestowal of democratic rights on all South Africans regardless of race, creed, or gender.[6]

Blacks as a group have expressed overwhelming opposition to the principle of racial exclusiveness favored by the ruling white minority. Even blacks who operate within the co-optation politics of South Africa often publicly advocate the elimination of racial discrimination. The current white leaders of the minority government, at best, favor a policy of "co-optative domination" that would "reform" apartheid and retain white minority "leadership." A significant amount of academic debate has focused on defining white supremacy in the South African setting as: either (1) essentially a racial capitalist phenomenon—therefore the result of a class-based society that deftly manipulates the race issue for its own ends; or (2) a racist, atavistic structure exploiting neutral capitalism as a tool to create a race-based utopia built on permanent black subordination. We should note that the end product is the same for blacks—varying levels of exploitation, exclusion from central decisionmaking, and recurrent repression of organs of black protest.[7]

Most blacks support the goal of eliminating the current political system of white domination (as do a minority of whites, such as the groups of Afrikaners who participated in the Dakar discussions in July 1987 with a group from the ANC). Disagreements, where they exist, arise over appropriate strategies, tactics, and methods to be employed. The dynamics of black politics center on the articulation and implementation of policies and actions that would: (1) bring about fundamental change; or (2) at the least provide a viable black defensive response to the cyclical repressive acts of the white minority government before fundamental change is implemented. There are various political, economic, and ideological factors that complicate these straightforward objectives and influence the dynamics of black politics. I shall confine my discussion to the "urban–rural dichotomy" that sets the stage for understanding zonal dynamics.

Let us first consider how the dynamics of black politics in urban and rural settings have come to differ. Second, we shall discuss black political realignments in 1987 using a generalized approach. Finally, we will combine the discussion of rural and urban politics within an integrative framework of zones. That discussion will demonstrate the usefulness of a zonal approach to a study of dynamics of black politics in South Africa.[8]

The Urban Dynamics

Urbanization and industrialization in South Africa since the 1880s has created a new social milieu that is multilingual, multiracial and multiethnic. The majority of the Indian and coloured sections of the black community were already urbanized by 1946, and the African group was in the process of moving into the cities and towns in large numbers; this created a black majority of residents in every major city except Pretoria by 1951.

The African population that moved to work in the towns and in the mines created new social groupings of urbanites who were: (1) male and female residents in the townships; (2) male and female residents of "hostels"; or (3) temporary male residents of the compounds who worked as migratory laborers. Out of these groups emerged a new *Humsha* (urban-dwellers) leadership class, which joined with the petit bourgeois "elite" educated in the mission schools. These leaders spearheaded the politics of "militant integration" and the struggle for equality of status. Some black leaders who struggled to be included in the privileges of white society occasionally displayed an avid and uncritical attachment to European culture and institutions. By the late 1920s, together with the petit bourgeois *Humsha* and *Kholwa* (Christian converts) leaders, black workers had organized fledgling trade unions, raised questions about fair wages and working conditions, and began an association with radical whites who espoused anticapitalist social change objectives.[9]

When the African National Congress was founded in 1912, its *Kholwa* and *Humsha* leaders made a conscious effort to link an urban-based African political movement with rural movements and constituencies. Thus, they could address the immediate economic and social needs of an emerging and assertive urban constituency without ignoring the rural constituencies who were being impoverished.

Urban-based black leaders seeking radical integration and equality with whites after World War II ran into the stubborn opposition of the Afrikanercontrolled Nasionale Party. The Nasionale Party was seeking to protect the interests of its white constituents who were recent migrants in the urban areas, and who were also led by a petit bourgeois group that had migrated from the rural areas to the cities. The Nasionale Party, from its "government" vantage point, responded to the competition for jobs and neighborhoods in the towns by instituting a rigorous policy of segregation called apartheid, using the state as the instrument of power. Apartheid subsequently became highly visible to the Western press and the outside world for two reasons: first, the proximity of events in the towns to news reporters, photographers, and, later, TV crews; second, the increasingly frequent use of English as a medium of political communication by blacks within a multilingual setting, which made it easy for analysts to "peek" into the discussion of issues. Journalists and academics, in a long list of outstanding books and articles, have studied, emphasized, and analyzed this Anglophone phase of black South Africa's political process since the publication of Gwendolen Carter's classic neoliberal study, *South Africa: The Politics of Inequality*, in 1958. Because the book employed a "liberal" perspective, it was optimistic about meaningful change in the future. However, there was and still is a critically important dimension of black politics that is centered in the rural areas of South Africa.[10]

The Rural Dynamics

The rural areas of South Africa contain a constituency of black politics that has a revolutionary potential equal to the urban groups. Until recently, this aspect of black politics had not received the primary in-depth research it deserves, except by political activists, preservist anthropologists, and a few social historians. This is ironic since, historically, blacks in the rural areas of South Africa have suffered gross expropriation of their resources in the form of removals, stock confiscation, and naked dispossession of land. This "underdevelopment" process during the nineteenth and early twentieth centuries, which constituted "official" dispossession by white-controlled governments, continued with the 1913 land act, the act that laid the basis for allocating 13 percent of the land to Africans who made up 70 percent of the population of South Africa.

The subsequent economic development of South Africa, based on migratory labor, shifted the burden of subsistence onto the backs of rural residents who were mostly black women and *especially* African women. Yet this rural dimension of black exploitation did not attract public attention or concern by predominantly white liberal and conservative scholars of South Africa until recently. Only studies by Marxists and neo-Marxists emphasized, in a generalized fashion, the exploitative aspect of South Africa's racial capitalism. Some liberal economists noted the cheap labor factor in South Africa's industry without tracing the ultimate black female source of this economic subsidy.[11]

The exclusion of black women from political participation in the white states was consistent until the 1960s. In the Cape, during the nineteenth century, black males enjoyed limited political participation in the new organs of central decisionmaking for the colony by voting for, and theoretically standing for office as, members of the Colonial Parliament. In the course of the twentieth century, first African, then coloured male residents of the Cape Province lost these limited rights while white women acquired them. Black women never acquired such rights until the *bantustan* (residual reservations for Africans, which the minority white government later renamed "homelands") days of the 1960s. The Nasionale Party government that came into power in 1948, with the goal of dichotomizing black politics, offered Africans the homeland alternative of local government in the 1950s, based on haphazard ideas of ethnicity and territoriality. These local bodies were reclassified as "national" states, and in the 1970s some of them supposedly chose to be "independent" states. In the late 1980s, nonindependent homelands were again reclassified as "self-governing" states. The Transkei, the Ciskei, and Bophuthatswana have all experienced transformation or attempted transformation from civilian to military dictatorships since 1985, demonstrating the abject failure of the bantustan social experiment to create honest and democratic local governments for these areas.[12]

USE AND MISUSE OF ETHNICITY IN SOUTH AFRICA

Ethnic diversity has been used by South Africa's white minority to justify the denial of political rights to blacks or to grant them substitute rights within areas set aside for specific ethnic and "national" groups. In response to this official misuse of ethnicity, some urban black leaders reject any mention of ethnicity, viewing it as a return to the "dark" days of "tribalism." This is due in part to the fact that the South African government represents ethnic groups as fixed and permanent divisions of the South Africans to be accommodated in permanent political structures. While not denying the negative use of ethnicity in some parts of the world, there is another way to view ethnicity. Like families, ethnic groups can become legitimate social and cultural building blocks for a national cultural ethos. Because they are receptacles of grassroots culture and an emerging transculture of resistance, expressed most often in vernacular languages, they can provide the symbols of affirmation for collective liberation and the points of articulation for political and economic interests. In this context, ethnicity is merely the result of "objective conditions of existence, mediated by [cultural] systems of symbolic representation." Within the South African imperial state, overarching ethnic diversity is a multiethnic commonality of the black experience with repression and oppression.[13]

South Africa's bureaucrats attempt to arrest and freeze ethnic identification as permanent and thereby distort an essentially fluid historical process. A glaring example of this fixity and myth is the often-quoted leadership of Gatsha Buthelezi over 6 million Zulus—without noting the historically based nature of this "leadership" and the political differences among the Africans in Natal, including KwaZulu itself. Neither do advocates of the "6 million Zulu" myth draw a distinction between IsiZulu-speaking people (language adherents) in Natal and the Transvaal and the people of KwaZulu (territorial residents). Such nuances are usually lost even to reporters when they do not speak IsiZulu. Even Chief Minister Gatsha Buthelezi has never publicly laid claim to the "6 million Zulu" myth, but only to supporters who are members of Inkatha, the "cultural liberation" movement that he leads.

We can conclude that there are soft and firm areas of support for Buthelezi, even in KwaZulu, and that only an open political competition can isolate areas of firm support from areas of soft support. Under the current foggy social definitions, when unresolved historical conflicts between advocates of local autonomy and representatives of the KwaZulu homeland government who represent a central authority flare into violence, or when supporters of Inkatha and the UDF fight over turf, news organizations report the incidents under the amorphous rubrics of "faction fighting" and "Zulu Wars."

Equally baffling is the illogical application of ethnicity in the case of the Eastern Cape. Outside the framework of continuous change, it is not possible to explain in a logical manner why IsiXhosa-speaking inhabitants of the transposed Ciskei are entitled to a separate "nation" from the IsiXhosa-speaking inhabitants of the Transkei.[14]

Ethnic identity can have a positive and progressive role if we view ethnic groups as the building blocks for liberation during the twentieth century. When the ethnic mosaic of South Africa is viewed through the prism of historical agreements, beginning with the formation of the ANC in 1912 and supplemented by later developments, we can detect the rise of a new consciousness. The collaborative process that led to the creation of (1) trade union movements such as the Industrial and Commercial Workers' Union in the 1920s and the Congress of South African Trade Unions (COSATU) in the 1980s; (2) the Congress Alliance after World War II; and (3) the ideological underpinnings of the Black Consciousness Movement in the 1970s, has affected consciousness and self-definitions. All the above organizational developments, ideological trends, and movements set in motion new and complex levels of self-definition, identification, and cooperation in the urban and rural areas that continue to constitute a vital element in the zonal dynamics of black politics. The Freedom Charter of 1955, for example, was a self-conscious attempt to grapple with and to define a common vision of South Africanhood, and in the 1980s the charter still represents an important point of departure for grassroots debate on a variety of issues. The charter can also be viewed as a basis for self-definition, and a reference point for subsequent identification as numerous organizations adopt it in the 1980s. However, there are important segments of blacks who oppose declarations in the charter that refer to black and white rights in South Africa.

THE GENERALIZED VERSUS THE ZONAL APPROACH

Scholars have analyzed the dynamics of black politics in South Africa using a generalized approach that, among other things, identifies "moderate" and "radical" leaders or movements without factoring in the zonal context of these leaders or movements. The reader is never sure whether the "moderate" leader is a local favorite son or daughter, or a national figure whose support cuts across zones and parochial concerns. Adding a zonal approach to a research paradigm offers a fruitful method of identifying transcendent pressing issues facing South African organizations and yields a comparative insight on the relative merits of constituencies that are working for a South Africa free from apartheid. However, as an additional theoretical element in a research model, the zonal approach should be tested; it must be able to explain similarities as well as dissimilarities across zones and across time within each zone. The zonal approach should provide the reader with a prism through which to understand the crux of developments in South African black politics, within a coherent framework and over short and long periods. We will attempt this, but first we will turn to the generalized approach.

THE GENERALIZED APPROACH

There is much to be said in favor of the popular generalized approach to black politics in South Africa: it retains a conceptual unity of the whole country and reads national meaning into all developments, even if they are confined to one zone. The major weakness of this approach is that it fails to exploit the historical significance of certain zones for national political development and invites invidious analysis based solely on "ethnic differences." Equally disturbing is the faint suspicion that the premises of the generalized approach often represent unfiltered "transplants" of useful analyses regarding political phenomena from the much smaller white community to the larger and more complex black community. However, since a great deal of literature on South Africa is based on this approach, we will summarize the emerging realignments of black politics in South Africa before the banning in February 1988, in order to demonstrate the efficacy of this approach.

The realignments that are significant for the future have emerged in the last quarter-century; they have crystallized into seven types of movements that advocate fundamental change. The exiled liberation movements led by the African National Congress of South Africa, headquartered in Lusaka, Zambia, represent a constituency of black politics that is committed to the use of all necessary means, including armed struggle, to further the cause of freedom and human rights in South Africa. This external constituency of liberation politics is the most free to:

1. Articulate without fear the grievances of South Africa's oppressed majority
2. Seek various kinds of material and moral support from every potential source in the world
3. Project an "inclusivistic" vision of a future South Africa that contrasts sharply with the "exclusivistic" vision of the ruling white minority
4. Openly debate the political, educational, cultural, economic, social, and intellectual options of South Africa

This external grouping, though not unified, is extremely important to a balanced understanding of the dynamic of black politics. It also includes the remnants of the Black Consciousness Movement organizations, the Pan-Africanist Congress, the Unity Movement, and the South African Communist Party (SACP) (which is allied to the ANC though distinct from it).[15]

The internal antiapartheid movements are involved in protest and liberation politics outside the legal political framework of the South African state. They are invariably committed to a nonviolent strategy. Three types of organizations have arisen to represent this constituency:

1. Organizations that are predominantly black but encourage multiracial and multiethnic membership in both theory and practice in the struggle against the white supremacist state; the United Democratic Front is an example of this type of organization.

2. Organizations that represent black interests, are committed to multiethnic membership, and pursue a publicly stated objective of creating a nonracial society but exclude, for tactical reasons, white South Africans from membership; for example, the National Forum and the Azanian People's Organization.

3. Ethnic organizations that represent one regional group distinguished by language, culture, or history but include members of other ethnic groups. One example is Inkatha, which is dominated by IsiZulu-speaking people and identifies itself as a national "cultural liberation" movement separate from the KwaZulu homeland legal structure.[16]

The trade union movement is the third major constituency to crystallize since the illegal Durban strikes of 1973. The power and influence of black organized workers have grown, and their demands have gone beyond the bread and butter issues to a call, after 1977, for the abolition of apartheid. There are three discernible ideological constellations in the present trade union movement:

1. The Congress of South African Trade Unions, created in 1985 under the leadership of Elijah Barayi of the United Mine Workers Union: COSATU espouses a philosophical position close to that of the United Democratic Front (UDF) and encourages multiracial and multiethnic affiliates to the labor federation.
2. The Council of Trade Unions of South Africa–Azanian Confederation of Trade Unions (CUSA-AZACTU) is another labor federation founded in 1985 that reflects Black Consciousness in the trade union field.
3. The United Workers' Union of South Africa (UWUSA) was established as a brainchild of Inkatha in May 1986. Its policies and its opposition to the militancy of the other black and multiracial trade unions correlates with the policies of Inkatha.

The fourth major constituency to crystallize revolves around the rise and the sustained impact of a militant *youth movement* such as the Azanian Students' Movement (AZASM), created in 1983 to replace the Azanian Students' Organization (AZASO), which had in turn changed its name to South African National Students' Congress (SANSC). In 1987, the South African Youth Organization was created, and its policies closely parallel those of the UDF. These organizations are successors to the banned student movements that originated with the Black Consciousness–inspired student protest movement that preceded the Soweto uprising of 1976.[17]

An additional group in the struggle to dismantle apartheid is the Black-led antiapartheid church movement that finally issued the historic Kairos Document in 1985. This document supported activism by the clergy to dismantle the institutions of racial oppression in South Africa. Archbishop Desmond Tutu and Doctor Allan Boesak are highly visible members of this new movement, which has played a critical role since the banning of the activities of the UDF and other direct action groups in February 1988. The South African government continues to threaten the activities of this group.

Another important crystallization that emerged in the 1984–1987 period was the phenomenon of the localized grassroots organizations such as street committees, peoples' committees, community action groups, popular councils, and grievance committees that supported the demands articulated by the militant youth. The National Education Crisis Committee and the Detainees Parent Support Committee are examples of organizations that have become prominent.[18]

The final black groups that "officially" oppose apartheid are more problematic to characterize. These are organizations operating within the co-optative participatory framework set up by the South African state. They represent the classical co-optative politics referred to earlier. The now moribund Transkei National Independence Party and the still active Coloured Labor Party in South Africa's tricameral Parliament are prominent examples. Elected councillors in township municipal councils may fit into this category as well. Spokespersons for these groups, such as the Reverend Alan Hendrikse, argue that change in South Africa can be brought about by working from within the system in a sort of "internal constructive engagement." The apology that Hendrikse had to make to President Botha after wading into a "Whites Only" section of the Port Elizabeth beach in 1986, and the initial unceremonious dismissal of Inkatha's Natal Indaba proposals by Botha before the May election of 1987, demonstrate the "self-peripheralizing" nature of this approach for blacks in the context of the present South African political crisis.[19]

THE ZONAL APPROACH

For our purposes, liberation and protest politics since 1945 suggest four regional zones that we can use to analyze black politics between 1983 and 1987:

1. A *Southwestern zone*, anchored by the City of Cape Town and extending to the surrounding areas;
2. a *Southeastern zone*, which stretches from the Port Elizabeth area to the Natal border south of the escarpment and includes the Transkei;
3. a *Central zone*, which takes in the Northern Cape, the Transvaal Province, and the Orange Free State and is centered around Johannesburg, Welkom, Bloemfontein, and Kimberley; and
4. an *Eastern zone*, which encompasses Natal and KwaZulu and is anchored by Ulundi, Durban, Pietermaritzburg, and St. Lucia Bay.

These zones fade into one another and, in some instances, do not represent the total "geographical" area. However, each zone includes one of the four major metropolitan areas of South Africa and possesses a core area of interaction that gives character to the zonal dynamics, depending on the

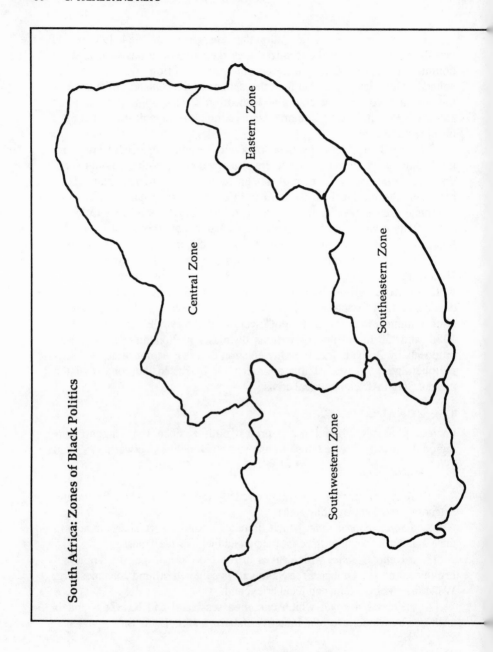

South Africa: Zones of Black Politics

relative political weight of urban and rural constituencies. In some zones, urban politics dominate the nexus of the zonal dynamics, in others it is rural politics, and in still other zones rural and urban constituencies share equal or alternating positions of leadership and initiative.[20]

We should emphasize that the zonal approach does not provide an independent paradigm but rather forces analysts to "zonalize" their investigations first and then to transzonalize their conclusions by synthesizing zonal developments. By so doing they can differentiate between the strength of transzonal organizations and the political razzle-dazzle of zonal operators. They can distinguish between organizations that provide viable national alternatives to postapartheid South Africa and opportunistic localized freelance "liberators."

The 1984–1987 Crisis

We have selected one of the four political crises in South Africa since 1945 to demonstrate the utility of the zonal approach. The three earlier crises that set the political and social stage for the crisis of 1984 to 1987 were: (1) the Defiance Campaign of 1952; (2) the Sharpeville crisis of 1960; and (3) the Soweto crisis (the uprising of the youth) of 1976. The constitutional (and liberation) crisis of 1984–1987 was dominated by the energized role of labor and the death-defying challenge of black youth in the streets. We will focus on the zonal manifestations of the crisis and examine salient political developments among blacks immediately leading up to the crisis. In addition, we will examine black responses to issues and developments during and after the crisis in each of the four zones.[21]

Although blacks protested actively in all four zones during crisis periods since 1945, culminating in the upheavals of the 1980s, we must review popular reaction in each zone within the context of the cultural and historical factors that distinguish political participation of the people in that zone.

In each zone, the formative years of Afro-European interaction influenced the nature of black political affirmation and resistance, the extent of resource dispossession, and the resulting socioeconomic alignment that became the basis for human coexistence and interaction. The social structures and formations that influenced events in earlier periods in each zone continued to impinge on black politics up to 1988. There are also elements of black politics that emerge from intrablack alignments, black–white interaction, and the relations of black groups to resources and to the environment in each zone. It has often been easy for outside scholars to gather information on the urban aspects of this socioeconomic dynamic while ignoring its rural and semirural aspects. Part of the reason is that information about the dynamics of urban black politics in places such as Soweto, and the socioeconomic setting of its residents in the Johannesburg area is easy to gather and to document.[22]

The continuing fate of the rural populace in which black women are disproportionately represented, and the tremendous economic price that has been exacted from this segment of South Africans in order to build "modernized" South Africa, often escaped the attention of scholars before the advent of the "underdevelopmentalist" approach and the concern about women. But the issue is more than economic exploitation; it is at heart a question of cultural genocide. Interestingly, South Africa's white minority government officials, in private correspondence, identify their most challenging problem not as the granting of "rights" to the urban blacks they consider "co-optable," but as their fear of the influence of "socialistic" rural blacks. These private admissions, which do not necessarily tell the whole story, present an intriguing counterpoint to prevailing conventional wisdom that views the urban areas as the main spearhead of the movement for fundamental change because of the historical urban-based activist challenge to the policies of the white minority government. That South Africa's government functionaries view urban blacks as less a future threat than are rural blacks is an aspect that requires further study and elucidation; the overthrow and attempted overthrow of black ruling classes by the "military" in both the Transkei (1987) and Bophuthatswana (1988) may mark an important refocusing of the dynamics of black politics for the next decade.[23]

For each zone the balance of influence in black politics between rural and urban constituencies, as well as the interaction between these two, is critical. The example of how quickly Winnie Mandela was able to build support in the small town of Brandfort in the Orange Free State belies statements that blacks in small towns, on farms, and in rural areas are passive and lack political interest. In fact, in these communities there is usually deep-seated resentment against racial discrimination, segregation, and ill-treatment. There is also a stream of vibrant cultural interaction with urban politics (the unintended result of the migrant labor system) that is too often unknown and unreported by the big-city presses, and inaccessible to foreign journalists because of language and distance barriers. In other words, issues of black politics are not solely urban-based, and are not always debated in an English or Afrikaans medium. Some of the most important and critical issues are debated in IsiXhosa, IsiZulu, SePedi, SeSotho, SeTswana, and "Cam-Cam."

Since we have to understand the dynamics of each zone in its own historical context, and as a response of its black people to the continuous onslaught of the white minority–controlled South African state and economy on the lives of black people, it is important to review the history of each zone.[24]

Southwestern zone. With the oldest history of black resistance to white supremacist rule, and also the longest history of black–white cooperation (no matter how uneven), the Southwestern zone is the primary home of black people classified as "coloured" in South Africa. With incidents of challenge to the unilateral imposition of European power dating back to 1510, when the Portuguese sailors accompanying Francisco D'Almeida tried to kidnap African children, this region experienced great strides in allowing black males to enjoy limited political participation during the nineteenth century. Black occupants of this zone also witnessed the gradual and relentless elimination of those political rights in the twentieth century. The Southwest is the zone where immense military struggles between black and white for the control of the land in the eighteenth and early nineteenth centuries were transformed into an immense political struggle by blacks for civil rights in the twentieth century. Out of this struggle came the first African–coloured collaboration for freedom in 1902, when Doctor Abdurahman founded the African People's Organization. Abdurahman was followed by Clements Kadalie, who founded the powerful Industrial and Commercial Workers' Union in 1919, which represented cooperation in the trade union field.

For this zone, segregation against blacks, outside the control of resources, was less severe before 1948. African males could vote before 1936, though under restrictive conditions. This was a zone where urban blacks, rural blacks on the farms, and rural blacks on scattered official residential areas called "locations" at first practiced the tedious politics of accommodation until they discarded it and chose the politics of confrontation after 1945. Countering the quasi integration of the coloureds into the white community, Africans in this area emerged as the supporters of Black Consciousness in the 1970s. Black Consciousness reoriented the thinking of the coloured community from desiring to integrate into white society to identifying with Africans.

Despite a changing kaleidoscope of leaders, movements, and philosophies, black people in this region displayed the ability and the will to organize and to resist what they considered an unjust system. From the universities of Cape Town, Fort Hare, and the Western Cape, from the townships, villages, farms, and cities, emerged black men and black women who would challenge the underlying tenets of white supremacy over and over again in this zone, where blacks speak Afrikaans, English, and IsiXhosa.[25]

Southeastern zone. Representing the original areas of intensified conflict over land with advancing European settlement in the western frontier of the AmaXhosa, black people of the Southeastern zone bore the brunt of resistance for a hundred years as they fought and lost wars to preserve their territorial independence. White military victory under the auspices of the British Empire gradually moved Africans eastward. Second only to the Southwestern zone in its early resistance to European encroachment, this zone includes the area misnamed the Transkei and, in its major cities, supported complex and sophisticated forms of resistance coordinating both the urban and the rural areas. Some of the most spectacular and innovative forms of struggle in South Africa have emerged from this region, especially from the townships of its two port cities of Port Elizabeth and East London. This was the zone where the policy of British integrationism turned into one of settler discrimination when Africans threatened to dominate the "politics" of the region. Here also, the national struggle of black unions and black political movements often found its greatest degree of support.

The Southeastern zone gave rise to some of the giants of the South African Black Resistance Movement at the national level, because rural and urban life here was one continuous form of black resistance. It is also a zone where black advocates of the need to compromise and advocates of the honor of resisting faced each other in fierce debates and created alternative movements. This is a region of diffuse sources of authority that made multiracial constellations and multiethnic alliances a necessity for political existence. The political debate is carried out in English and IsiXhosa; often both languages are used at the same time. Inhabitants of this region experienced the worst effects of centralized, arrogant, and uncompromising application of white supremacist principles after the Afrikaner-dominated Nationalist Party assumed power in 1948.

Eastern zone. The Eastern zone is an important region that differs markedly from all other zones, because it was the one that provided the setting from which a fabulous imperial and military state, KwaZulu (called "Zululand" by the British), emerged to cast its long political, social, and cultural shadow over the political developments in all lands east of the Undi River and its vicinity. The rise of this centralized black state in the nineteenth century challenged the survival of, and created the counterresponse to, self-direction and local autonomy among the fiercely independent clans among the IsiNguni-speakers. Used to a loosely enforced authority, black advocates of clan autonomy took to arms against the new controls of the regional imperial structure, whether it was led by blacks or whites.

Not only has the political and cultural dominance of KwaZulu over all of Natal continued into the twentieth century, but it has been consolidated by Gatsha Buthelezi through the Homeland Government Structure on the one hand, and the Inkatha ye Sizwe movement that Buthelezi controls on the other. Inkatha was originally an attempt to create a political refuge for former members of the banned ANC in Natal. The ANC had enjoyed massive support in Natal during the 1950s, partly influenced by the leadership role of the popular Albert Luthuli. Inkatha's close association with the dominant white business leadership in Natal follows a zonal tradition and follows also the tendency to look for answers to human problems by consolidating authority structures at the top and imposing agreed-upon solutions on the populace, rather than entrusting power to grassroots structures to solve problems using a "bottom-up" perspective.

In contrast, urban-based political coalitions of the 1980s, represented most visibly by UDF activists, advocate the empowerment of local grassroots organizations and power-sharing between the local centers and the rural-based political center of this zone. This intrablack struggle (encouraged and abetted by the embattled white minority state officials) has exacted a heavy price in black lives. Yet, in theory, all sides support the struggle for black liberation. In addition, this zone is the primary home of South Africans of Indian descent (80 percent of them live here), and their presence creates an added ethnic complexity to the struggle for local autonomy. The Eastern zone has nurtured towering visionaries of black politics such as Seme, Gumede, Gandhi, Dadoo, Champion, and Luthuli. Blacks communicate through IsiZulu and English, though some use Hindi and Tamil.[26]

Central zone. From its early history, the Central zone, one of mining, agriculture, and large human settlements, has given rise to a special balance between rulers and those who are ruled. With the advent of European imperialism and industrial mining, the temporarily wealthy interior attracted foreign economic developers, humanists, and parasites. In the last 100 years, mining and urbanization have created novel multiracial and multiethnic communities dominated by the African social presence and the European political presence. Blacks in the Central zone have envisioned and crafted into existence national multiethnic organizations, secular and religious, to meet the challenges of the new black social reality.

The growing value of land in this zone since the 1880s has exacerbated the expropriation of African lands. As white-controlled mining companies and industries created worldwide renown for themselves with their "legendary wealth," blacks who inhabited the rural sections of this zone, because their land was so close to the "dynamic economic centers," have borne the brunt of land expropriation, peasantization, and forced removals. Blacks in the countryside have been impoverished and radicalized. Blacks in the urban areas also experienced brutal suppression but not the constant, long-term, systemic deprivation and impoverishment of the men and women of the rural areas.

Black organizations, because they were invariably multiethnic, always carried a national message that addressed the concerns of all zones. Because the growing industrial complex pulled workers from all over Southern Africa, labor leaders proposed solutions and articulated a vision that applied to all of South Africa, and all of Africa in their Pan-African ideals. The African National Congress was founded in this zonal context in 1912 and has represented since then not only the creation of a political coalition but also a solemn historic agreement of Africans, of blacks, and ultimately of South Africans of all races to work for a common future. This phenomenon, which we can call the African National Congress movement, has dominated black politics to the present. This movement should not be confused with its manifestations—disagreements over tactics, criticisms of leadership style, and other day-to-day problems.

In no other zone can the vicious nature of ethnic particularism demonstrate its empty reward for a multiethnic and multiracial people. From 1983 to 1987, the organizations that were strongest in this zone grew out of the multiethnic towns, townships, and villages to carry a message of cooperation and unity for freedom and justice in such languages as SeTswana, SeSotho, SePedi, SeKgatlha, IsiNdebele, IsiZulu, IsiSwati, IsiShangane, IsiXhosa, English, Afrikaans, and "Cam-Cam."[27]

Leaders and Movements in the 1984–1987 Crisis

When we attempt to review the latest political crisis and its zonal dynamics we face two sobering problems. The first is the obvious issue of information sources and the documentation of incidents outside the urban areas, which the major foreign and domestic newspapers do not routinely pick up as news. Thus, we know more about events that took place in and around major cities such as Cape Town, Durban, East London, Port Elizabeth, Johannesburg, Pretoria, and Bloemfontein, and their satellite townships of Katlehong, Vosloorus, Tokoza, Tsakane, Kwathema, Daveyton, Duduza, Tembisa, Soweto, Langa, Nyanga, Kwamashu, New Brighton, and Zwide. Very little is reported outside these "stringer centers," unless it involves spectacular events such as the removal of the people in the northern Transvaal. This tendency creates a theoretical bias that favors an urban-based nexus for zonal dynamics.

A second and related problem has to do with the language used in these areas. Most outside reporters (including those from South Africa) are sometimes blind to words and opinions expressed through the medium of African languages. The unproven assumption is that black leaders are, of necessity, English or Afrikaans speakers, and this is a grave distortion of South Africa's reality.[28]

The 1984–1987 political crisis in South Africa grew out of the consequences of the "Reform Constitution" of 1983. The constitution gave a section of the blacks (so-called coloureds and Asians) token representation in a tricameral Parliament ultimately controlled by the white minority. The "reformed constitution" completely left out the African majority, perhaps on the assumption that the subsidiary participation of Africans in the limited local government of township councils and in the much publicized homeland arrangement adequately addressed the needs of this group for the time being. In short, the "new dispensation" kept the country's white supremacy complex intact by offering political "rights" to the two black groups (coloureds and Indians) who would become automatic "minorities" within the white constituency. The majority of blacks in these two groups rejected this offer of peripheral participation in what they considered to be "tokenist" structures, with only 20 percent of the coloureds and 30 percent of the Indians taking part in government-sponsored elections in 1984.[29]

Two significant antiapartheid alliances also emerged to oppose the new constitution in 1983. The United Democratic Front, described earlier in this chapter, came into existence during a meeting of 12,000 delegates in Cape Town in August 1983. The UDF embraced an ideological stance that was multiracial and that publicized the Freedom Charter of 1955. The National Forum Committee emerged even earlier in June 1983 when 800 delegates convened in Hammanskraal near Johannesburg. The forum issued the Azanian Manifesto in 1985 and adopted an ideological position closer to that of the Black Consciousness Movement and the Pan-Africanist Congress.[30]

However, the two most influential social catalysts for black political dynamics during this period were the black youth and the black workers. The black youth risked and laid down their lives in a continual confrontation with the police and state-supported vigilantes over a thirty-month period (September 1984 to March 1987), while the black workers, through their energized trade union movement, launched a series of labor challenges to the economic institutions of the South African state from 1985 to 1987.

A zone-by-zone analysis of the events unfolding between 1984 and 1987 still relies on impressionistic data, but certain general trends stand out. The first and possibly the most significant trend is the active participation of black workers and their organizations, and the concomitant political urgency to articulate the special status and place of the worker and the peasant in a free South Africa. The issue of the relations between capital and labor, the nature of the economic system, and the rights of the workers have now become as much forefront issues to be addressed in black politics as is the question of voting and access to facilities and opportunities for South Africa's fledgling black middle class. Although they differ in many significant ways, the Freedom Charter and the Azanian Manifesto both emphasize the importance of issues that relate to the political economy, and both affirm the centrality of social justice and worker participation.[31]

The Southwestern zone was extremely active in the political crisis of 1984 to 1987. The event that signaled major participation of activists in this zone was the march on Pollsmoor prison in 1985 to demand the release of Nelson Mandela and other political prisoners. The march led to riots and boycotts involving black and white students and other activists. The banning and restrictions of seventeen antiapartheid organizations in February 1988 led to another march in Cape Town (this time to present petitions to Parliament), led by clerics such as Nobel Laureate Anglican Archbishop Desmond Tutu and the Reverend Alan Boesak.

However, it was the Southeastern zone that produced some of the most dramatic and spectacular developments of this crisis period. First, the elimination of informers through the "necklacing" technique began in this zone. Antiapartheid activists set up viable "peoples'" committees to run the "liberated zones" in the locations and townships after the white government was rendered "blind" to these developments by the elimination of its agents and informers from the townships. Here blacks used rent strikes successfully and mounted an economic boycott around Port Elizabeth that forced white merchants to respect the impact of black consumer power.

The Central zone also initiated rent strikes, as well as boycotts of stores in the Vaal triangle area, especially around Sebokeng Township. These tactics financially strangled the operations of government-supported local bodies and those black businessmen and women notorious for their political fence-sitting.[32]

Once more, the Eastern zone proved to be the most difficult for the UDF and AZAPO to organize successfully outside the urban area, because of the alleged obstruction and intimidation by supporters of Inkatha. The KwaZulu homeland government was given powers with the belated creation of the Joint Executive Authority in November 1987. Organizations representing various urban interests that have sprung up in Natal have been forced either to negotiate a public or private truce with Inkatha and its leader, Buthelezi, or to engage in a protracted field and street struggle with Inkatha's supporters. This confrontation and the secret intervention of the minority government's security agents exacerbated conflict and violence, leading to the overseas impression of massive, ongoing "black-on-black violence" in Natal. The nature of news coverage belies the massive resistance of the countryside in this zone, resistance often triggered by the wholesale removal of Africans and the consequent systematic and deepening impoverishment of this group—a group that is already at the bottom of South Africa's economic ladder, and whose womenfolk, especially, bear the brunt of poverty.

News reporters continued to concentrate on developments in the towns, until a series of stringent states of emergency was introduced, beginning with the one of June 12, 1986. These were geared to forestall the coverage of events leading to the celebrations of the tenth anniversary of the Soweto uprising. The commemoration itself was forbidden.

Beginning on December 12 further restrictions of press reports by the government deprived analysts of any meaningful day-to-day national resistance reports in the urban and rural areas and virtually turned news reporters into agents of the government's information department.[33]

The white minority government's banning of yet another set of resistance organizations in January 1987 and February 1988, the heavy-handed tactics used to stop the tenth commemoration of the Soweto uprising in June 1986, and "The Christmas against the emergency" boycott in December 1986, testify to the political resilience of black opposition to the South African minority government. The severe measures adopted by the minority government also point to their failure to dissuade black political activists from following ANC's call to make the country ungovernable. This testifies to the effectiveness of a myriad of grassroots organizations associated with liberation movements, including groups of resisters with ideological tendencies closer to Black Consciousness and the PAC. Other grassroots opposition groups are local, with no relation to any other political group outside their zone and setting. These independent grassroots organizations were accommodated by the ANC's functional policy of "unity in action."[34]

There is a growing tendency toward radicalization in the rural population because of their growing impoverishment. This impoverishment is a result of the white minority government's policy of repression and its harshly applied policy of forced removal of blacks from white areas. The corruption among many of South Africa's black leaders in the subordinate houses of Parliament and in local authorities, and their reported disregard for human rights, have become legendary. The presence of spacious white farming areas adjacent to congested black settlements and resettlement areas in the rural areas is a continuing irritant to the black masses who bear the brunt of these policies.[35]

Inkatha continues to employ antiapartheid rhetoric but alleged actions of its supporters, directed against the youth, the UDF, and other progressive black groups, contradict its leader's public pronouncements. Finally, allied with the white business establishment in Natal and dedicated to a policy of survival, Gatsha Buthelezi and the Inkatha movement, despite its claims of impressive membership, has yet to mobilize its followers into action and to challenge the odious aspects of apartheid in a manner similar to organizations affiliated with the UDF or the National Forum. With its strategy of survival, Inkatha so far appears to have employed only carrots in its dealings with the white minority government, reserving its stick, according to some observers, for black organizations that oppose it.

The latest proposal sponsored by Inkatha, the Indaba/Natal Option, was first dismissed out of hand by the Botha regime. Botha successfully received a ringing endorsement from Natal's white electorate in May 1987, before taking another look at Inkatha's proposals and instituting the largely ceremonial Joint KwaZulu-Natal Authority in November 1987. Given the current rightward shift of white politics, it is difficult to see why the government would wish to make major concessions to an organization that will not mount a serious threat against the apartheid state.

Inkatha may not, strictly speaking, qualify to be included among the antiapartheid forces in South Africa, though its rhetoric and posture have always been essentially antiapartheid. What is more significant is that the rural nexus at Ulundi still controls the outlying urban areas of the Eastern zone and, under the circumstances, democratic formations that will empower the village and the town vis-à-vis the power of Ulundi and Pietermaritzburg face an uphill battle in the future of KwaZulu and Natal at this time.[36]

THE FUTURE OF BLACK LIBERATION POLITICS

The zonal dynamics of black liberation politics in South Africa have been affected by the imprisonment of UDF leaders since June 1986 and will certainly be affected by the banning of the seventeen antiapartheid organizations in February 1988 (most of which have been mentioned earlier in this discussion). Some innovative people's democratic structures have been dismantled by repression, others survive, and new ones will arise to continue the struggle and to sustain the spirit of resistance that lives on among the people in the form of a culture of resistance.

An important group of the political leadership of the antiapartheid movement and liberation politics has emerged from the educated elite, comparable to what Gramsci calls "organic intellectuals." This group has become the prime target for recruitment by the minority regime in South Africa in order to make co-optative domination operational. These black leaders and "intellectual workers" are also targeted by those local and foreign business interests who wish to alienate the middle class from the rest of the blacks. It is this group of black South Africans who could assist Anglo-American chairman Gavin Relly in the creation of a "good multiracial oligarchy" to control the country for the primary benefit of business interests. Such a co-opted black leadership would also dovetail with the goal of conservative administrations in the United States to create a black middle class, committed to "free enterprise" and willing to support U.S. economic and "globalist" interests in Southern Africa, as does the current minority government in South Africa. However, the pace, direction, and nature of South Africa's protest and liberation politics after 1983 made co-optation of these groups difficult, because a sizable number of them identified with the objectives of the black workers and the black youth who challenged the apartheid state between 1984 and 1987.

Another significant group of black leaders reemerged out of the new and independent grassroots community organizations of the 1980s, whether these organizations were associated with or independent of national liberation movements. The strength of this leadership cadre was enhanced by its ability to operate successfully without the glare of press publicity.[37]

The dilemma facing the minority government is that in order to lure enough middle-class blacks, whites who control South Africa's political and social system have to change the basic *racial class nature* of the system and make its distribution of benefits "multiracial." That development, by diverting long-held resources from white constituents, would destroy the present regime's strong political base of support in critical segments of the white minority constituency. Since the authority of the state rests squarely on continued "public" support of racism, any attempt to offer "enticing" benefits to the black middle class alters the politics of South Africa as we know it today. Any such leftward development is very unlikely in the near future, especially after the election of May 6, 1987 and subsequent by-elections, which signaled a significant rightward shift in the white electorate.[38]

On the black side of the equation, the attainment of autonomy and the reacquisition of African land lost during the military conquests of the nineteenth century are clear objectives for blacks in the rural areas of South Africa, where there are not the sources of cultural confusion that sometimes bedevil the social objectives of urban black politics. In order to blunt a potential ground swell of black political assertiveness and rural–urban collaboration in the early 1950s and to bifurcate black politics into disconnected urban and rural movements, the white minority government of South Africa decided to restore secondary political functions to traditional rulers. Complaisant "chiefs" became the linchpin of the "Bantu Authority" system. Given the rising level of protest activity in the urban areas, and militant black resistance to government policies at that time, the white minority government also sought ways to extract from the rural communities, or to contain, progressive elements among the traditional elite, such as Albert Luthuli in Natal and Dalindyebo Sabata in the Transkei. Accommodationists such as Kaiser Matanzima of the Transkei stepped in and assumed the new peripheral political roles offered within the homeland system.

As if to disprove the much publicized apathy of the rural areas, serious challenges to the authority of the South African government occurred in the Eastern Transkei and the Northern Transvaal in the 1950s and 1960s. Additionally, the weakness of the secondary political edifice has been demonstrated by the coups of 1987 in the Transkei and the attempted coup of 1988 in Bophuthatswana.[39]

After 1983, a new agenda of black politics in South Africa appeared, despite fluctuating fortunes of various leaders and organizations. The first clear objective is the attainment of majority rule, which at minimum means an effective black voice in government affairs. The second publicized objective is the release and empowerment of political prisoners (such as Nelson Mandela), coupled with the legal recognition of the ANC, the PAC, and other organizations. The third and final objective of black politics is the elimination of the homeland option (as it currently stands) with its implication for black peripheralization or the possible repartitioning of South Africa.[40]

Within the black communities of South Africa at home and abroad, the major debate is over strategy and tactics rather than over the goal of political and personal freedom. Even the most ardent "homeland leader" (when cornered off the record) admits that the current system is a necessary evil and not a positive good. The homelands, these leaders argue, are the best that can be accomplished at this time. None agrees with the implied partition of South

Africa under current circumstances, none accepts a permanent inferior role for Africans, and most admit privately that they are often "frustrated by the Boers." This may not be operationally significant for liberation politics at present, but it does suggest a soft spot in the support of the apartheid state and a basic lack of black ideological identification with the current system. We can characterize the rationale of some homeland leaders as opportunistic, but they will argue that their policies are pragmatic.

Arguments concerning the efficacy of moral persuasion versus protest, petitions versus demonstrations, and boycotts and all the foregoing versus armed struggle usually center on the questions of feasibility and the pragmatic considerations of liberation movements outside the country. Similarly, black leaders inside South Africa—such as Desmond Tutu, Nthato Motlana, and Alan Boesak—publicly advocate nonviolent resistance: two of these three leaders are affiliated with churches.

However, the publicly stated major goal of all black political movements is to create a society free from racism, a society that will address the issues of social justice either through a welfare state, a socialist economy, or a mixed economy. Together with white organizations, and individuals and groups opposed to the racist and exploitative nature of South African institutions, black organizations represent an antiapartheid consensus of the *majority* of South Africans.

Although the antiapartheid majority has no current political clout to implement new policies, these South Africans are opposed to the ruling regime and its policies. The political nuances within this South African majority are what a zonal dynamics approach seeks to elucidate. In the future, it may be necessary for analysts to shed the generalist approach to the study of South African politics and to come to terms with the zonal dynamics of black politics in South Africa, because these dynamics will set the stage for the "fire next time."[41]

The zonal realignments alert us to expect differing responses from various regions based on their long history of struggle and to respect the diverse methods by which people often participate in the struggle for change. To appreciate this diversity, we have to understand the traditional democratic structures that governed village life in most of precolonial South Africa and the transformation of these traditions into the new grassroots committees. The nature of the "traditional constitutions" and their philosophies is enshrined in the values of *Batho\Ubuntu*, expressed in the languages of the people of South Africa. The left-wing ideologies that have become popular share similar elements with those earlier values. But the traditional ready-made cultural institutions that embody the symbols of resistance have yet to be fully exploited and publicly integrated into the people's struggle for liberation as effectively as was done in the days before the banning of the ANC and the PAC.[42]

South Africa's black youth and workers have called for fundamental change to apartheid and racial capitalism and have supported this demand with boycotts, strikes, and even their lives. The privileged white ruling classes have found it difficult to yield on the issues of significant political participation without endangering their monopoly of control over political and economic institutions of the country. The white electorate endorsed this essentially white supremacist position in the May 1987 elections. White South Africa dreams of a constitutional compromise that will maintain white hegemonic control over politics, economic resources, and culture through a process it calls "evolutionary change." So far, this slow-paced "reform" program has radicalized more blacks and, as the circle of confrontation and repression continues to expand, more blacks and some whites are drawn to support the pursuit of liberation for the *control* of the state.[43]

Some serious reservations should be made concerning the published literature on South African politics. Popular analyses of black politics constantly repeat the mistakes that were made in analyzing the struggle for Zimbabwe. Despite the Zimbabwe example, many analysts fail to recognize the central role of African cultural symbols of resistance in the struggle for liberation. In the case of Zimbabwe, they neglected to examine the central role of *Nehanda*, the spirit medium, during the fourteen-year *Chimurenga* (the liberation war). The strength of the Zimbabwe African National Union-Patriotic Front (ZANU-PF) in the countryside in its struggle against the Smith regime was based in large part on its ability to identify itself with these powerful cultural symbols of resistance. Although the Zimbabwe African People's Union-Patriotic Front (ZAPU-PF) had a well-equipped and disciplined army, its activists did not infiltrate as large an area of the countryside with the cultural symbols of resistance as did ZANU-PF. Many analysts missed this phenomenon as it happened and thereby failed to realize that a massive victory for ZANU-PF was a foregone conclusion months before the election of 1980.[44]

A great deal of discussion has appeared in the literature on South Africa about the social contradictions inherent in having the black petite bourgeoisie as leaders of black resistance. Yet, resistance, accommodation, and social contradictions can be found in every society, with only the degrees of contradiction and commitment to social change differing. Cabral's call for the national bourgeoisie of Guinea–Bissau to commit "class suicide" and to identify with the struggle of the masses applies to South Africa as well. Out of this continued effort to bring about fundamental change would emerge a "people's culture of struggle," but this "culture of struggle" has to reject both the symbols of success and the symbols of legitimacy adopted by South Africa's ruling class. During South Africa's political crisis of the 1980s, clear indications of black commitment to fundamental change rather than reform emerged. But the progressive African symbols of cultural resistance have yet to be successfully merged with liberation politics outside the Southeastern zone.[45]

Another special problem that seems to be neglected has been the confusing role of the Christian church in the struggle against apartheid before the publication of the Kairos Document in 1985, and the prominence of church-based leaders in the struggle against apartheid. In the past, the Christian church as a whole has been divided between support and opposition to apartheid and has been slow to embrace fundamental change for South Africa. This vacillation engendered confusion of objectives and confusion of cultural identity down the line. People often wondered whether the struggle in South Africa was to create another version of a Christian South Africa, or a truly free South Africa. This issue becomes critical because the current minority government also employs Christian cultural symbols to justify its power and its hegemonic vision of a "just" South African state.[46]

The failure of urban-based activists to capture the cultural symbols of resistance in the countryside may explain why Buthelezi can successfully merge a zonal-based culture of resistance in rhetoric and exploit the potential support from the countryside, while some narrow-minded urban-based leaders are quick to denigrate these powerful symbols of cultural resistance as "backward." This was not always the case. We should note in this regard that the national leadership appeal of a Nelson Rolihlahla Mandela and of an Albert Luthuli was always partly based on combining the twin symbols of resistance: (1) the appeal of the modern ANC; and (2) the historical appeal to the symbols of cultural resistance among the rural grass roots. (The late Dalindyebo Sabata embodied a similar twin appeal.) We should also note that Oliver Tambo, president of the ANC, has often been criticized as a "conservative" by Eurocentric "radical" analysts. These analysts do not appreciate his respect for cultural symbols of resistance and his intimate knowledge of the awesome power for change that can be generated when the symbols of resistance from the town are combined with the symbols of resistance from the countryside to create a "culture of struggle" that bridges the bifurcation. For, in the final analysis, it is identification through culture and history that leads individuals to sacrifice themselves for the vision of future freedom for a people, not subscription to rampant individualism that often facilitates co-optation for personal gain.[47]

Whether one employs the Marxist or liberal paradigm to explain the current South African crisis, we must emphasize the independent intellectual and cultural variables of black politics in South Africa, which can only make sense within a context of zonal dynamics. Otherwise, it is difficult to explain recent political developments in places such as Kwandebele, Bophuthatswana, and Transkei, where the old white government–supported leadership has recently been discredited by rampart corruption and "coups." It is equally impossible to explain the ongoing personal sacrifices of many blacks at home and in exile who are dedicated to the creation of a truly free South Africa. We should note that both the Freedom Charter and the Azanian Manifesto implicitly support transzonal unity and call for social justice in the political economy.

Observations of developments in the four zones in this study bring out conclusions that demonstrate the connective interdependence of a comprehensive approach with a zonal approach in analyzing the dynamics of black politics in the transition phase of the 1980s.[48] The zonal approach also allows us to pinpoint some major changes in the composition of the antiapartheid elements, and shifts in the support base for change, among blacks.

For example, during the crises of the 1950s and the 1960s, organized hostel residents supported protest and resistance to apartheid, but during the crises of the 1970s and 1980s, some of the hostel dwellers in the Southwestern, Eastern, and Central zones became part of a "reactionary vigilante" or *impi* element. Whether this was due to their isolation from township politics or because the organizers of protest looked upon them as unimportant or peripheral may be difficult to gauge with the insufficient information at hand. Yet, this same class of people has been successfully organized by clusters of trade unions such as those in COSATU and CUSA. Whatever the final explanation of this unfortunate turn of events, it demonstrates an important change in the relationship between hostel dweller and township dweller since the ANC and kindred organizations were banned from legal operation in 1960.

During the crises of the 1980s, the Southeastern zone presented a unique cooperation of rural and urban constituencies, while the Central, Southwestern, and Eastern zones experienced conflicts among "vigilantes," *impis*, and the young "comrades," which provided a buffer of diffusion for the South African apartheid state. Police instigation is not enough to explain why hostel dwellers in Soweto were never recruited into liberation politics while successful organizational work was done with the same group by the new trade unions. More research work needs to be done to pinpoint the underlying causes of this phenomenon. Did the young "comrades" ignore cultural symbols among a people still wedded to age-grade classification of society regarding rights, privileges, and responsibilities? Obviously, in the case of Natal, the role of Inkatha alone, or the alleged lack of consciousness among the hostel dwellers, does not fully explain this new and disturbing factional phenomenon that divides the worker-peasant from the worker.[49]

We have indicated that the dynamics of black politics in South Africa are influenced by the wide variety of population, tradition, culture, and history in the four zones of South Africa. South African politics is indeed complex because of the national issues involved and the ways these issues are affected by zonal context. But we have also indicated the unifying influence of mining, industrialization, politicization, and the urban experience. To all this we should add the vast substratum of African cultural norms leavened by the new experiential dynamics and the "coloured" cultural contribution in the Southwestern zone. (We should also add the varying impact of the European cultural input in all zones to get the full picture, but in this article we have purposely restricted ourselves to blacks and the dynamics of their politics.)

This picture of human and cultural diversity should underline the need for political and social movements that are *transzonal*, integrative, and transformative in order to be positive influences at the national level. Zonal organizations and movements, no matter how impressive their membership and charismatic their leadership, can play a positive transformative role for a free South Africa only if they are *part* of a national transzonal alliance. These transformative and transzonal movements must also act as an elastic social cement that can embrace all the constituent peoples of South Africa. The transzonal organization that had such a broad base within South Africa in 1987 was the United Democratic Front, followed closely by the organizations of the Black Consciousness Movement, such as the National Forum. Among banned organizations, the ANC is clearly the most transzonal movement, with significant levels of support from all zones, all races, and all ethnic groups. Elements of the Black Consciousness Movement and the reduced PAC represent the other potential transzonal entities.

The rightward shift of white politics that occurred after the May 6, 1987 election may retard the "lebanonization" of black South Africans that "separate development" has nourished in the last two decades. The emergence of such zonal "strongmen" in the homelands will be the hallmark of a country deteriorating into a form of warlord politics. The future of South Africa may yet depend on the direction and dynamic of black politics moving away from the "lebanonization phenomenon" in the coming decade.[50]

Further, any long-term challenge to the apartheid state through black politics will need a viable and independent cultural underpinning now that majority rule, rather than reform and civil rights, has become the priority of black politics. Transzonal leaders and organizations that will integrate different parts of the country as they transform certain segments and institutions in society are now urgently needed in internal activist roles more than ever. Given the zonal peculiarities of South Africa, the political achievements of the ANC as the premier transzonal integrative and transformative movement should be appreciated. Meeting the growing needs of the urbanized masses and relieving the acute suffering of the folk in the countryside—the vision that was incorporated into the consciousness of the ANC at its formation—should once again be placed high on the agenda of priorities for liberation politics. Without the support of, and sensitivity to, the needs of the town and the countryside in the various zones, there is little hope for a sustainable fundamental change in South Africa in the foreseeable future. Rural–urban bifurcation and the absence of a strong transzonal leadership on the ground only guarantee a painful and prolonged fundamental crisis.[51]

NOTES

1. Edward Roux, *Time Longer Than Rope: A History of the Black Man's Struggle For Freedom in South Africa*, 2d ed. (Madison: University of Wisconsin Press, 1964), pp. 45–77; Sam C. Nolutshungu, *Changing South Africa: Political Considerations* (Manchester: Manchester University Press, 1982), pp. 1–6; Motsoko Pheko, *Apartheid: The Story of a Dispossessed People*, 2d rev. ed. (London: Marram Books, 1984), pp. 1–10; Thomas Karis, "Black Politics: The Road to Revolution," in Mark A. Uhlig, ed., *Apartheid in Crisis* (New York: Vintage Books, 1986), pp. 113–148; Alan C. Isaak, *Scope and Methods of Political Science: An Introduction to the Methodology of Political Inquiry*, rev. ed. (Homewood, Ill.: Dorsey Press, 1975), pp. 16–19.

2. Tom Lodge, *Black Politics in South Africa Since 1945* (London and New York: Longman, 1983), pp. viii–ix; D. A. Kotze, *African Politics in South Africa 1964–1974: Parties and Issues* (New York: St. Martin's Press, 1975), pp. 1–23, 77–98.

3. The political culture that will survive into the twenty-first century will be one embraced by the majority of the people of South Africa. Pheko, *Apartheid*, pp. 156–159; F. Van Zyl Slabert, *The Last White Parliament* (London: Sidgwick and Jackson, 1986), pp. 144–174; Martin Legassick, "South Africa in Crisis: What Route to Democracy?" *African Affairs* 84 (October 1985), pp. 587–603; Tom Lodge, "The African National Congress in South Africa, 1976–1983: Guerrilla War and Armed Propaganda," *Journal of Contemporary African Studies* 3, no. 1/2 (1983–1984), pp. 153–180. While recognizing the contributions of European–South Africans and Asian–South Africans, this framework emphasizes the central importance of African aspirations and adopts a world view that affirms and emphasizes the special role of an Africanized political culture for South Africa.

4. Alison Todes and Vanessa Watson, "Local Government Reform, Urban Crisis and Development in South Africa," *Geoforum* 17, no. 2 (1986), pp. 251-266; Philip Frankel, "Political Culture and Revolution in Soweto," *Journal of Politics* 43 (August 1981), pp. 831–849; Baruch Hirson, *Year of Fire, Year of Ash: The Soweto Revolt: Roots of a Revolution?* (London: Zed, 1979), pp. 3–9.

5. Nolutshungu, *Changing South Africa*, pp. 116–143; Pheko, *Apartheid*, pp. 77–90, 145–159; J. Gus Liebenow, *African Politics: Crisis and Challenges* (Bloomington and Indianapolis: Indiana University Press, 1986), pp. 4, 7–11, 37–44.

6. Karis, "Black Politics," pp. 144–147.

7. John S. Saul and Stephen Gelb provide an informed Marxist analysis in "The Crisis in South Africa: Class Defense, Class Revolution," *Monthly Review* 33 (July–August 1981), pp. 9–44. Bernard Makhosezwe Magubane's presentation is illuminating in *The Political Economy of Race and Class in South Africa* (New York and London: Monthly Review Press, 1979), pp. 258–

330. Ben Turok posed important theoretical questions in *Strategic Problems in South Africa's Liberation Struggle: A Critical Analysis* (Richmond, B.C., Canada: LSM Information Press, 1974), pp. 7–8.

8. Karis, "Black Politics", p. 146.

9. Saul and Gelb, "Crisis in South Africa," pp. 63–83, 91–93; David Yudelman and Alan Jeeves, "New Labour Frontiers for Old: Black Migrants to the South African Gold Mines, 1920–85," *Journal of Southern African Studies* 13 (October 1986), pp. 104–124; Jordan Ngubane, "South Africa's Race Crisis: A Conflict of Minds," in Heribert Adam, ed., *South Africa: Sociological Perspectives* (London: Oxford University Press, 1971), pp. 11–16. Rural residents become *Abantu abasemakhaya* ("people of home").

10. Saul and Gelb, "Crisis in South Africa," pp. 92–94; Jill Natrass, *The Dynamics of Urbanization in South Africa,* Development Studies Unit, Working Paper No. 2 (Durban: Centre for Applied Social Science, University of Natal, 1983), pp. 8–15; Gwendolen Carter, *The Politics of Inequality: South Africa Since 1948* (London: Thomas and Hudson; New York: Praeger, 1958).

11. Saul and Gelb, "Crisis in South Africa," pp. 94–97; Jenna Marichild, "Fighting with Bare Hands: South Africa's Homeland Policy Kills," *Commonweal* 113 (February 28, 1986), pp. 104–107; Julie Frederikse, *South Africa: A Different Kind of War* (Johannesburg: Ravan Press, 1986), pp. 176–177; Francis Wilson, "Mineral Wealth, Rural Poverty," *Optima* 33, no. 1 (1985), pp. 25–28; Cheryl L. Poinsette, "Black Women Under Apartheid: An Introduction," *Harvard Women's Law Journal* 8 (Spring 1985), pp. 93-119; James North, *Freedom Rising* (New York: Macmillan, 1985), p. 170; William Beinart and Colin Bundy, eds., *Hidden Struggles in Rural South Africa: Politics and Popular Movements in the Transkei and the Eastern Cape 1890–1930* (Los Angeles and Berkeley: University of California Press, 1987). (These struggles may have been "hidden" to the Anglophone world, but they were always known to the Africans who lived through them. The thrust of Beinart and Bundy's book is another exercise in Eurocentric hegemony.)

12. The multiethnic, multiclass broad base of the political struggle in South Africa is cogently argued by John D. Brewer in "Black Protest in South Africa's Crisis: A Comment on Legassick," *African Affairs* 85 (April 1986), pp. 283–294, and in North, *Freedom Rising,* pp. 169–196. However, it is important to emphasize that the 1912 Convention of Unity at Bloemfontein, which created the South African Native National Congress, later to be known as the African National Congress, provided a mechanism to represent rural as well as urban constituencies of all ethnic groups by electing as honorary presidents King Lerotholi of colonial Lesotho (Basutoland Protectorate) and the queen regent of colonial Swaziland, Indlovukati Nabotsebeni. The continuing participation of such "historical" rural leaders within South Africa itself would become impossible after 1923, when the Smuts white minority government barred "chiefs" from belonging to political organizations. From its beginnings, therefore, the ANC emphasized its commitment to a multiethnic as well as a rural–urban constituency. The participation of rural leaders from the historical and traditional elite in the ANC continued into the postwar period, as the examples of Albert Luthuli from Natal in the 1950s and

Dalindyebo Sabata from the Transkei in the 1980s concretely demonstrate. (Subsequently, the ANC expanded its scope to a multiracial constituency in the generation after 1950.)

13. Govan Mbeki, *South Africa: The Peasants' Revolt* (Hammondsworth, England: Penguin Books, 1964), pp. 111–134; Liebenow, *African Politics*, p. 54.

14. The name Transkei (Latin: *Trans* = across) and Ciskei (Latin: *cis* = this side) are based on a Eurocentric perspective. The point of reference for Transkei is Cape Town and the west rather than the African areas east of the Kei River. To affirm themselves, the people in the "Transkei" should at least transpose the names. See Brian M. du Toit, "Introduction," R. C. Adams, "The Coloureds of South Africa," and Wilf Nussey, "The Future of Ethnicity in Southern Africa," in Brian M. du Toit, ed., *Ethnicity in Modern Africa*, Westview Special Studies on Africa (Boulder, Colo.: Westview Press, 1978), pp. 1–11, 253–270, 282–301. Also see Archie Mafeje, "The Ideology of Tribalism," *Journal of Modern African Studies* 9 (August 1971), pp. 253–261; Peter C. W. Gutkind, ed., *The Passing of Tribal Man in Africa* (Leiden: E. J. Brill, 1970); and Liebenow, *African Politics*, pp. 50–67.

15. Andrew Prior, "South African Exile Politics: A Case Study of the African National Congress and the South African Communist Party," *Journal of Contemporary African Studies* 3 (October 1983–1984), pp. 181–196; Robert Fatton, Jr., *Black Consciousness in South Africa: The Dialectics of Ideological Resistance to White Supremacy* (Albany: State University of New York Press, 1986), pp. 63–80; "The African National Congress of South Africa: The Limitations of a Revolutionary Strategy," *Canadian Journal of African Studies* 18, no. 3 (1984), pp. 593–608; "Rejoinder" by Thabo Mbeki of the ANC, pp. 609-612; "South Africa: The ANC," *Africa Confidential* 27, no. 25 (December 10, 1986), pp. 1–4.

16. Mokubung Nkomo, *Student Culture and Activism in Black South African Universities: The Roots of Resistance* (Westport and London: Greenwood Press, 1984); Steven MacDonald, "A Guide to Black Politics in South Africa," *CSIS Africa Notes* 36 (November 5, 1984), pp. 1–7; "Unionists Form Historic Confederation," *Africa News* (December 16, 1985), pp. 5-6; "South Africa: The U.D.F.," *Africa Confidential* 28, no. 2 (January 21, 1987), pp. 4–6; "South Africa: Inkatha," *Africa Confidential* 28, no. 1 (January 7, 1987), pp. 2–3.

17. Pheko, *Apartheid*, pp. 165–170; Fatton, *Black Consciousness*, pp. 99–102.

18. Steven Mufson, "The Fall of the Front," *New Republic* (March 23, 1987), p. 19.

19. Kai Nelson, "South Africa: The Choice Between Reform and Revolution," *The Philosophical Forum* 18, no. 2/3 (Winter–Spring 1986–1987), pp. 228–236; Kotze, *African Politics*, pp. 144–187.

20. G. Carter Bentley, "Ethnicity and Practice," *Comparative Studies in Society and History* 29, no. 1 (1987), pp. 24–27.

21. In another historical study, I have divided South Africa south of the Zambezi River into eight historical zones based on issues affecting resources,

geography, history, and culture. South Africa's current black politics makes sense only when viewed from a perspective that integrates history and geographic regions into zones. After designating zones based on historical and cultural criteria, it also became clear that each zone enclosed one of the four major metropolitan industrial axes: (1) Johannesburg-Kimberley-Welkom in the Central zone; (2) Pietermaritzburg-Pinetown-Durban in the Eastern zone; (3) Port Elizabeth-East London-Uitenhage in the Southeastern zone; and (4) Cape Town and environs in the Southwestern zone.

22. South African Council of Churches and South African Catholic Bishops Conference, *Relocations: The Churches' Report on Forced Removals* (Johannesburg: SACC and SACBC, 1984), pp. 4–62; P. W. Cunningham, "Trade Unions and Politics in South Africa," *South African Journal of Sociology* 16, no. 2 (1986), pp. 43–48; Ben Roberts, "Black Trade Unionism: A Growing Force in South African Industrial Relations," *South Africa International* 13, no. 4 (1983), pp. 290-298; Dan Ncube, *The Influence of Apartheid and Capitalism on the Development of Black Trade Unions in South Africa* (Johannesburg: Skotaville Press, 1985), especially pp. 1–91; David Lewis, "Trade Unions and the Political Struggle," *The Philosophical Forum* 18, no. 2/3 (Winter–Spring 1986–1987), pp. 214–220; "South Africa: Black Consciousness," *African Confidential* 28, no. 3, (February 4, 1987), pp. 5–6; MacDonald, "Guide to Black Politics", pp. 8–9.

23. See Eddie Koch, "Without Visible Means of Subsistence: Slumyard Culture in Johannesburg 1918-1940," in Belinda Bozzoli, ed., *Town and Countryside in the Transvaal: Capitalist Penetration and Popular Response*, History Workshop 2 (Johannesburg: Ravan Press, 1981), pp. 151–175, and Kevin Shilington, "The Impact of the Diamond Discoverers on the Kimberley Hinterland: Class Formation, Colonialism and Resistance Among the Tlhaping of Griqualand West in the 1870s," in Shula Marks and Richard Rathbone, eds., *Industrialisation and Social Change in South Africa: African Class Formation, Culture and Consciousness 1870-1930* (New York: Longman, 1982), pp. 99–118. The work of Charles Van Onselen in *Studies in the Social and Economic History of the Witwatersrand 1886-1914*, 2 vols. (New York: Longman, 1982) also focuses on this phenomenon.

24. Neville Alexander, "Aspects of Non-Collaboration in the Western Cape 1943-1963," *Social Dynamics (Rondebosch)* 12, no. 1 (1986), pp. 1–4; R. E. Van der Ross, *Coloured Viewpoint: A Series of Articles in the Cape Times 1958-1965*, compiled by J. L. Hattingh and H. C. Bredekamp (Bellville: Western Cape Institute for Historical Research, 1984).

25. R. L. Cope, "Political Power Within the Zulu Kingdom and the Coronation Laws of 1873," *Journal of Natal and Zulu History* 8 (1985), pp. 11–31; Stuart Romm, "Political Conflict, Role Differentiation and State Formation: A Case Study of the Zulus," *Social Science Information* 25, no. 3 (1986), pp. 607–645; Molefe, "Buthelezi: The Politics of Reformism," *African Communist* 104 (1986), pp. 41–49; John Kane Berman, "Inkatha: The Paradox of South African Politics," *Optima* 30, no. 3 (1982), pp. 142–177.

26. Tore Jansen, "A Language of Sophiatown, Alexandra and Soweto" (Afrikaans-based creole), *York Papers in Linguistics* 11 (1984), pp. 167–180.

The relevant studies would certainly include Van Onselen, *Studies in Social and Economic History*, 2 vols.; Bozzoli, *Town and Countryside*; and Marks and Rathbone, *Industrialisation*.

27. Frederikse, *South Africa*, p. 176. "Cam-Cam" is a changing lingua franca of urban black youth in places such as Soweto. It is derived from a potpourri of African and European languages.

28. Along with its neo-Marxist orientation, a new revisionist school of South African history gives attention to rural development, especially the development/underdevelopment theories. See Belinda Bozzoli, "Introduction: History, Experience and Culture," in Bozzoli, *Town and Countryside*, pp. 1–47. Marks and Rathbone's *Industrialisation* is another example of this genre. See also J. E. Spence, "South Africa: Between Reform and Retrenchment," *World Today* 40 (November 1984), p. 472; Barry Streek, "Apartheid Under Siege," *Africa Report* (January–February 1985), pp. 54–55; and Johnson, *How Long Will South Africa Survive?* (London and New York: Oxford University Press, 1977), pp. 191–194, 196–200.

29. Pheko, *Apartheid*, pp. 181–183; Brian Lapping, *Apartheid: A History* (London: Grafton Books, 1980), pp. 171–176.

30. Karis, "Black Politics," pp. 127–129.

31. Glenn Adler, "The March Stay-Aways in Port Elizabeth and Uitenhage," *South African Labour Bulletin* 11, no. 1 (1985), pp. 86–120; Philip Black, "Boycott Strategies in the Eastern Cape," *South Africa International* 17 (July 1986), pp. 32–37; Mufson, "Fall of the Front," pp. 18–19; Lapping, *Apartheid*, pp. 173–174; Karis, "Black Politics," pp. 128–130.

32. Clifton C. Crais, "Gentry and Labour in Three Eastern Cape Districts, 1820–1865," *South African Historical Journal* 18 (1986), pp. 125–146. See Colin Bundy's *The Rise and Fall of the South African Peasantry* (Berkeley and Los Angeles: University of California Press, 1979), and Beinart and Bundy, *Hidden Struggles*.

33. Karis, "Black Politics," pp. 130–135; Lapping, *Apartheid*, pp. 173–175, 182; Nielsen, "Reform and Revolutions," p. 227.

34. Marichild, "Fighting With Bare Hands," pp. 104–167; *Human Rights in the Homelands: South Africa's Delegation of Repression* [...the Political Role of Homeland Chiefs] (New York: Fund for Free Expression, 1984); Lapping, *Apartheid*, pp. 174–175; Fatton, *Black Consciousness*, pp. 139–140.

35. William Finnegan, "A Reporter at Large: Getting the Story," *New Yorker* (July 13, 1987), pp. 31–41.

36. Ari Sitas, "From Grassroots Control to Democracy: A Case Study of the Impact of Trade Unionism on Migrant Workers' Cultural Formation on the East Rand," *Social Dynamics* 11, no. 1 (1985), pp. 32–43. Gavin Relly is quoted in Joseph Lelyveld, *Move Your Shadow: South Africa, Black and White* (New York: Times Books, 1985), p. 234, and in Brewer, "Black Protest," pp. 283–284.

37. Brewer, "Black Protest," pp. 290–294.

38. Bentley, "Ethnicity and Practice," pp. 24–27.

39. Mufson, "Fall of the Front," p. 17.

40. Berman, "Inkatha," pp. 174–176; Karis, "Black Politics," pp. 135, 142–143; Lapping, *Apartheid*, pp. 179–180; Richard Leonard, *South Africa at War: White Power and the Crisis in Southern Africa* (Westport, Conn.: Lawrence Hill and Company, 1983), pp. 48–51; Roger Southall, "A Note On Inkatha Membership," *African Affairs* 85 (October 1986), pp. 574–578, 586–588; Lodge, *Black Politics*, pp. 355–356.

41. Mufson, "Fall of the Front," pp. 17, 19.

42. Liebenow, *African Politics*, pp. 102–128.

43. A classical statement of this phenomenon is in the speech by Amilcar Cabral issued as *On Identity*, Document No. 2 (Philadelphia: Institute of African and African American Affairs, Temple University, 1986), pp. 3–15.

44. Owen Cranshaw, "Theories of Class and the African 'Middle Class' in South Africa, 1969–1983," *Africa Perspective*, n.s., 1, no. 1/2 (1986), pp. 3–33; *North, Freedom Rising*, pp. 220–223, 236–254.

45. See the historic *Challenge to the Church: A Theological Comment on the Political Crisis in South Africa*, The Kairos Document (Braamfontein: The Kairos Theologians, 1985), especially pp. 22–25, and Liebenow, *African Politics*, pp. 84–86.

46. Karrim Essack, in *The Road to the Conquest of Political Power in South Africa* (Dar Es Salaam: Continental Publishers, 1986), pp. 15–20, recognizes the importance of a worker–peasant alliance but decides that the worker is going to be the "leader" of the alliance. The South African Defence Force, alert to the potential challenge of such an alliance, adopted a "hearts and minds" campaign in the countryside, discussed in "South Africa: The Security Line Up," *Africa Confidential* 28, no. 12 (June 10, 1987), pp. 2–3, and in Nolutshungu, *Changing South Africa*, pp. 124–126.

47. "Security Line Up," pp. 2–3.

48. Karis, "Black Politics," pp. 127–129.

49. Leonard, *South Africa at War*, pp. 48, 58.

50. Mufson, "Fall of the Front," p. 19.

51. Martha Murray, *South Africa: Time of Agony, Time of Destiny. The Upsurge of Popular Protest* (London: Verso, 1987), pp. 398–400, 436–439.

6

The Black Trade Unions and Opposition Politics in South Africa

PEARL-ALICE MARSH

One of the more important social and political changes in South Africa since the Nationalist Party came to power in 1948 has been the development of a new African trade union movement, which has had a profound impact on South Africa's political economy. Black labor's strength in the industrial sectors became an increasingly important factor, in large part because of demographic changes in the composition of the workforce. As early as the 1950s, African labor represented 75 percent of the manufacturing labor force.[1] At the same time, the manufacturing sector doubled in size. This was more than the combined strength of both agriculture and manufacturing. Not only did the racial composition of the manufacturing labor force begin to change, but the type and availability of labor needed change as well. New industries demanded labor with mobility, education, and skills; and a class of industrial workers that could command wage levels sufficient to produce and sustain domestic markets.

Beginning in the early 1970s, black workers forged a redistribution of power in industrial relations and utilized collective bargaining processes to establish a new economic power base for the black community. Unlike earlier years, when collective bargaining for blacks was virtually illegal and unheard of, blacks were able to force government and industry to "reform" labor policies in order to incorporate blacks into the process.

Since 1973 (when South Africa experienced its first trade union strikes since the 1950s) the crisis of apartheid has escalated to phenomenal proportions. The decline in the effectiveness of institutional controls over the black population forced Prime Minister P. W. Botha to adopt a two-pronged strategy for maintaining white domination. On the one hand, he engaged in "reforms," designed to eliminate ineffective regulatory practices and streamline others. On the other hand, he restructured the "security" apparatus, creating a new system of "security management and control."

Botha's agenda was dictated by the emergence of a new black politics in the 1970s and 1980s. Black politics, more militant during these two decades, adopted new forms and strategies designed to make South Africa ungovernable. As a former president of the United Women's Organization (UWO) said, "When the police would come through the townships in the 1960s, the children would run and hide; now in the '80s, they throw stones."[2] This organizational tactic of the new movement was designed to introduce into the black community new structures of self-governance to serve several purposes: (1) to lay the basis for challenging the authority of the South African government both at the township and national levels; (2) to establish and maintain political order and social control in the community; (3) to build structures of communication for strengthening and expanding these new organizations; and (4) to "practice" democracy on the ground.

The two most important branches of this new movement have been the political organizations, beginning with the "civics" (local block political organizations) and culminating in the formation of national bodies, and the independent trade unions. Both have emerged, side by side tactically and in collaboration strategically, developing an agenda for restructuring South African society. This is obvious in the continuing strong relations between community and labor groups.

This chapter chronicles the development of the relationship between these two powerful movements and analyzes a debate that emerged around that development. Much of the political discussion of the 1980s finds its origin in the 1950s, when the South African Confederation of Trade Unions (SACTU) conducted work stoppages and general strikes on behalf of community antigovernment activities as an integral part of the Congress Alliance Movement (CAM).

The debate centered on two issues: (1) the emergence of an ideological basis for trade union development and internal affiliations; and (2) the development of formal relations between the trade unions and political groups. While opposition to the ideology of white domination and the government's apartheid policies was unanimous among the new independent trade unions, there was not a consensus among them concerning the ideological underpinnings of the new movement, or its potential political nature.

The South African government has assessed the political nature of the independent trade union movement. In 1982, shortly after P. W. Botha heralded the new labor reform legislation, National Party parliament member C. J. van der Merwe stated:

> The [global community] onslaught is also being made through the South African Congress of Trade Unions, which is another partner in this so-called alliance for liberation. We also find this in the sphere of trade unionism, about which we shall hear a great deal more in the

near future. The right climate is being created there as well. Trade unions are being infiltrated in order to recruit people for eventual actions according to the aims of the ANC.[3]

This assessment by van der Merwe reflected the government's fears of the emergence of political linkages between the black majority in South Africa and the exiled movements, and the potential political nature of the trade unions themselves as a part of an internal black majority opposition. Convinced of the external origins of both community and trade union resistance to apartheid, the government calculated that by destroying the leadership cadres of both groups—the "agitators"—it could maintain domestic peace. As the new trade union and community organizations began to take form, the government began a concerted campaign of surveillance, violence, and repression against trade unionists and community activists. The arrest of trade union leaders went hand in hand with arrests of political leaders.

As innumerable economic, organizational, and industrial strides have been made by black trade unions over the past fifteen years, their role in the mass struggle for overt political power has emerged at a slower pace. At question has been their ability (at times interpreted as their will) to use their new power to constrain the use of the repressive power of the state and to further the political objectives of mass political organizations. Indeed, the actual power of the trade unions to engage successfully at this time in protracted political conflict has been overestimated. However, a system of community organizational structures has emerged nationally, and the potential for concerted labor and political activism has become more viable.

Constructing a timetable for change in South Africa is an almost impossible challenge. However, educated speculation is possible. We can discuss South Africa's future by focusing on those in South Africa engaged in forging new alliances and strengthening antiapartheid institutions. Two political movements directly affected the regeneration of the trade union movement—the Black Consciousness Movement and the "democratic student movement." In this chapter we look at the role of political organizations (e.g., student and community) in forging the trade union movement and at the role of the trade union movement in the politics of South Africa in the 1980s.

BLACK CONSCIOUSNESS AND TRADE UNION MOVEMENTS

In the late 1960s and early 1970s, when black trade unionists began to recover from the anti-black labor government policies of the 1950s, black politics, and specifically the South African Confederation of Trade Unions (SACTU), began to re-emerge. A significant voice came from young black university-based intellectuals. As early as 1967, black members of the multiracial National Union of South African Students (NUSAS) began assessing the political relations of blacks in South Africa—beginning with their own alliance with white students in NUSAS. Because of their relative advantage for matriculation at university, whites formed the majority of the organization. Among black students, the idea of all-black organizations and an all-black movement began to take hold. By July 1969, the South African Students' Organization (SASO) was inaugurated, and Steven Biko, a medical student from Natal University, was elected president. In an attempt to define the cause and nature of the student movement, Biko and associates attacked white liberals and the "nonracial" approach to antigovernment politics. In "Black Souls in White Skins?" in SASO's newsletter dated August 1970, Biko argued:

> In adopting the line of a nonracial approach, the liberals are playing their old game. They are claiming a "monopoly on intelligence and moral judgement" and setting the pattern and pace for the realization of the black man's aspirations. They want to remain in good books with both the black and white worlds. . . . They vacillate between the two worlds verbalizing all the complaints of the blacks beautifully while skillfully extracting what suits them from the exclusive pool of white privilege.
>
> One sees a perfect example of what oppression has done to the blacks. They have been made to feel inferior for so long that for them it is comforting to drink tea, wine or beer with whites who seem to treat them as equals. This serves to boost up their own ego to the extent of making them feel slightly superior to those blacks who do not get similar treatment from whites.[4]

While the merits of this nascent "black consciousness" qua "black power" construction have been debated heavily over the subsequent two decades, it lit the spark that ignited political activism in the black community. Biko and SASO leaders started from the premise that oppression is fundamentally a psychological problem of the oppressed, and that the first line of attack on the system of white domination was the denigration of the notion of black inferiority. To those who questioned the correctness of focusing on psychological oppression as opposed to economic oppression, black consciousness advocates contend that while the color question has its origins in economic interests, after generations of segregation, discrimination, and exploitation, the whites had developed a belief in the inferiority of black people. Likewise, those oppressed for so long had grown to believe the myth. Therefore, while economics lay at the root of the racial problem, the psychological problems of oppressor and oppressed had taken on lives of their own and become problems in their own right.

The priority task of black people was to create a new image, a new identity formed on the foundations of African pride. And, while Black Consciousness did not resolve the conflicts in relations between white liberals/activists and blacks, it developed a basis for the emergence of mass—instead of minority—intellectual, black political activism in South Africa and established a new dialogue between whites and blacks over politics, political behavior, and political mobilization and leadership.

The early Black Consciousness Movement denounced "class analysis" as an ideology that divided rather than united the black community; it laid no strong basis for organizing among workers as a separate body. Further, early Black Consciousness stressed the cultural and psychological aspects of black liberation, therefore limiting its capacity to foster successful political action campaigns designed to redress specific grievances—rent increases, housing shortages, job security, wages, etc. Quoting Sekou Touré, Biko wrote in 1970, "To take part in the African revolution, it is not enough to write a revolutionary song, you must fashion the revolution with the people. And if you fashion it with the people the songs will come by themselves."[5] Implicit in this reference is the later tendency among Black Consciousness organizations to place the practical tasks of organizing second to the ideological tasks.

But the well-intentioned rhetoric did not overcome the physical distance between the universities, where Black Consciousness was thriving, and the urban townships, where the problems were; nor did it overcome the identity distance between students and township dwellers. Though the idea of Black Consciousness was attractive on a visceral level in the community, the students' militancy was by and large alien to the majority. The students were perceived as youthful and energetic, with their hearts in the right place, but offering no practical strategy for dealing with the day-to-day problems of living with apartheid.

The Black Consciousness idea did find its supporters among some black intellectuals and community leaders. In mid-1972, the Black People's Convention (BPC) was inaugurated and embraced Black Consciousness as its motivating ideology. BPC set as its first task organizing nationally, and by 1974 reported that it had forty-one branches nationwide—but the number of branches belied the general weakness of the organization. By attempting to spread so rapidly, BPC leaders neglected the tasks of building and strengthening local organizations. However, the rhetoric of Black Consciousness was heady and the enthusiasm it generated among its adherents unsurpassed. After a decade of political dormancy, the black political voice was again awakening. To criticize in hindsight the Black People's Convention for its organizational weakness overshadows its significance as the first post-1950s repression attempt to mobilize blacks politically. Indeed, it may be that had they proceeded with more caution, the voice of the movement would not have been heard so broadly.

The state took immediate action to destroy the BPC. Through its usual tactics of intimidation, detentions, and police attacks, the government successfully crippled the BPC as a political organization. On October 19, 1977, eighteen organizations were banned, including virtually all of those linked to Black Consciousness. Members not in detention tried the next year to form the Azanian People's Organization (AZAPO), but, owing to subsequent detentions, they were unable to complete the organization until September 1979.

The BPC leadership did attempt to organize trade unions during its brief period of activities. In 1971, following an African bus drivers' strike in Johannesburg, the BPC formed the Sales and Allied Workers' Association (SAWA) with the intent of being an umbrella organization for all black trade unions emerging in Johannesburg. Drake Koka, a founding member of the BPC, became the first general secretary. Koka announced that SAWA would hold a conference in early 1973, to which black workers and black businesspeople would be invited to lay the foundation for a trade union movement. His rationale for inviting black businesspeople was articulated through his definition of "black workers." According to Koka, the very nature of any black person's relations to whites in South Africa made him or her a "worker" even if that person was a shopkeeper, since all African labor, wealth, and economic power had been usurped to serve white people's interests.

SAWA was unable to hold its mass workers' conference in 1973, because of governmental intimidation. However, it continued to function as an organization allied to both the BPC and SASO. The three organizations convened a conference in 1974 to articulate and express, publicly, their position regarding government policies toward the African community. A number of leaders were arrested during the conference. Following the meeting, SAWA changed its name to the Black Allied Workers' Union (BAWU) and called for the recognition of black trade unions. It severely criticized the attempt by white unions to assume roles as bargaining representatives for African workers.

BAWU's original goal was to organize a nationally based workers' movement. Consistent with the "mass-base" nature of the Black Consciousness ideology, it chose to adopt an organizing strategy that did not establish job or labor function as a criterion for membership in the organization. "Black workers are not being oppressed, exploited, or discriminated against because they are miners, salesmen, engineers, teachers, doctors, or road diggers. They are simply deprived of their rights because they are black."[6] Expressing its primary goal in its statement of aim and purpose, BAWU claimed:

> The aim and purpose of BAWU is to organize and unite all black workers into a powerful labor force that can earn the respect and *de facto* recognition by both the employers and the government; to educate black workers and make them aware of their power and

significance at work; to build them into a "oneness"—the spirit of solidarity and unity is essential for the workers' [familihood], based on the philosophy of black consciousness and black communalism. It is from this position of strength that black workers could bring about a change in the labor and economic system in view of a political change. Thus, *BAWU is a workers' unit for the liberation of blacks in South Africa. Other things, such as workers' rights, privileges, job opportunities, fringe benefits shall automatically follow. This includes legal recognition by the government.*[7]

BAWU's principal organizing strategy was mass-based, as opposed to industrial or "shop floor," in orientation. Thus, reporting on his banning order, which restricted him from industrial premises, Koka could chide the government and claim that "thanks to God," he could continue the work of BAWU.

A major issue for BAWU concerned membership and leadership within the new trade union movement. Consistent with the ideas of Black Consciousness, BAWU claimed that because racism and segregation in South Africa had been directed primarily at the African community, Africans had to form organizations for themselves with membership and leadership of Africans. Thus, they not only rejected but also attacked the prominent role of white activists in key positions in other unions in South Africa.

BAWU had recurring problems within its leadership ranks. In February 1973, the executive suffered a major crisis when four of the nine members resigned, claiming that Koka acted too independently in making decisions and public statements involving the union. However, Koka and the five remaining members continued to work to build the union. By 1974, BAWU claimed 2,700 members, which increased to 6,000 by 1975 and to 20,000 by 1980; the reported membership in 1981 was 51,000, organized into fourteen separate unions.[8]

With the government's heavy assault on the Black Consciousness Movement, the BAWU leadership was banned in the early part of the 1970s. Then, during "Black October," in 1977, the entire BCM leadership became the object of South African security operations and left but a remnant of the original leadership to continue the organization. Koka and the other leaders found themselves exiled in neighboring Botswana and, for a while, attempted to manage and direct BAWU from there. At that time, they undertook an international campaign to gain support, as did other Black Consciousness organizations driven into exile.

Despite the heavy criticism directed toward BAWU for its lack of shop floor strength (which created its industrial weakness), BAWU did spawn several important breakaway unions that became independent unions or federations in the post-1977 period.

The major breakaway union was the South African Allied Workers' Union (SAAWU), which operated in Natal, the Eastern Cape, Transvaal, and the Ciskei/Transkei border areas, and broke away from BAWU in April 1978. The bases of the split were the questions of organizing strategies for building the trade union, and of Black Consciousness versus nonracialism. After pursuing the Black Consciousness mass-based organizing agenda and experiencing major attacks from the government, SAAWU became concerned about its lack of concentration on shop floor organization, where it believed its actual power base was concentrated. SAAWU did not wish to abandon its community activism, however. In response to the government's attack on SAAWU for not being a bread-and-butter union—a "normal" union—SAAWU adopted a slogan: "There can be no normal union in an abnormal society."

SAAWU's basic organizational principles were: (1) nonracialism; (2) links with community struggles; and (3) shop floor strength. On the racial issue, Sisa Njikelana from the East London branch stated in 1981: "We are not struggling against a particular race, creed or religion. We are toiling against the exploiters and oppressors irrespective of color."[9] Organizationally, SAAWU focused on its worker membership and adopted a principle of "mass participatory democracy," which meant that

> hand in hand with the formal organizing task, the union is attempting to raise the consciousness of workers and preparing them to be self-sufficient in the task of representing their own interests, so this knowledge does not remain entirely in the hands of union officials.[10]

The purpose of the organizing principal was twofold: to safeguard against an elite leadership, which might estrange itself from its membership, forming in the union; and to ensure that when the government attacked the leadership of the union with bannings, detentions, and persecution, as it had in the past, a vacuum would not be created, leaving a leaderless and ill-informed union with no organizational capacity to carry out its industrial and political work.

Though initially SAAWU was a single union, formed of a number of different committees, it later evolved into several independent unions with SAAWU acting as the umbrella organization. SAAWU's popularity among workers and the African communities of the Eastern Cape made management and government perceive it as both an industrial and a political threat. A circular passed "privately" by members of the security police to employers in the East London area alleged that the contributory causes of labor unrest came from pressure groups with political motives. The memorandum raised the issue of the "agitators" in strike situations, whom it identified as "white agitators," and the "intellectual black workers." The security police then detailed strategies for curtailing the growth of the trade union movement under SAAWU's leadership. Despite this opposition, and deadly harassment against SAAWU officials, its membership grew to 70,000 by May 1981.

The influence of Black Consciousness on the trade union movement suffered another blow in 1980 when the General and Allied Workers' Union (GAWU) broke away after expressing dissatisfaction with the ideological leadership of BAWU. By 1980, the nonracialism in the trade union movement had gained wide acceptance, particularly in light of the practical achievements of "nonracial" unions. At the commemoration on June 15, 1980, GAWU joined the Congress of South African Students (COSAS) and the Azanian People's Organization (AZAPO) in strongly criticizing Black Consciousness ideology on the basis of its racial exclusiveness. More fundamental was the criticism of the logical and tactical inconsistencies of the movement. For example, Black Consciousness unions and organizations did not view capital as a necessary enemy of the labor movement and sought and received support from (white) multinational corporations, the same ones engaged in labor discrimination against black workers. To the growing body of militant black workers this amounted to collaboration with management. In a direct attack, Reavell Nkondo of AZAPO accused Black Consciousness political leaders of being "black liberals," not concerned with the day-to-day political work but primarily concerned with symbolic events. GAWU followed the lead of SAAWU by concentrating on shop floor strength rather than mass-based community support.

BAWU continued to exist as an umbrella union and in 1981 claimed sixteen affiliates active, for the most part, in Natal and the Free State.[11] It vowed to continue its commitment to Black Consciousness and to working through the labor movement to achieve political change. By 1984, it claimed 86,000 members organized into nineteen affiliates.

However, through its insistence on placing ideology over organization, BAWU lost the claim to being the guiding organization for trade unions committed to Black Consciousness. A much more pragmatic Black Consciousness union movement began its growth out of the Durban strikes of 1973.

The Trade Union Council of South Africa (TUCSA), the majority white union federation, played a strong role in destroying black unions in the 1950s. For its own purposes, it had participated with the government in criminalizing African unions by setting up separate councils, with no collective bargaining power, to which African, Asian, and coloured unions could affiliate. In 1959, TUCSA supported the establishment of the Federation of Free South African Trade Unions (FSATU), to incorporate black trade unions into their organization on apartheid terms. In 1968, the African Affairs Section (AAS) of TUCSA completely disbanded under pressure from the government. Disaffected members of the AAS formed a new organization, the Urban Training Project (UTP), to serve as an advice bureau and general service organization for African workers. The belief of the UTP organizers, both black and white, was that leadership of African workers belonged in the hands of black people. Following two years of operation, the UTP formed the Consultative Committee (CC), which was a loose coordinating body for the trade unions seeking affiliation with the UTP.

In 1978, trade unionists and support organizers held a formal meeting in Durban to begin discussing the formation of a national federation that could act as a coordinating body for all independent trade unions. A number of key participants were white student and labor activists who had been involved in the 1973 Durban general strike. Black leaders complained that the Durban participants were led by white academics. They further observed that the black participants from Durban did not participate in the discussions. A black caucus during the meeting expressed concern that white academics might misdirect the new movement of black workers, and that the struggle might be confused if white liberals and/or radicals led it. Following the caucus, the CC leadership announced that "white input into trade union matters should be supplementary and not directive or dominating."[12] CC leadership further argued that it was important for leaders, in formulating a strategy for workers, to consider that their personal life may be affected by the situation, hinting that radical white academics could afford to be more adventurous than black workers in formulating union strategies. Based on this position, several unions were expelled from the meeting. Charges were alleged from both sides at the meeting, between the black-led CC and the white-led groups from Durban. While the CC charged the white-led unions with being radically oriented toward the state, without regard for consequences for black workers (particularly vis-à-vis social and economic insecurities, with their tenuous residential rights) the CC was accused by the more militant trade unions of being "liberal" and conciliatory to both management and the state.

After the discussion with the Natal black workers, CC participants decided not to participate in the discussion regarding the formation of a federation. Those CC unions that chose to continue to participate in the talks were expelled from the CC for breaking rank.

Following the Durban meeting, the Black Consciousness leaders proceeded to propose a new African trade union body—the Association of South African Black Trade Unions—to replace the Consultative Committee. It was felt that the CC had lost its effectiveness and could not provide the leadership to deal with the growing needs of the fledgling trade unions. On September 14, 1980, after one year of deliberation, the Council of Unions of South Africa (CUSA), composed of nine trade unions, was inaugurated. CUSA had several TUCSA unions cross over to join it. CUSA welcomed this shift, believing that as the trade union movement grew more and more militant, there would be less likelihood that black unions would want to stay with TUCSA. (By "black," CUSA means all people of African, Indian, and "coloured" origin.)

Though CUSA did not affiliate with any Black Consciousness national political body—e.g., Black People's Convention or AZAPO—it did adhere strongly to the principle of Black Consciousness for black trade unions—but on a more pragmatic line than its Black Consciousness predecessor BAWU. CUSA narrowly limited its Black Consciousness objectives to (1) reserving leadership positions for blacks; and (2) supporting black unions that wanted to register with the government. In 1981, CUSA claimed a signed membership of 49,000 workers, with 18,000 paying members. During that same year, CUSA signed 17 recognition agreements and anticipated signing 19 more. By 1983, CUSA claimed 12 affiliates.[13]

Also in 1981, CUSA began to make public statements, condemning government actions on influx control, migrant workers, and the government's antiblack housing policies. It supported the Soweto Anti-Community Councils Committee in its call for residents to boycott town council elections in Soweto, based on its own belief in a common citizenship for all individuals. CUSA downplayed any potential "ideological differences" with community organizations and instead found common ground on political issues. CUSA was the only major federation to join the UDF at its founding. Perishaw Camay, general secretary of CUSA, also served on the National Forum committee, convened by AZAPO in 1983 to establish a forum in which black organizations could mobilize. The chair of the National Forum, Saths Cooper, also stated that there were "no ideological preconditions to being invited to the National Forum" and that differences were being "unnecessarily played up."[14] CUSA's policy on black leadership was stated as follows in 1982: "CUSA operates in a country which is racialist, undemocratic and which exploits the larger Black community. Racially disadvantaged [sic] people need re-education and training so that they can take their rightful place in their community."[15]

In summary, CUSA provided an institutional focus among trade unions in which the ideas of Black Consciousness, vis-à-vis trade union leadership, could be tested ideologically and practically. While there was no substantial evidence supporting the thesis that black leadership was essential to the development of the trade union movement, there was equally no evidence supporting the opposing thesis—that the issue of black leadership was neutral, not particularly affecting the development of a strong rank and file organization.

The influence of Black Consciousness continued to be felt, primarily throughout the Eastern Cape, though virtually all unions had now turned for practical reasons from mass appeals to shop-floor organizing. Emerging out of the extensive auto industry strikes of 1979 came the Motor Assembly and Component Workers' Union of South Africa (MACWUSA). Though not a "black consciousness union" per se, MACWUSA leadership felt a strong pressure to respond to "community needs" in ways the unions less influenced by Black Consciousness did not. From the outset, MACWUSA identified itself as a "community-based" union. Thus, it drew much of its leadership and membership from political ranks within the Port Elizabeth community. However, as an open community and labor-oriented organization, it began to attract small groups of individuals from other industries, as well as unemployed workers. Knowing from experience the deleterious effect such a diverse membership could have on the union, MACWUSA formed a second branch, the General Workers' Union of South Africa (GWUSA), to accommodate non-auto industry–related members. The two-pronged union became known as MACWUSA/GWUSA.

MACWUSA/GWUSA was organized with the explicit purpose of being responsible for and responsive to the African communities in the Port Elizabeth area, including addressing their welfare needs. According to members of its executive committee, "shop floor issues stem from the community."[16] MACWUSA and GWUSA, while autonomous unions, shared the same leadership. Thus, while the functional identity of the unions was separate structurally, any real separation barely existed.

The community orientation of MACWUSA/GWUSA stemmed both from the political tradition of the Eastern Cape and, according to the executive committee, from the fact that while most, if not all, of the motor industry workers were Section 10 (having permanent urban status), many of their neighbors, relatives, and friends were not and were therefore caught in a cycle between the relocation areas and the industrial areas.

MACWUSA/GWUSA's extensive community ties were second only to SAAWU's. However, because of its extensive community involvement, including counseling on the "Black Sash" model, the union was not able to carry through any organizing that it had done in the factories. Union leaders who should have been spending time organizing workers and establishing bargaining strategies were preoccupied with trying to meet the immediate and pressing welfare needs of their community members.

MACWUSA argued the political position for more community involvement in every trade union forum to which it was invited. Later, it affiliated with the United Democratic Front as a response to political demands.

NONRACIALISM AND THE TRADE UNION MOVEMENT

The major alternative ideology to Black Consciousness in South Africa is nonracialism. The unfortunate implication of this is that Black Consciousness is "racist." To the contrary, the principle of Black Consciousness, applied to trade union and community organizations, is very complex. The term identifies a redress approach to organizational strategies and leadership development based on an assessment of historical racial inequities in organization and leadership training. Black Consciousness comes out of historical intellectual and political tradition in South Africa committed to developing through organizations the means of reclaiming black authority in politics. The Pan-Africanist Congress followed this tradition.

Nevertheless, nonracialism proved to be a compelling ideology for the majority of black South Africans, in both the community and trade union movements. The degree to which this can be attributed to the Congress Alliance of the 1950s cannot be measured empirically. However, the maxim, "You can kill a movement but you can't kill an idea," resonates in the South African case. While early in the 1980s many analysts attributed the public sympathy for the African National Congress and Nelson Mandela to their historical emotional appeal, no one made that same argument by the end of the decade.

A study conducted in June–July 1984 by the Human Science Research Council found that in the Pretoria/Witwatersrand/Vereeniging and Port Elizabeth areas, the ANC was supported by 27 percent of the population; AZAPO and AZASO by 6 percent; Inkatha by 14 percent; and the UDF by 11 percent.[17] Over the next four years, as the UDF and its affiliates adopted the Freedom Charter as the guiding document for South Africa's political future, much of the ANC's support was drawn its way.

Concern about relations with the community formed the basis of major contentions between the emerging trade unions. Opposed to the Black Consciousness community model were the unions following out of the tradition of the South African Confederation of Trade Unions (SACTU). In the 1950s, SACTU had emerged as the body representing outlawed African trade unions. Despite heavy repression, in 1957 it claimed membership of 15 affiliates. This number grew to 22 in 1958, representing 10,875 signed workers.[18] By 1961, SACTU could claim 38,791 union members, or 64.7 percent of all organized African workers. Even after its virtual banning in 1963, it boasted 54 union affiliates.[19] After that time, African unions were virtually defunct until the early 1970s.

Though SACTU represented African unions solely, it was strongly affiliated to the Congress Alliance. Nonracialism was the fundamental premise on which the Alliance and the Freedom Charter were based. Thus, nonracialism heavily influenced the trade unions of that time. As the new unions began to emerge, the organizing history of SACTU attracted many workers to their ranks. Ever-present was an energetic corps of former SACTU union organizers ready to apply their skills toward developing the new movement. Likewise, in the black townships, several decades of political dormancy had not obliterated the political legacy of the Alliance. Thus, the black community was prepared overwhelmingly to embrace the principle of nonracialism. Important assets to the nonracial trade union movement were the research bodies that grew out of the predominantly white "democratic student movement."

The Black Consciousness Movement pulled black students out of the national students' organizations and turned their attention toward constructing a new consciousness among black people. The split between the black and white members of the National Union of South African Students (NUSAS) generated a major crisis in white progressive politics. After the split, NUSAS attempted to form an alliance with the newly formed black South African Students' Organization (SASO) but met with strong rebuff. In 1972, SASO leaders told Stellenbosch University students to "keep your hands off" black campuses and sent an official message to the NUSAS Forty-eighth Congress "reaffirming its policy of non-cooperation with NUSAS and wished the organization the best in its fight for its own battles."[20] Struggling with this rejection, NUSAS's president claimed that their problem lay "thus not in our failure to represent the aspiration of black students. . . . This option (if it was ever a real option) is no longer open to us—it lies somewhere in the white society and it is there we must seek to resolve it."[21]

Thus, white students turned their attention toward educating the white community regarding the plight of the African population. The government retaliated by arresting and prosecuting hundreds of white students involved in protest campaigns. NUSAS leaders were further harassed. One student leader's house was fire-bombed, and pamphlets that attacked the leadership were circulated. In February 1972, the prime minister announced that he would investigate, through a select committee of Parliament, the objectives, activities, and financing of NUSAS and other white liberal organizations.

Being rebuffed by SASO and thwarted in its work in the white community, NUSAS began practical work in the black community. In 1971, the National Union of Students' Welfare Department (NUSWEL) of NUSAS decided to campaign for equal pay for equal work as a part of its national program. Wage and Economic Commissions (WEC) were set up on all white, English-speaking university campuses, and, in 1972, they began issuing reports and presenting evidence regarding the failures of the industrial relations system in terms of African workers. White students were able to work with the black trade unions because of the latter's strong legacy of nonracialism and because the student research groups had useful skills to offer.

Prime Minister B. J. Vorster's investigatory committee, the Schlebusch Commission, found that NUSAS, as a whole, was a relatively harmless student group, but that it had been "misguided" by a group of eight activists who had political links with overseas organizations. The eight were accused of furthering the aims of communism, banned, and prevented not only from participating in NUSAS/NUSWEL but from attending educational institutions to further their education. NUSAS issued a "counterreport" and denied that it was a revolutionary organization, that it was controlled from overseas, or that it advocated violence as a means of changing the system.

In spite of political assault directed at the student movement by the government, NUSAS/NUSWEL continued its wage commissions and its research and continued to give evidence at wage board hearings regarding the wages and working conditions of African workers. In 1972, the Durban Wage Commission and the left wing of TUCSA formed the General Workers' Benefit Fund (GWBF), an organization designed to aid workers and, ultimately, to help them by promoting the formation of African trade unions.

In 1973, a wave of strikes hit Natal. Black workers, facing high inflation rates, suppressed wages, intolerable working conditions, and nonresponsive management, flexed their muscles in ways reminiscent of the black trade union movement in the 1920s. African workers struck illegally, demanding wage increases and recognition agreements for newly formed unions.

The extreme divergence in ideological, normative, and political interests and beliefs made cohesion and cooperation in the industrial relations system among government, business, and black labor highly problematic. The apartheid government played a major role in industrial relations matters. It had increased its role through the 1968 Planning Act, in order radically to reorient the distribution of labor vis-à-vis the homeland policy and permanently to deny blacks a labor voice. For several decades, the government had maintained industrial peace. However, the unrest of the 1970s proved that the new industrial policy was inadequate to control African workers.

As black labor quiescence dominated the industrial scene during the 1960s, labor militancy and rebellion characterized the 1970s. Black workers expressed their grievances against low wages, bad working conditions, disrespectful behavior on the part of managers and supervisors, and, more importantly, the right to organize and bargain collectively. From 1970 to 1980, the government reported 1,800 known strikes and work stoppages involving a total of a quarter-million black workers (see Table 6.1). The most immediate cause of strikes, accounting for 92 percent, was low wages, according to the minister of labor.

The question of whether or not to recognize African trade unions consumed a large part of the debate among industrialists during the first half of the decade. Entrusting labor disputes to independent and autonomous African trade unions did not seem acceptable to most industrialists. After studying the strike situation in Natal in 1973, the South African Chamber of Industries reported that "agitators" were an important element in fomenting worker unrest in the Durban area. To charges of "agitation," TUCSA's Harriet Bolton responded, "As for agitation, this was, as has been said before, in the belly of the workers. They did not need telling they were badly off."[22]

These "agitators" represented the first signs of the emerging relations between labor and white activists. "Agitators" were by and large students, though black community workers were also involved. Although many strikes

Table 6.1 Work Stoppages in South Africa: 1970–1980

Year	Number of work stoppages	Number of employees involved		Number of employee hours lost	
		All workers	Black workers	All workers	Black workers
1970	76	4,168	3,210	4,528	—
1971	69	4,451	4,067	3,437	—
1972	71	9,224	8,711	14,167	—
1973	370	98,378	90,082	229,281	—
1974	384	59,244	57,656	98,583	95,327
1975	274	23,323	22,546	18,709	18,275
1976	245	28,013	26,291	59,861	22,014
1977	90	15,304	14,950	15,471	14,987
1978	106	14,160	13,578	10,558	10,164
1979	101	22,803	15,494	67,099	16,515
1980	207	61,785	56,286	174,614	148,192

Source: Survey of Race Relations, 1981 (Johannesburg: South African Institute of Race Relations), p. 208

during this period were spontaneous, they were not the result of blind impulse. Black workers, becoming increasingly aware of their relative deprivation within the economy, began to rely heavily upon student support groups, whose primary purpose was to interpret complex industrial legislation as it affected African workers.

The academic training and access to research facilities shared among progressive white students provided a significant resource to the trade union movement. Had these same facilities and levels of training been available to black university students, the same sort of support for black workers probably would have emerged among them. While the number of white students active with the trade unions was small relative to their overall numbers, their actual numbers available to staff research bureaus far outstripped the numbers of university-level black students available for the same purpose. Also, it should be noted that, while a significant number of white students suffered tremendously at the hands of the government for their involvement, the aggressiveness with which the state security apparatus assaulted black students and black organizations was not evident on the same scale among whites. Likewise, black and white students did not share equally social and economic advantages.

After the 1973 strikes, the GWBF formed the Trade Union Advisory and Coordinating Council (TUACC) with the explicit purpose of organizing African trade unions. In addition, the Institute for Industrial Education (IIE) was organized by NUSAS's economic commission in Durban to provide education resources to the new trade unions. In 1974, a group of black workers founded the Industrial Aid Society (IAS) in Johannesburg, with the primary aims of disseminating information, offering training and information services to workers and organizers, running a complaint and advice bureau, and managing a small benefit fund for death and retirement. The goal of the organization was stated to be strong shop floor organization for African workers. The following year, IAS made a major organizational adjustment and handed all grievances and complaints over to shop floor organizers.

In 1976, the Durban student organizers who had gone to the Johannesburg area formed the Council for Industrial Workers of the Witwatersrand (CIWW) as a coordinating body for trade union activities of the IAS and the new Metal and Allied Workers' Union (MAWU-Transvaal). By 1977, there were a known twenty-six unregistered African unions holding membership in these and other service groups. In March, these unions and service groups met to discuss the possibility of forming a federation of registered and unregistered trade unions. At that time, a feasibility committee was established to draw up a draft constitution for the federation.

Many issues divided the meeting and impeded progress. The Western Cape unions decided it was premature to set up an umbrella organization before the unions were solidly placed in the factories and were firmly and democratically controlled by workers. Former Black Consciousness unions objected to the leadership of whites in the federation movement. One of the major challenges concerned the relations between the emerging trade union movement and opposition politics in the black communities. The primary conflict arose between the Eastern Cape and Johannesburg unions.

Despite the lack of consensus, the Federation of South African Trade Unions (FOSATU) was formed in 1979, and though Eastern and Western Cape and CUSA unions stayed out, they agreed to continue "unity talks." Responding to charges that FOSATU was insensitive to the community struggle of the black majority, Joe Foster, acting general secretary, claimed that FOSATU was, in fact, sensitive to community issues and envisioned as its aim a society in which workers control their own destiny. However, he harkened back to the 1950s when SACTU engaged in popular political struggles and was destroyed by the government. According to FOSATU, the time was ripe for building an independent working-class movement, which was the fundamental *political* task.

Although FOSATU did not modify its fundamental position on community activism, the death of trade unionist Neil Aggett while in police custody and the growing political militancy of some of FOSATU's strongest unions (including the Metal and Allied Workers' Union) forced the federation to reconsider its unwillingness to get involved more openly and aggressively in the public debate about political matters affecting the African community. In the immediate aftermath of the Aggett crisis, FOSATU made a point to speak out against the homeland policy of the government and called for a one person–one vote democratic government.

Another union central to the community debate was the General Workers' Union (GWU) of the Western Cape. In its policy statement GWU took a more open stance toward community activism while maintaining its primary responsibilities to the shop floor:

> In our relationship with other organizations of the workers and people of South Africa, we commit ourselves to cooperating and working constructively with all organizations which are committed to the same basic democratic principles and aims. In this way, we commit ourselves to carry forward the interests of the workers and people of South Africa towards a democratic future.[23]

Despite the debate among trade unionists, community groups were unswerving in their support of labor groups. This was demonstrated most directly through consumer boycotts engaged to bolster sagging strikes by black workers. Two such boycotts were conducted in 1979 and 1982, respectively, in the Eastern and Western Cape areas in support of the Africa/Food and Canning Workers' Union (A/FCWU) and the South African Allied Workers' Unions.

In 1978, the registered A/FCWU attempted to use the Industrial Conciliation process to press for a R40/40-hour work week. However, management of the company involved, Fatti's and Moni's, refused to respond and, during the year, fired most of the workers who had signed the complaint. As the union continued to press its demands, workers involved in organizing or showing interest began to be laid off. This was interpreted by the union as a form of reprisal. In April 1979, five coloured women workers presented grievances to management regarding low wages and inadequate benefits; the grievants were fired immediately. Management made it clear to the union that its demands would not be met or even considered.

In response, the union called a strike, and the entire milling section went out. Replacement workers were hired, and those striking African workers who were on contract and resident in the hostel were told to leave the Cape area according to law.

During the eight months of the strike, the workers' families suffered severe hardships. At one point, members were living on 14 cents' food rations per day. Several families lost children because of illness and lack affordable medical treatment.

As the conflict between the union and Fatti's and Moni's escalated, a consumer boycott was initiated in support of the strike. In a matter of weeks the strike gained widespread national support. At one point, shopkeepers from the Western Cape Traders' Association (WCTA) refused to put Fatti's and Moni's products on their shelves, thereby making them totally unavailable to a large number of consumers. After the boycott had gotten under way nationally, the company management acknowledged in the press that it could not withstand a nationwide boycott for more than a two-week period and would be driven into bankruptcy. In the meantime, competing firms enjoyed a period of prosperity. Finally, as a direct result of the boycott, the company was forced to soften its position. At that time, the union issued a letter to management calling for a negotiated settlement. Management agreed to meet, and, finally, a tentative agreement was drawn up.

At this point, the union faced a problem with the consumer boycott. The community, students, and shopkeepers, intensely engaged in the strike effort through the boycott, opposed the settlement and attempted to broaden the issues beyond wages, working conditions, and union recognition. Quite sympathetic to the broader interest, the union recorded its appreciation for the support but chose to settle with management. Without the boycott, the union would probably have lost the strike.

A second, though less successful, boycott in the Eastern Cape involved Wilson Rountree, a British-held company. Although plagued by organizational problems and unable to consolidate the strike and boycott efforts, this episode also illustrated the communities' willingness to sacrifice for the sake of the workers' movement.

Despite "community" (e.g., student and activist) support, a number of the major trade unions were still defensive about their position on the "community issues." Somehow, there was an implicit quid pro quo that the unions were not fulfilling. Much of the pressure for more active political involvement came from inside the trade union movement itself. Rank and file members, including a sizable number of older and more vocal individuals with experience in SACTU, were quick to confess their ultimate desire for politically related actions. Within the ranks of the movement, some unions were identified as more "militant" than others, usually meaning they shared characteristics of militancy vis-à-vis management and on community issues. In 1982, in response to criticism from "militant" unions, A/FCWU issued the following statement:

> Our viewpoint is that a union should not split the struggle of the workers in the factory from struggles outside the workplace in community and political issues. However, we do believe that separate forms of organization are needed for these struggles. A union which tries to be a community or political organization at the same time cannot survive.[24]

In the same statement, FOSATU committed itself to working with community groups.

Despite the organizational and "racial" debates that emerged during the formative period of the trade union movement, the desire for unity was expressed unanimously, at least in principle. Faced with hostilities from both government and industry, and having the entire state security apparatus turned against it, unionists agreed that the movement would be better off if some basis of unity was laid and adhered to. In spite of the failure to reach such unity at the first federation congress, the unions agreed to hold talks again in 1981. The purpose of the meeting was to see if the unions, nationwide, could find ways to resolve their differences and unite in a common cause.

The unity meeting failed. While most unions attended, none came prepared to relinquish its position regarding the major issues. As the meeting drew to a close, however, the unions agreed to continue considering unity talks at a regional level; Neil Aggett was dispatched to the Transvaal to serve the A/FCWU. He also began informal talks with the federations and the independent unions regarding another unity conference. Within hours after news of Aggett's death, trade unionists from each federation and independent union agreed to meet to work through a united response to the tragedy and, subsequently, to another round of unity talks. The meeting was convened in Johannesburg in April 1982. As the meeting got under way, the old divisions became apparent. CUSA refused to attend and did not send a message to the conference. MACWUSA/GWUSA challenged the FOSATU unions and demanded that those registered with the government agree to deregister before the meeting could convene. The FOSATU unions refused to comply and MACWUSA/GWUSA walked out. The remaining unions eventually agreed that unity was a good thing, something to be strived toward, but adjourned to their regions to continue informal talks with no commitment to a future meeting date or agenda.

In the meantime, the unity talks had failed to produce a single federation and in November 1985 FOSATU, SAAWU, the General Workers' Union, FCWU, the General and Allied Workers' Union, MACWUSA, and the Municipal and General Workers' Union launched a new super-federation, the Congress of South African Trade Unions (COSATU).

Thirty trade unions representing about 650,000 members launched the new organization. COSATU leaders pledged to "play an important role in transforming South African society into one acceptable to everybody and which would eventually become nonracial, classless, and democratic."[25] The first president, Elizah Barahi, called for the abolition of the pass law and nationalization of mines and major industries, and supported disinvestment of foreign companies. In his inaugural speech, he gave the government six months to abolish pass laws or face massive strikes. At the same time, opposition politics were emerging on a national level.

While unity remained a desirable goal among trade unionists, differences over ideology, leadership criteria, and relations with communities continued to hamper progress. FOSATU and CUSA, as the two contending federations, differed most strongly on all three accounts. FOSATU continued to charge community groups with being undemocratic formations. Though their aims and general politics were progressive, they were not elected bodies and did not answer to anyone except their voluntary constituents. The real fear was over control. If unions formed a close liaison with community groups, would they be subject to popular control and, if so, would that result in an aborted trade union movement? FOSATU believed the answer to that question was "yes." This position was held by at least half of the major independent unions in the country, particularly those in the Western Cape.

Regardless, community pressure was strong. And when FOSATU attempted to organize in the Eastern Cape among auto workers, it found itself having to respond to community pressures. As one FOSATU leader put it in 1982, "We were losing ground among the non-worker groups who supported unions. We felt we couldn't put our heads in the sand."[26] From this period forward, FOSATU began seeking ways to accommodate community pressure while still maintaining the organizational integrity of the trade unions.

CUSA, though more pragmatic than ideological, still maintained a stance favorable to Black Consciousness. Though several white members were admitted to one of its unions, it still reserved leadership positions for blacks. And, though not a "community-based" trade union, it showed more accommodation toward community groups than did FOSATU. CUSA's stance toward Black Consciousness, however, was not satisfactory to the major Black Consciousness organization, AZAPO. After the failure of the Black Consciousness Black Allied Workers' Union (BAWU), AZAPO continued trying to organize worker organizations and in 1984 nine Black Consciousness unions formed the Azanian Congress of Trade Unions (AZACTU).

In 1982, concerning its role in the community, CUSA wrote: "CUSA believes therefore that we need to develop a leadership which serves the community. We believe in developing the awareness and consciousness of the black community which has been denied its rightful leadership role in South Africa."[27]

It was clear at this point that lines between the Black Consciousness unions and COSATU had been drawn clearly and that a separate federation would emerge. In October 1986, CUSA and AZACTU formed the federation CUSA/AZACTU and in 1987, formally changed its name to the National Congress of Trade Unions (NACTU).

THE TRADE UNION MOVEMENT AND
OPPOSITION POLITICS IN SOUTH AFRICA

One of the major concerns for the trade union movement as it emerged in the 1980s related to its overall orientation vis-à-vis the broader social situation. The debate over these issues, at times, involved vociferous verbal and written engagement within and outside the movement. Some unions were accused of being too interested in their own development, to the detriment of the African community, while others were accused of being too interested in "politics," to the detriment of the trade union movement.

It should be noted that unions anywhere are not just economic institutions. Throughout labor history, unions have always represented extraeconomic interests. In Western Europe, trade unions have been associated with political movements, religious organizations, political parties, national movements, and in some cases, management itself. In the Soviet Union, trade unions brought about social revolution. In the United States, the absence or presumed absence of politics in union organization is as interesting as the strong political nature of labor in France, Italy, and throughout the Labour Party in Britain.

While political economy has focused on the role of trade unions in social change and the structural relations between trade unions and political organizations, it is interesting to understand the motives and perceptions of the trade unions themselves, since how they perceive themselves, how they act and interact, and what motivates them to act affect what we call the "objective conditions" of particular situations. The "subjective" is the domain of actors. While general theory provides insight into labor in the broader context, behavioral theory seems necessary to gain insight into the motives, perceptions, beliefs, etc., of trade unions and their activities as ongoing phenomena in the political world.

The imposition by the government of massive rent increases and bus fare hikes, and the imposition of Community Councils provided the basis for the formal growth of community organizations. Resident associations, "civics," and other community groups—e.g., of women or youths—began to emerge, particularly around 1979. In Soweto, the Soweto Civic Association, with thirty branches, was founded in 1979.

In the Eastern and Western Cape, the civic emerged as a new mass-based community organization. The Port Elizabeth Black Civic Organization (PEBCO) was heavily involved in community and trade union struggles in the 1979 strike period. The civic organizations concerned themselves with housing problems, electrification, rent increases, bus fare hikes, and other issues that affected the household. Civics were heavily involved in opposition to the relocation policies under separate development. In 1981 in Durban and the Western Cape, Housing Action Committees were formed to engage the government over rents, electrification, garbage, sewer, and the general improvement in the living conditions in the townships.

Within the civic movement in all areas were activists from the Congress movement of the 1950s. The civic movement had close relations with the trade unions, since many community issues affected workers and their families. The civics were very important in organizing economic support for the trade unions, particularly in the case of the nationwide boycott of the Fatti's and Moni's firm during the FCWU strike in 1979. However, the relations between the trade unions and the civics were problematical for the unions. On the one hand, close relations provided a kind of "protection" in the community and an immediate source of support in the event of a "mass action." The community organization that developed around the Neil Aggett memorial in Johannesburg brought 20,000 participants from around the country. On the other hand, the civics would like to have received direct support from the trade unions for their demands. For example, when rents were increased the civics would have liked to ask the unions to strike to help them demonstrate the plight of township residents. However, it was virtually unanimous among the independent trade unions that this kind of action was inappropriate at the time. The major problem was to support community groups while retaining the integrity of the trade unions.

Concerning the relations of the GWU with the community, organizers within that body stated that the trade unions entered the community as an organization and as members of an ad hoc community-based coalition. Most workers found that the community lacked the muscle of the unions but were not eager to let union members take up leadership or participate actively in community work. The GWU insisted that the trade unions must be democratically involved along with the other organizations, meaning they should share an equal voice in determining the political strategies of the civic association.

Problems arose when community organizations had different structures or perceptions of intergroup "democracy." They usually were very involved in ad hoc campaigns and did not understand the procedures that unions had to go through to get direction from their membership in order to participate and take a position. The unions had a more formal structure, as opposed to the community organizations' more ad hoc structures. In order to avoid estranging the civics, the unions provided them primarily with services, such as transport, and issued public statements in support of their work. Mutual education regarding the significance of issues and the nature of support occurred continuously. Also, union members were present as members of the civic organizations and were able to assert the trade union perspective on any particular debate in which the demand for trade union action was considered appropriate.

The civic was not a phenomenon in the Transvaal, though the Soweto-based Committee of Ten did act, to some degree, as a "community"/munici-pal organization. Explanations for the absence of mass-based community groups included the fact that Soweto is heterogeneous, where the Cape communities are not. Soweto is the third largest city on the continent of Africa, after Cairo and Lagos. Consequently, there was no sense of a close-knit community. Because of its high degree of urbanization, "ethnicity" was not an organizing factor in the Transvaal as it was in the Cape. Finally, because the population in the Johannesburg area was made up primarily of permanent urban residents, there was not the strong demand for a vigilant ongoing community group, as there was in the Cape. When rents were raised or bus fares hiked, spontaneous organizations emerged and were able to affect matters on an issue-by-issue basis.

FOSATU had developed a series of arguments against its involvement in community affairs. It claimed that FOSATU did not want to be taken over by petit bourgeois elements in the community (as CUSA had been) or take up "radical" political issues in the community (as MACWUSA did).

However, FOSATU, as a national federation, was not immune from community demands. According to FOSATU officials, relations between the union and the community varied from region to region and were dependent on the historical and political circumstances under which they organized. For the National Auto and Allied Workers' Union (NAAWU), the auto trade union operating in the Eastern Cape, community demands were so strong that NAAWU had agreed to sit on community committees. To protect the unions from succumbing to strong community demands, FOSATU had tried to foster "union–community" relations between the federation offices and the community. Like the GWU, NAAWU had a transport committee and a community health committee. However, like the other unions, FOSATU believed that while the tendency to become more "political" had increased as the pressure on the community had increased, political action was still peripheral and occurred around ad hoc protests rather than constituting long-term engagement strategies. Thus, FOSATU unions were able to respond without getting entangled. Indeed, in retrospect, it could well be argued that those calling for the use of trade union muscle for community actions were acting prematurely. Community organizations, like the trade unions, needed to develop independent bodies with structures sufficient in breadth and depth to sustain political actions independent of worker power. Not that unions would not or could not support civic issues, but the intermingling of labor actions with community actions and organizational development would have made it much more difficult to build the strong, national bodies that later emerged.

The major problem in this debate was the development of a litmus test that implied that anything short of formal trade union affiliation in the opposition movement, and engagement in strikes called either by or at the behest of community groups, meant the trade unions were denying the communities their muscle. This placed the trade unions in an untenable situation. Despite their clear agenda in support of political processes to make South Africa a majority-ruled country, their reluctance to affiliate formally with "democratic political forces" placed them on the defensive.

The most important development in South Africa in the 1980s was the emergence of the aboveground black political movement. In opposition to government-planned elections, the United Democratic Front was launched in 1983, composed initially of 600 organizations, including women's groups, civic associations, youth/student groups, religious organizations, and a few trade unions. Virtually all independent trade unions sent representatives, and thirteen union groupings joined immediately. However, the most powerful federations and two of the largest unaffiliated unions decided not to join, though they gave their support (see Table 6.2).

FOSATU's general secretary, Joe Foster, argued that his organization could not join UDF because its collective memberships did not identify with a single political organization. Second, FOSATU was busy trying to form a union federation and had to make this responsibility to the workers its first political agenda.

Terror Lekate, former GWU organizer and the new national publicity secretary for the UDF, summed up the other position:

> The struggle of the working class does not end at the factory floor. When workers who face management leave the factory they come up against the problems of high transport costs, rents, and inadequate community facilities—all of which eat into our wages. To strengthen the community organizations is to improve the conditions of the working class; to fight high rents and bus fares is to fight the struggle of the working class. Unions must take up community struggles if they are to represent the interests of workers.[28]

In response to a question as to whether or not unions could take up community struggles without joining the UDF, he responded, "The role of the UDF must not be to substitute organizations at the local level. Its strength lies in the strength of its member organizations. The UDF's role is to coordinate and give direction to the struggle."[29] Although attempting to clarify his political position, Lekate still left no doubt as to who should dictate the direction of political (and trade union, one can conclude) actions.

Responding somewhat defensively, the GWU in 1983 stated:

> We take issue with claims and resulting criticism that we do not support the UDF or that we are not interested in politics. We support any organization opposing the new constitution and other laws which deny the majority of South Africa democracy. Our support obviously extends to the UDF. We have stated our willingness to participate jointly in campaigns and give our general support in a variety of ways.[30]

GWU leaders continued, however, to argue that they had "real difficulty" with single workers' organizations affiliating to the UDF. Instead, they envisioned a national union federation affiliating to a national political body.[31] They vowed to continue encouraging members to join organizations affiliated with the UDF and, "should our members rise to become even a leader of the UDF," they would not view that as "inconsistent with union policy in the slightest. In fact, it would probably be a source of great pride to the union."[32]

The GWU went to great lengths to explain its position on the UDF.

Table 6.2 UDF Unions

Unions Joining UDF	Unions Not Joining UDF
CUSA	FOSATU
SAAWU	A/FCWU
GAWU	GWU
Orange Vaal GWU	Cape Town MWU
M & GWUSA	
MACWUSA	
GWUSA	
SATWU	
MWASA	
Johannesburg Scooter Driver Association	
CAW	
NFW	
AWA	

Without question, the GWU supported the launching of the UDF, committed itself to supporting UDF campaigns, and looked forward to joint campaigns in the future. But, the GWU also made credible arguments for not formally affiliating with the UDF, thereby failing the litmus test. Briefly, the GWU had involved itself with a local organization in the Western Cape—the Disorderly Bills Action Committee (DBAC)—and had found the experience frustrating on a number of points. First, the DBAC was fraught with conflict among its member organizations. Second, individuals were engaged in power struggles over the leadership of the organization. Third, the objectives of the organization were clearly lost at some point. But, after some unofficial experience with the UDF, the GWU shook off the ill effects of the experience with the DBAC and pledged full support to the UDF.

The concerns raised by the GWU seem wholly legitimate for at least three reasons. First, GWU's members had differing opinions on various UDF political affiliates and on the political agenda of the day for any particular group. Thus, to embroil the union in the issues taken up through UDF affiliates, and at the national level, had the potential of disrupting relationships within the organization and confusing the focus of the union. Second, as in any coalition or federation, the UDF member organizations varied in membership orientation and issue focus, and might differ from time to time on strategies and tactics of the movement. Once again, it could have threatened the cohesion of the trade unions to have had their members drawn into conflict over matters that could distract them from the goals and purposes of their trade unions. By analogy, the trade unions argued that women's organizations might choose to work on women's issues. Throughout the country, this had dictated a particular kind of organizing strategy, because women had been heavily victimized by removal policies and other laws affecting their freedom and their residential status. What if, as was likely the case, women's organizations chose to develop a political base among highly vulnerable women by organizing self-help projects, child care co-ops, and health clinics. It might be considered premature by these same organizations to engage themselves, in their political infancy, in militant political actions determined by other political groups or, in this case, other UDF affiliates. And third, the trade unions jealously guarded the decision to engage in strike action. This has not precluded them from calling strikes in support of political causes; but these actions were taken as decisions of the union membership. By analogy, when SAAWU called for a boycott of Wilson Rountree confectionary products, the communities, locally and nationally, were not in a position to pull off the boycott successfully. Yet, because of SAAWU's request, they tried and failed. Likewise, political organizations could call for unions to strike when unions were not in a position to do so. Such action, too, would probably fail.

The unions were on less solid ground when they argued that the strictly political nature of the "oppressor" in the community group's mind, e.g., the state, is not the same as the "oppressor" in the trade union's mind, e.g., industrialists and economic actors. While this is true on one level, on another level the South African government is very much involved in industrial and economic affairs that affect and are affected by the trade unions. If this were not so, the government would not have responded so strongly to trade union activism from 1948 onward. It is conceivable that trade unions could strike on behalf of overt political issues and then demand to negotiate directly with the state. But this is to be tested. The problem is: who determines the political issues over which the unions could strike? This is where the unions have their legitimate concern.

Explaining its reasons for joining the UDF, the Municipal and General Workers' Unions of South Africa (MGWUSA) argued that four political issues affected workers and needed to be addressed: (1) the increasing push toward *bantustan* independence for all the homelands; (2) the attempt to push through new pass laws that would tighten up the control of all workers; (3) the community council elections that were to be held later that month (1983); and (4) the "New Deal" being pushed by the government in the forthcoming constitution.[33] MGWUSA explained that the first line of obligation of the trade unions, as organizations of workers, not of political parties, is the defense of workers. Unable to take on political issues effectively, MGWUSA believed that the best way to address these issues was to form alliances with political organizations. It defined the UDF as a "rallying point" more than an organization. It continued to describe it as "a form of unity in action—but not in structure/form or detailed policy."[34] It also acknowledged the symbolic value of the UDF as a focal point of national determination to end oppression.

MGWUSA saw as the main limitation on trade unions their structure and "way of operating," which focused them exclusively on economic issues. The only way to overcome "economism" was to associate with the political organizations that already existed. By participating in the UDF, the unions could: (1) oppose the tendency toward economism by stating their commitment as trade unionists to the broader struggle for freedom; and (2) influence that struggle's direction and goals by actively participating.[35] In conclusion, MGWUSA stated:

> We believe that it is impossible to separate off apartheid from the capitalist system it has fed. A truly committed opposition to apartheid (and its consequences) will lay the foundation for a fundamental change in the entire system of South Africa.
>
> It's up to the unions and all other progressives to ensure that the organized workers are fully involved in the process of struggle—that worker leaders emerge and take up positions amongst the political leadership—that progressives unite to ensure a struggle for truly fundamental change in South Africa.[36]

Sisa Njikelana argued yet another perspective, that the working class needed to lead the broad democratic struggle against apartheid and could only do that by taking up leadership of democratic political organizations such as the UDF.

THE UNGOVERNABILITY OF THE TOWNSHIPS

Immediately following the implementation of South Africa's new "reform" constitution in September 1984, the most intense and dramatic uprisings since the Soweto rebellions began. Unlike Soweto, the new rebellion was broadly based and rooted deeply in the political anger of the black community. Opposition to rent increases, service charges, the imposition of government structures, and the new "reforms" fueled the anger. Instruments of opposition included petrol bombs, consumer boycotts, demonstrations, stayaways, and political organizing. The government responded with deadly force, arrests, and detentions, plunging the country into an escalating civil war. Thousands of UDF, COSATU, and other leaders were held in detention. The African National Congress, through its president, Oliver Tambo, called for the people to "render the townships ungovernable."

> We must begin to use our accumulated strength to destroy the organs of the apartheid regime. We have to undermine and weaken its control over us, exactly by frustrating its attempts to control us. We should direct our collective might to rendering the enemy's instruments of authority unworkable. To march forward must mean that we advance against the regime's organs of state power, creating conditions in which the country becomes increasingly ungovernable.[37]

This call to action was followed one year later by an ANC appeal for South Africans to "replace the collapsing government stooge councils with people's committees in every block which could become the embryos of people's power,"[38] and began a period of massive resistance and the building of alternative structures in the community to take over the governance of the townships, to build grassroots resistance, and to develop self-help/self-reliance projects.

What can be defined as the new antiapartheid movement began with "hit-and-run" meetings designed to decrease the violence in the townships committed by *kabasa* and *comtsotsis*, or "false comrades," in response to the mass uprisings. Mandela's "M-Plan" in the 1950s had called for a street-cell system to inform the community of important decisions without having to call large public meetings or distribute circulars. Instead, street committees used messengers, small meetings, and whistle blowing and light flashing to signal distress in the neighborhoods. By October 1985, there were 102 cells in the Western Cape alone.

The ANC's call for "ungovernability" coincided with antigovernment campaigns already emerging in the country. This period tested the will of the trade unions to engage the political issues. In October 1984, FOSATU issued a statement to employers questioning their attitudes toward the new constitution. FOSATU explained its strong opposition and vowed to use its strength on the factory floor to oppose the government. CUSA took a similar stand against the new constitution. A reading of trade unions seems to demonstrate their capacity to maintain a strong stance in support of opposition politics. In April 1986, COSATU called for a May Day nationwide strike to support the following political issues:

- A 40-hour work week and a living wage
- The right of all workers to join democratic unions
- Democratic student representative councils
- An alternative system of people's education
- The release of all political prisoners and the unbanning of organizations
- An end to pass laws and influx control
- Decent housing and affordable rents
- A paid public holiday on May 1
- The declaration of June 16—the anniversary of the Soweto uprisings—as a public holiday

The May Day strike was 70–100 percent effective in industrial centers around the country. It is estimated that 1.5 to 2 million workers stayed out. On June 16, the strike was 95–100 percent successful in the Pretoria-Witwatersrand-Vaal region, and 80 percent effective in the Cape.

As the government declared its states of emergency, trade unionists were targets along with political activists. Over 2,000 trade unionists were arrested after the first declaration of the state of emergency. Of these, 269 were office holders. Four SAAWU leaders were put on trial for treason; they were subsequently acquitted. The government did not distinguish between trade unionists and other activists during its attack on antiapartheid opposition. It used the Riotous Assemblies Act to break up strike meetings and publicly linked the trade union movement to the African National Congress. This public assertion followed the "total onslaught" theory pushed by the government in the early 1980s. Union leaders were detained, tortured, and charged under the Terrorism Act and Internal Securities Act. Trade unions were also the target of the "Intimidation Act," which came into force in 1982 to halt union recruitment of new members and to prevent strike solidarity.

While trade union involvement with recently organized "progressive politics" appeared cautious based on some very narrow criteria, trade unions, in fact, maintained a high level of activity in and loyalty to opposition politics. Workers were encouraged to join political groups. Oscar Mpetha of the A/FCWU was elected vice president of the New Democratic Forum (forerunner to the UDF). The first president of the UDF was a trade unionist, and, throughout the development of the civics, trade unionists have been active as individual members.

Government repression was particularly severe from the first declared state of emergency through 1988. The Law and Order Minister Adriaan Vlok reported that between July 1985 and June 1986, 508 members of the ANC and PAC had been "eliminated."[39]

In May 1987, COSATU House in Johannesburg was hit by two powerful bombs, virtually destroying the building. Terrorist attacks, attributed to no organization or individuals, but deadly nevertheless, hit COSATU very hard during early October 1987. During the week of October 15–22, COSATU organizer Amos Tshabalala's body was found in the East Rand township of Tsakana; in Natal, regional secretary Matthew Oliphant was shot at several times; and a bomb destroyed the home of former COSATU Northern Transvaal regional chairman, Jerry Thibedi. Thibedi and his wife and children miraculously escaped with minor injuries. During the last week of October, four COSATU offices in Kimberly were fire-bombed, bringing the total number of bomb attacks to nine over a period of less than two months. The government had no lead on any suspects. The assault on COSATU was so heavy during this period that it called a "Hands Off COSATU" campaign to bring national and international attention to the rash of attacks on offices and personnel. COSATU faced severe repression, deaths, and detentions under an onslaught from the state, employers, and vigilantes.

In fact, the heavy government repression of the 1980s, in reaction to the growing strength and confidence of the trade union movement, the radicalization of the black majority, and the growth of strong community-based organization created the new political order through which stronger linkages between trade unions and political organizations could be forged.

In the winter of 1987, at COSATU's second annual congress, the organization adopted the Freedom Charter as a guiding political document. This adoption followed two years of discussion and negotiation with the UDF over strategies, organizing techniques, and—more centrally—how COSATU related to democratic organizations based in the townships. Speaking for COSATU in response to the repression and violence directed toward its leadership, information officer Frank Meintjies made the following statement in January 1988:

> There is a great deal of rethinking and strategizing going on in the Congress of South African Trade Unions.
>
> A clearer sense of direction would only emerge once the federation finalized the structure or the shape of the united front which COSATU and the UDF have been discussing.
>
> I think that the main area of weakness was our slowness in building solidarity action between the different unions and our failure to quickly build solidarity action at the community level with other democratic organizations and townships.[40]

He acknowledged for the union that "COSATU has not built solidly enough the links with democratic allies in the townships. This is an area which we have to attend to and correct as a matter of urgency this year."[41]

If there were any questions about the reserve power of the unions, however, they were resolved with the stayaway called in June 1988. Observers predicted that repressive conditions under which the union had suffered would prevent any sizable showing and, in fact, would illustrate the absolutely weakened condition of the labor movement. The stayaway, the largest in South Africa's history, brought 3 million workers off the job, costing industry some R5 billion. The manufacturing sector averaged a stayaway rate of 77 percent; the retail sector 55 percent. Bobby Godsell, speaking for Saccola, had predicted, "You can take X number of people away from work for three days, but when the sun rises on Thursday morning what has changed?"[42] Though recanting later, the labor minister offered to suspend parts of a proposed amendment to the industrial conciliation act.

As the organizational sophistication of the trade union and antiapartheid movements has grown, the trade unions and democratic community organizations have become increasingly more comfortable with formal relations. Among the trade union federations, there still exists some distance between COSATU and NACTU. However, the differences have not been as deadly and severe as those with the United Workers' Union of South Africa (UWUSA), a construct of Gatsha Buthelezi's Inkatha organization.

In fact, the major political problem in the trade union movement has to do not with its identity with the progressive political movements but with the major competing political movement, the Zulu, Natal-based organization, Inkatha. Though ideological differences exist between the UDF and AZAPO, the organizations consider themselves part of a larger pro-majority movement and have not exhibited the degree of hostilities demonstrated by Inkatha. In fact, some organizations and unions are affiliated to both the UDF and AZAPO's National Forum. In 1984, the UDF issued a statement that it did not see itself as a rival to any group, and participated in some joint actions in Johannesburg with AZAPO. However, violence has characterized the rising tensions between the UDF and Buthelezi's Inkatha movement.

As the trade union movement began to develop in the early 1970s, Buthelezi had made overtures to trade unions to join the Inkatha movement. There were obvious differences between the trade union movement and Inkatha from the beginning. The first and most obvious was the predominance of Buthelezi, the individual who clearly wanted to exert himself as the head of any new black worker organization. The trade union movement was second to the political movement in his mind, and the only legitimate political movement was Inkatha. Another difference was the issue of the unions' relations to capital and the disinvestment movement. Buthelezi established himself as the moderate in the minds of overseas capital. He strongly opposed disinvestment and supported moderation in industrial matters. He supported business-sponsored codes of conduct where the independent trade unions opposed them. Furthermore, Buthelezi's penchant for launching verbal attacks on organizations and individuals not conducting themselves to his liking made any negotiations or discussions with him and Inkatha virtually impossible. Buthelezi's clear agenda was either to control or eliminate what he perceived to be opposition.

Buthelezi and his associates created a hostile and often deadly environment for both UDF and COSATU leaders. The violence emerged as UDF-supporting youth congresses and union organizers began to appear in areas of Natal where Inkatha's support had not been traditionally high. In response, Inkatha launched a violent two-pronged strategy: (1) terrorism, to rid the area of UDF/COSATU activists; and (2) intimidation of local residents, in an attempt to convince them to join Inkatha.

On May 1, 1986, Inkatha formed the United Workers' Union of South Africa (UWUSA) as a direct response to COSATU. During its first year, it claimed a membership of 100,000. UWUSA sought and received support from the African-American Labor Center (AALC)—a regional organization attached to the American Federation of Labor-Congress of Industrial Organizations (AFL-CIO). Other trade unions had shunned numerous overtures from the AALC, after years of suspicion regarding its alleged links with the U.S. Central Intelligence Agency (CIA). Where other unions had established informal rules of competition among themselves for recruiting members in key industrial areas,[43] UWUSA engaged in open and aggressive competition, including finding replacements for fired workers from other unions. Competition was at times deadly. In 1987, two UWUSA organizers were accused of murdering a National Union of Mineworkers organizer. By the end of 1987, over 150 lives had been lost to "union warfare" in the Pietermaritzburg area alone.

In spite of attempts by UDF and COSATU leaders to end the violence, Buthelezi consistently launched impetuous, irrational, and vituperative attacks against their organizations. His political motives seemed quite clear— to maintain his own territorial and political base in Natal/KwaZulu. But his attacks were often ill-timed, out of context, and deliberately designed to fuel anger and violence. According to reports in October 1987, Buthelezi launched two separate verbal attacks on UDF president Archie Gumede at the very moment the latter had been conducting delicate cease-fire negotiations between UDF/COSATU and Inkatha members.

In one October speech released to the press at the time the local Chamber of Commerce was sponsoring talks between warring factions, Buthelezi claimed the UDF and COSATU were "not worthy of reconciliation." He went on:

> I am now coming closer to believing that the only reconciliation there will ever be in this country is the reconciliation of the most powerful with those who pay homage to the powerful. We are talking about a life and death struggle. We are talking about all-or-nothing victories. We are talking about the final triumph by good over evil."[44]

To stage his accusations, Buthelezi demanded at the conference sponsored by the Chamber that the UDF and COSATU repudiate an article in the journal *Inquaba Yabasebenzi*, published by the Marxist Workers' Tendency, a group purged by the ANC in 1985. The UDF and COSATU, feeling Buthelezi had raised a non-issue, refused to do so. Blaming the UDF and COSATU, Buthelezi gave license to the Inkatha youth to continue the violence against their opposition. In a fiery statement he continued to fuel the conflict: "I must say rather bluntly that the UDF and COSATU are not worthy of the status of organizations to whom we need to be reconciled. It is their choice that death keeps us apart and death is keeping us apart."[45]

The response by the state to the violence appeared to favor Inkatha. Routinely, UDF and COSATU activists were arrested and placed in detention. It was not until the evidence against Inkatha activists began to damage both Buthelezi and the government that the government moved to halt some of the violence. In January 1988, two temporary interdicts were served on Inkatha restraining their "warlords" from killing, assaulting, threatening, or intimidating local residents. This brought the total number of interdicts to seven. However, the individuals served were free to move about.[46] Later that month, UDF, COSATU, and the Chamber of Commerce became convinced that Inkatha had scheduled a "Doomsday attack." Though that "attack" did not take place on the appointed date, armed youth—alleged Inkatha supporters— raided neighborhoods, attacking pedestrians and shoppers.

By March 1988, six Inkatha members had been found responsible for the deaths of three people. The members had been trained at a paramilitary camp run by Inkatha. Buthelezi acknowledged the paramilitary regimentation but compared the school to the Boy Scouts and Salvation Army.[47]

Sensing the political liability, particularly overseas, of those convictions and the other accusations, Buthelezi announced in his presidential address that it was very important for Inkatha to counter "politically and diplomatically the accusations that Inkatha commits political atrocities against black brothers and sisters in the struggle for liberation."[48] He claimed to be "uneasy" with the corrupt and violent behavior of some of his members and proposed watchdog committees to assure that Inkatha rid itself of the image of violence against fellow black South Africans.[49] Nonetheless, Inkatha activists will probably still be extremely hostile to UDF and COSATU workers, and future violence is more likely than not.

CONCLUSION

The existence of Black Consciousness–oriented unions and "nonracial" ones is not an aberration in South African politics. Both types of movements follow a long tradition of this same divergence within the politics of the black community. In a more formal political setting, one could envisage them constituting a "two-party system." The fact exists that despite the differences, there have not emerged deadly hostilities between the two tendencies. As the political environment in South Africa has become more repressive and the political movements more mature, there have been fewer denunciations of one another's ideas and motives, and more statements of cooperation. Black Consciousness unions, though fewer in number, will continue to exist as long as they serve a political and social need among some black workers. In the meantime, those supporting the two ideologies, represented by trade union and community groups, will continue to build structures opposing the government and continue to find common ground between themselves.

The black trade unions have overcome earlier criticism that they were resistant to affiliating formally with opposition political organizations. The issue of "formal affiliation," used earlier as a litmus test to determine political involvement, ignored the real commitment of the trade union movement. Trade unions had to develop their organizational structures along lines compatible with their "turf"—the industrial environment. Likewise, mass movement organizations had to develop their structures along overt political lines. As both movements have matured (and the political situation in South Africa has become more radicalized), they have moved toward closer formal alliance. Their "structures," organizational systems based on grassroots and rank and file democracy, have potential for guiding the movements toward increasing pressure on the government and, over the longer term, toward negotiated political change.

NOTES

1. Stanley B. Greenberg, *Race and State in Capitalist Development: Comparative Perspectives* (New Haven: Yale University Press, 1980), p. 177.

2. Personal interview, Anonymous, Guguletu (Cape Town), South Africa, February 16, 1982.

3. *Hansard*, verbatim parliamentary record, South African Parliament (Pretoria: South African Government Printer, 1982), p. 1093.

4. Steven B. Biko, "Black Souls in White Skins?" *SASO Newsletter* (August 1970), p. 15, and in Gail Gerhart, *Black Power in South Africa* (Berkeley: University of California Press, 1978), p. 264.

5. Steven B. Biko, "We Blacks," *SASO Newsletter* (September 1970), p. 18, and in Gerhart, *Black Power*, p. 291.

6. *Working for Freedom*, unpublished document (Johannesburg, n.d.), p. 28.

7. *Ibid.*, p. 28 (emphasis in original).

8. Shirley Miller, *Trade Unions in South Africa, 1970–1980*, Saldru Working Paper No. 45 (Capetown: University of Capetown, April 1982), p. 74.

9. Editorial: "Workers Struggle in East London," *Work in Progress*, no. 17 (April 1981), p. 6.

10. *Ibid.*, p. 7.

11. *Survey of Race Relations* 1981 (Johannesburg: Institute of Race Relations), p. 107.

12. Editorial: "Workers Struggle," p. 7.

13. *Survey of Race Relations* 1983, p. 176.

14. *Ibid.*, p. 54.

15. Council of Unions of South Africa, *Policy Document on Some Issues* (unpublished, 1982), p. 1.

16. Personal interview, Perishaw Camay, general secretary, Council of Unions of South Africa (CUSA), Johannesburg, March 17, 1982.

17. *Survey of Race Relations* 1984, p. 58.

18. *Survey of Race Relations* 1957, p. 220.

19. *Ibid.*

20. Personal interview, Government Zini, organizing secretary, Motor and Components Workers' Union of South Africa (MACWUSA), Port Elizabeth, April 9, 1982.

21. *Survey of Race Relations* 1972, pp. 391–392.

22. *Survey of Race Relations* 1974, p. 327.

23. General Workers' Union, "Relationships with Other Organizations," *General Workers' Union Policy and Constitution* (Capetown, 1980), p. 4.

24. Food and Canning Workers' Union, "Search for a Workable Relationship," *South African Labour Bulletin* 7, no. 8 (1982), p. 55.

25. *South African Labour Bulletin* 9, no. 9 (1984), p. 82.

26. Steven Friedman, *Building Tomorrow Today* (Johannesburg: Ravan Press, 1987), p. 437.

27. CUSA, *Policy Document*, p. 1.

28. *South African Labour Bulletin* 9, no. 9 (1984), p. 82.

29. *Ibid.*

30. General Workers' Union, "The GWU on the UDF," *South African Labour Bulletin* 9, no. 2 (1983), p. 47.

31. *Ibid.*, p. 52.

32. *Ibid.*, p. 57.

33. Municipal and General Workers' Union of South Africa, "MGWUSA on the UDR," *South African Labour Bulletin* 9, no. 2 (1983), p. 63.

34. *Ibid.*, p. 71.

35. *Ibid.*, p. 72.

36. *Ibid.*, p. 74.

37. University of California Faculty Against Apartheid, Organizing Committee for a Free South Africa, "For a Free South Africa: A Tribute to Winnie and Nelson Mandela. Update: South Africa." Program for humanitarian concert, Berkeley, CA, September 14, 1986.

38. *Ibid.*

39. "Vlok's Arithmetic of Terror," in *Weekly Mail* 3, no. 2, (1986) p. 5.

40. "Battered COSATU Does a Rethink," in *Weekly Mail* 4, no. 3, (1987) p. 11.

41. *Ibid.*

42. Eddie Koch, "The Non-Strike Called by No-One Confounds the Critics Who Said: It Must Flop," in *Weekly Mail* 4, no. 22, (1987) p. 2.

43. This approach to union competition was best addressed in an unpublished 1982 CUSA document:

> Whilst the Council of Unions would prefer seeing industry-wide trade unions finally emerging, we recognize that in the present developmental stage, worker aspirations need to be expressed through their freedom to choose or create associations to protect and enhance their interests. It is only when sufficient trust and credibility is established between unions that common purpose will allow unions to adopt common stances or merge. The Council would also wish to develop a dispute procedure acceptable to non-affiliated union and other federations which may be used when issues need to be resolved between competing unions. (Quoted from CUSA, *Policy Document*, p. 2.)

44. "Buthelezi in Amazing Swipe at UDF," in *Weekly Mail* 3, no. 49, (1986) pp. 1–2.

45. *Ibid.*

46. Phillip van Nierkerk, "The Warlords Who Walk Free," in *Weekly Mail* 4, no. 3, (1987) p. 1.

47. "Six Inkatha Inquest Accused Attended 'Paramilitary' Camp," in *Weekly Mail* 4, no. 11, p. 3.

48. Carmel Rickard and Thandeka Gqubule, "Inkatha Poised to Clear Out Warlords," in *Weekly Mail* 4, no. 19, (1987) p. 1.

49. *Ibid.*

7

The White Mind, Business, and Apartheid

HERIBERT ADAM & KOGILA MOODLEY

No solution to the problems in South Africa is conceivable without realignments among the country's 5 million whites. They control the state and the economy with little loss of confidence, despite a severe crisis. Unless this ruling group splits or loses its morale, the basic power equation is unlikely to change in South Africa.

The role of white business seems crucial in such a realignment. What has been the response of capital to the unprecedented emergencies and outside pressure? What has come out of the contacts between liberal tycoons and the ANC? How have sanctions affected the white electorate, the economy, and the relationship between state and capital? What do recent election results reveal about new policies and shifts in the white mood? What does the increased militarization and rise of the security establishment indicate for future reforms?[1]

RESPONSES TO CRISIS: THE URBAN FOUNDATION

The political response of South African business to the Soweto crisis of 1976, the Urban Foundation, essentially represents corporate charity. It even comes relatively cheap, considering the huge profits South Africa still yields. Like charity everywhere, it provides a good conscience for the donors and reaffirms their moral superiority. Above all, critics of multinationals are fended off when corporate headquarters can proudly display how much they spend on "community development" and how hard they lobby Pretoria with pious resolutions. As an alibi for business-as-usual, the progressive efforts are well worth the outlay. That is the cynical evaluation, but it is not far from reality.

Only Marxist dogmatists view the Urban Foundation as a giant conspiracy to create a black middle class in defense of capitalism. South African capitalism is far too disorganized and fragmented to be capable of a conspiracy. Concerted action presupposes a minimal common understanding of long-term interests. Most overworked tycoons live by the day and the next balance sheet. Like politicians, they react to crisis rather than anticipate future costs.

Furthermore, the emergence of a black middle class is severely constrained by the racial division of labor. After three decades of talking about color-blind promotion policies and black advancement schemes, the results remain dismal. The page of the Sunday papers that pictures "People on the Move" still shows mostly white appointments (with few females at that). In the whole of Natal, there is hardly any position where an African gives orders to an Indian or white. The greatest indictment of racial capitalism lies in the following official statistic: out of a total of 256,000 managers and administrators, 10,802 are black. This figure means that less than 4 percent of persons in this category are black, and the ratio of black managers to workers is about 1 to 820. How could these few tokens be expected to hold the line against demands for state control of South African monopolies?

The extraordinarily high degree of capital concentration under the control of a few corporations also severely limits the chances of independent black businesspeople to carve out a niche of the monopolized market. Most will invariably end up as junior partners of existing conglomerates if they do not become bankrupt earlier because of a stifling bureaucracy, deficient loan facilities, or lack of expertise. But even if eventually there were to emerge a more substantial *African Bourgeoisie* (the title of a perceptive book by the liberal South African sociologist Leo Kuper, published in 1965!),[2] they would still be locked in the ghettoes by the Group Areas Act, politically excluded, and humiliated by the Race Classification Act. As all surveys show, it is this group of better-off and better-educated subordinates who most resent the system. They harbor psychological rather than material grievances. They are in the forefront of militancy, which the really downtrodden can ill afford. The more *material* interests are met, the more people's *ideal* interests come to the fore.

Herein lies the major fallacy of the Urban Foundation's development approach and the state's upgrading of townships: in the absence of political equality, "development" hopes to buy off dissent with material improvements. Better housing, as necessary as it is, does not solve the political crisis. Economic advance is no substitute for political rights. It is fatuous to assume that people with full stomachs will not care about politics. On the contrary: thinking about alternatives to mere survival starts when basic needs are fulfilled. The diffusion of class conflict in the Western democracies depended on political incorporation. The vote for powerful Labor parties preceded embourgeoisement in Europe. In South Africa, stability seems impossible without democratic equality, without equal citizenship, and without a legitimized state with which all can identify. Politicized blacks are suspicious of business not only for its silent support of an apartheid regime; an Urban Foundation, whatever its undoubted merit, is seen as cheating the victims out of the anticapitalist promise. Blacks resent being pacified. Even the most generous charity degrades. Sophisticated capitalist-sponsored self-help schemes are perceived as worse—inducing the victims to welcome their own degradation when they are entitled to equal life chances. Only the conquest of the state, they argue, can achieve this. Afrikaner nationalism has set an obvious precedent.

THE POWER OF BUSINESS

In her provocative *Capitalism and Apartheid*, Merle Lipton discusses four possible relationships between South African capital and the apartheid state: (1) capital has neither an interest nor the power to get rid of apartheid; (2) capital has developed an interest but still has no power; (3) capital has an interest as well as the power to dismantle apartheid; and (4) capital would have the power but has no interest to abolish apartheid.[3] Lipton argues that labor requirements and other costs have changed to such an extent that apartheid has not become dysfunctional for large sectors of South African business, even for commercial agriculture and mining.

Why then the complacency? Why the "deafening silence," which even Anglo board member Murray Hofmeyer deplored, lending support to the widely held belief that business pays only lip service to reform? The usual answer, according to Raymond Ackerman, the chairman of South Africa's largest supermarket chain, is that business has no power but instead tries everything behind the scene, where it is far more effective in a quiet way. As a liberal tycoon, Bob Tucker, however, has aptly characterized the difference between public and private behavior: "One wonders, for example, whether the extremely important FCI [Federated Chamber of Industry], AH [Afrikaanse Handelsinstituut], ASSOCOM [Association of Commerce] resolutions, and Project Free Enterprise conclusions, are even recognised, let alone reinforced in the process of direct interface between leaders and government." It is simply part of corporate mythology that South Africa represents the only capitalist country where business stands to the left of the government. While this may be true with respect to the abolition of certain apartheid measures, business unanimously stands to the far right of Pretoria as far as "free enterprise" and other neoconservative economic policies are concerned.

There are two crucial areas where business has the undoubted power to effect change and make its political mark. At the same time, they highlight the obstacles to a more progressive political involvement. The first task would be to transform the company environment into a model of a nonracial industrial democracy. Within the factory gates, business has almost total sovereignty and no excuse for feudal labor relations. Here the business/labor solidarity that the "Project Economic Participation" aims at would be a sensible beginning. If farsighted management were to adopt elements of the social-democratic German, Swedish, or Japanese industrial system of partnership (guaranteed union participation in all employee decisions, profit-sharing schemes, incentives, living wages), it would prove far superior to the current adversary principle of labor relations. However, apart from a hardware company (Cashbuild), there is not a single major enterprise that demonstrates the advantages of higher productivity through carefully fostered employee loyalties. If a reformed capitalism wants to weather the clamor for a peoples' dictatorship in a future postapartheid South Africa, it can only succeed through a deal with the unions in a genuine social democracy. In the transition, this must include protection of unions against assaults by the security establishment. If this ground is not cemented now, it may well be too shaky during the time of reckoning.

In a permanent emergency, it is the legal unions who carry the burden of the repressed political cause, often at great cost to themselves. Labor consultant Andrew Levy concluded: "Labour mobilisation during the past year has advanced the aims of the broader anti-apartheid movement far more than those of the labour movement, despite the fact it has focused on routine workplace issues. It has in part led to the ironical situation where industrial wars may have been lost, but political battles have been won."[4] South Africa is one of the few Western countries where union membership is still growing. Strikes have generally increased in length. The 9 million worker-days lost in 1987 was six times higher than in the previous year.

Business/labor solidarity would also entail strong efforts to bring recalcitrant companies into line. South African business as a whole, for example, cannot afford situations where parastatals, such as the South African Transport Services (SATS), endanger the fragile peace by supremacist management conduct. Similarly, the more enlightened mining houses would have to lean on Gencor or Goldfields lest they, too, risk being tarnished by the behavior of their backward associates.

The ANC and the major nonracial union federation, COSATU, on the other hand, must also consider the devastating implications of extreme union militancy. Increasingly, employers will trim their work force to the bone and mechanize. Given the still comparatively high employment rate per product or service, there is considerable scope for labor-saving devices in the South African economy. "Unreasonable" demands by politicized unions accelerate these trends toward labor substitutes and thereby cause worse black unemployment. In ANC terms, such a strategy would make sense only if greater unemployment leads to greater challenges to the state. However, unions will obviously be weakened by a huge surplus army of docile labor, steadily drifting into apathy, escapist religions, alcoholism, or crime.

PRESSING FOR POLITICAL SOLUTIONS:
BUSINESS AND THE ANC

A second arena of crucial business leadership lies in facilitating negotiations between Pretoria and the ANC. It is depressing to hear Gavin Relly, chairman of South Africa's largest conglomerate, backtracking with the statement: "I don't think that we have a role to get the government and the ANC together." Anthony Sampson records many more of such shortsighted attitudes in his informative account *Black and Gold.*[5] While business still wavers and presently retreats on mere contacts with the ANC, only a few have contemplated the more radical alternative: financing the revolution. Will the journeys to Lusaka ever be more than public relations exercises? Can new alliances be forged?

When the handful of progressive South African business leaders meet ANC representatives informally in London, Lusaka, or New York, both groups are usually surprised about the ease or even warmth with which personal relationships are established on the basis of a common South African background. Notwithstanding different political strategies and ultimate goals, the common aversion to National Party rule and anachronistic apartheid laws provides a backdrop of understanding, even solidarity, in some instances. However, these tentative personal alliances quickly fall apart when their mutual expectations are spelled out.

In the ANC strategy, progressive businesspeople serve the twofold purpose of splitting the enemy and providing clout to the broad antiapartheid forces. ANC strategists have no illusions that South African capital as a whole is prepared to throw its weight behind the organized resistance. In the perspective of progressive business leaders, on the other hand, the tentative alliances with the political alternative come to naught, when ANC spokespersons exhort that the war against enemy personnel be carried into the white areas, shortly after they have talked about finding solutions to violent escalation. The businesspeople feel compromised and manipulated as "useful idiots." The ANC military strategy therefore puts South African capital effectively into the government camp and counteracts the strategy to isolate the South African regime. On the other hand, without the militancy of organized resistance, South African business would have pursued its complacent course and not even contemplated the ANC alternative in the first place.

Since bank chairman Chris Ball was found responsible in 1987 for knowingly financing an ANC advertisement, Pretoria has successfully intimidated corporate heads with the threat of labeling them "friends of the enemy." Business has largely failed to educate its own organization for nonracial alternatives and negotiations outside government parameters. A conservative in-house constituency and lack of support among associates constrains even the handful of farsighted entrepreneurs. The "enemy" image also harms profits when prejudiced customers and public institutions withhold orders or transfer their accounts, as happened after the Ball case.

The ANC, on the other hand, would genuinely like to forge an alliance of antiapartheid forces, including capitalists. The two-stage theorists in the ANC explicitly acknowledge the role for private enterprise in the postapartheid order. Even Joe Slovo, the chairman of the South African Communist Party, emphasizes the need for a mixed economy for some time after apartheid. He implies a role not only for the small black business sector but also for managers and entrepreneurs of nonmonopoly private enterprise who are prepared to abandon racism. The SACP has put the socialist republic on ice for the immediate future because it sees a democratic transformation as far more promising. As with the armed struggle it is the Communist Party that acts as a restraining influence against far more radical tendencies inside South Africa. It is not the Communists who instigate the townships, but the politicized and brutalized products of Bantu education who radicalize the old-style Communists in exile. Will South African capitalists grasp this opportunity for a compromise?

It can almost be said that there now exists an unacknowledged and tacit new "social consensus" between both sides as far as the ANC is concerned. This consensus provides the basis for a further compromise between old-style free marketeers and traditional socialists. The compromise, as sketched in the Freedom Charter, includes an acknowledgement of responsibility by the state for social welfare programs and its role in the overall management of the national economy. Business, on the other hand, is guaranteed that nationalization and redistribution of private wealth in the socialist sense has been postponed almost indefinitely. Management prerogative in enterprises will be accommodated within a vaguely defined industrial democracy. Both sides accept the fundamental proposition that increases in the well-being of every social group, whatever its unequal position, are to be achieved by economic growth, in which the existing capitalist interests play a major part. This consensus differs substantially from the command economy of state-owned enterprises and central planning.

EFFECTS OF SANCTIONS AND DISINVESTMENT

The sanctions and disinvestment campaigns clearly impede current economic growth. However, according to Jay Naidoo, the general secretary of COSATU, the union federation has "recognised the need for economic growth in SA, and in fact we believe that economic growth is indispensable to making a non-racial democracy work in SA."[6] The simultaneous calls for sanctions and economic growth contradict each other.

However, advocates of sanctions would argue that sanctions are only aimed at abolishing apartheid quickly in order to stimulate normal growth thereafter. In fact, the short-term costs of sanctions as a form of "apartheid tax" are meant to motivate business to pressure the government into dismantling apartheid for higher long-term growth. Jay Naidoo explicitly states that "we believe that business has the power to influence the state to end repression and move towards a peace that is based on democracy and an end to poverty."[7] Neither the assumption that disinvestment leaves long-term economic growth unscathed nor the belief in the political role of business can be empirically upheld.

Once multinationals have withdrawn from a country, they will not return easily. The disinvestment moves have strengthened South African monopolies who could buy up the departing foreign companies at bargain-basement prices. Domestic capital is less susceptible to antiapartheid pressure than are foreign companies who are subject to public opinion at home. Above all, the sanctions campaign has not deepened the cleavage between primarily affected business interests and government, as its advocates had hoped. On the contrary, Pretoria has utilized the foreign pressure to remind business of its patriotic duty to stand behind a beleaguered state. Most South African businesspeople have accepted this rationale. Far from splitting with the government, South African capitalists, with some exceptions, moved closer to the government camp in the name of beating a hostile sanctions campaign. Some companies, if they were to remain profitable, had little choice other than to cooperate with state-sponsored designs to circumvent export restrictions and neutralize calls for the boycott of South African products abroad. In short, the well-intentioned sanctions campaign has proved counterproductive as far as splitting state and capital is concerned.

Moreover, almost all foreign firms that have withdrawn from South Africa have maintained their links with the South African market by supplying it with its products through new, independent local outlets (Kodac/Ford-Samroc) or from neighboring states (Coca-Cola). The withdrawal has negatively affected the social responsibility programs and labor codes with which various foreign interests rationalized their South African presence. Local management proves less susceptible to fair labor practices. Sanctions have marginally increased the already high black unemployment. In the general economic recession and restructuring of firms, the interests of white workers have been protected at the expense of blacks. Nonracial unions, though now numerically stronger than ever, have been weakened by the emergency, and a large surplus army of unemployed has been further increased. Although COSATU officially supports all pressure on the South African government, many shop stewards are ambivalent about further economic pressures, particularly disinvestment. Union officials fear that further black unemployment will depoliticize workers rather than make them take further political risks. While the ANC demands comprehensive mandatory sanctions, the sanctions drive, in Western public opinion, has lost momentum, and popular attention has turned to other "hot spots" (Israel,

Central America). This perception was reinforced by the failure of existing measures to change Pretoria's policy, as well as the realization of South African self-sufficiency and the dependency of Front Line States on the South African economy. Further economic measures are a dead issue for the time being because of Japanese, United Kingdom, and West German refusal to comply.

Some loss of Western markets for South African products has been substituted by the dramatic development of South African trade links with Pacific Rim countries, particularly Japan and Taiwan. Whether these new markets would also absorb a European Community ban on South African coal and fruit imports remains doubtful because of alternative close suppliers (Australia). South African exporters have made elaborate preparations for disguising the origins of their products by using Mauritius, Swaziland, and the Seychelles in particular. The withdrawal of foreign investment finance could pose a serious threat to a future South African expansion. However, at present the low economic expansion rate (+ or –2 percent) has limited the demand for foreign capital; the relatively stable gold price suffices to ensure an adequate flow of foreign exchange, and Swiss and German banks still continue to lend to South Africa. South Africa so far has kept its foreign debt repayment schedule that was negotiated with its debtor banks after the country defaulted in 1985. However, the forthcoming debt renegotiations provide the foreign banks with great leverage to press for political concessions. This bargaining will be a true test for the seriousness of external antiapartheid rhetoric.

POLITICAL ATTITUDES AMONG THE WHITE ELECTORATE

The short-term success of the emergency and the failure of outside pressure to move South Africa toward majority rule have led to divergent responses among the minority. Several prominent liberal business leaders (e.g., Tony Bloom, Chris Ball, Tony Williamson, and Gordon Waddell) have emigrated. Although the euphoria about imminent liberation has given way to a despairing pragmatism among black South Africans, the predominant white mood is optimistic again.

In an international Gallup poll, South African whites took fourth place among thirty-five nations in expressing optimism for 1988 (Korea, Sweden, and Portugal ranked above). Among South African blacks, only 30 percent believed that conditions would improve in the future, surpassed only by greater pessimism in Finland, Austria, Costa Rica, Ireland, and Peru.

Politically, the minority moved decidedly to the right. Of the 3 million white voters registered in the May 6, 1987 election, 67.97 percent cast their vote. Of the total votes cast, the National Party (NP) received 52.45 percent, the Conservative Party 26.37 percent, and the Herstigte Nasionale Party (HNP) 3.14 percent, giving the three status quo parties 82 percent of the popular vote. The 14 percent for the Progressive Federal Party (PFP), 2 percent for the New Republic Party (NRP), and 1.3 percent for independents, account for the 18 percent on the "left" of the ruling party. This means that South Africa's National Party has been voted in by roughly 5 percent of the country's total population.

During the past years, the white electorate has shifted in two contradictory ways: it moved to the left on apartheid issues but to the right on security. These moves are not unrelated. The more traditional apartheid fell into disrepute, the more law and order issues came to the fore. By manufacturing anxieties, the authorities lured doubting voters into their camp. By associating the PFP with the ANC, terrorism, and anarchy, the NP offered itself as the reliable guarantor of a basic human need.

For the first time, the NP attracted as high a percentage of English voters as Afrikaners. Its new constituency of conservative English whites and immigrants is hardly disturbed by the almost exclusive Afrikaner character of the party in terms of office holders and imagery. On the contrary, Afrikaner nationalists are seen by the majority of English whites as the most trustworthy guardians of security. English support for the NP during the 1983 referendum endorsed reform and power sharing; the current support for NP security was rather motivated by the opposite reason: to preserve white rights and endorse repressive policies.

The new NP constituency of the fearful English makes the party's support at the constituency level more volatile to swings in the national mood. In the past, Afrikaners supported the party because it was perceived as an emotional, ethnic home, resulting in a lifelong allegiance. The new support depends much more on efficient media manipulation, compared with the grassroots loyalty previously.

The right-wing support is difficult to classify in class terms since ideological issues predominate. However, the Conservative Party represents substantial sections of the Afrikaner lower middle class, an urban and rural petite bourgeoisie, and employees of state enterprises. The Conservative Party absorbed what is left of the Afrikaner working class by virtually wiping out the rival HNP. A right-wing union leader was elected on a CP ticket. While the NP has solidified its middle-class support in both ethnic groups, the CP's strength still lies more in rural areas and among the lower echelons of the civil service. Among the police, sympathies for the extra-parliamentary neo-fascist Afrikaner Weerstandsbeweging (AWB) prevail. The AWB operates in a loose alliance with the CP. The CP's strong showing is particularly significant in light of P. W. Botha's abandonment of reform, together with the declaration that it preempted and prevented an even further shift to the ultra-right.

However, it can also be argued that the results do not support explanations of a total right-wing shift. In terms of apartheid laws, the NP has moved into the realm that the PFP held in the past. The previous ideological currency of the PFP—negotiations, reform, and power-sharing—has been taken over by the NP, while the CP now stands ideologically where the NP stood during the 1970s. The PFP lost because it did not move further to the left in response to this NP invasion but rather tried to compete with the NP on the same terrain. Many voters on the left of the PFP deserted the party for its decision to stay in a racial Parliament and for watering down its human rights principles by a pact with the conservative NRP. This abstention lost the PFP marginal seats in university towns such as Cape Town, Pietermaritzburg, and Grahamstown.

While the middle-class English joined the NP, the upwardly mobile Afrikaner middle class deserted the party where there was an opportunity to vote for three independents. The independents fared well and contradicted the general trend. Worrall, Malan, and Lategan were wise to distance themselves from overtures by the PFP, still tainted with an English–anti-Afrikaner–capitalist image, even for Afrikaner dissidents. After losing the endorsement of the church, the NP now has been challenged by its intellectuals.

THE POST-BOTHA ERA: NEW TRENDS IN WHITE POLITICS

The most significant recent trend in white politics is the increased defection of Afrikaner professionals from the Nationalist Party orbit. Several meetings between Afrikaner dissidents and the ANC have been held, in Dakar (July 1987), Leverkusen (October 1988), and Harare (February 1989), organized by F. van Zyl Slabbert's Institute for Democratic Alternatives (IDASA). Prominent Afrikaner establishment figures have dissociated themselves in increasing numbers from their former political home. At Stellenbosch University (the Harvard of Afrikanerdom) it is hard to find one reputable academic supporting the ruling group, at least in the social sciences. The NP has clearly lost its former hegemony. While most Afrikaner dissidents have not formally joined opposition organizations, they are sympathetic to the broad aims of the democratic movement, particularly open-ended negotiations in good faith with the ANC and the legalization of the banned nonracial movements. In this respect the ANC strategy of peeling away layers of support for the status quo has been highly successful. It does not force wavering whites to choose sides or push them over the fence on which they sit. The strategy merely aims at neutralizing former government supporters. Obviously, this makes it easier to create new reference groups for those who doubt or feel the costs.

These trends have crystallized in the formation of a new political party in which the three existing parties to the "left" of the ruling group merged. The "Democratic Party" represents an amalgam of older liberals, English conservatives, concerned capitalists (both English and Afrikaner) and, above all, Afrikaner intellectuals and opinion makers. They are supported by roughly 20 percent of white voters at present, as against 45 percent for the Nationalist Party and 35 percent for the ultra-right Conservative Party. It is a soft constituency on which the white democrats rely, unified by little more than sentiments against old-style apartheid, seen as bad for business and the future stability of the country. A South African editorialist (*Cape Times* 4, no. 11 [1988]) has described the intellectual wellsprings and political motivations of Afrikaner dissidents as discomfort with English institutions and traditional liberalism: "If nothing else, they are recognising the pointlessness of trying to organise an English minority to overthrow an Afrikaner majority; their proper field of endeavor is Afrikanerdom itself. Nor are they liberals in the Anglo-Saxon mould but, at best, social-democrats in the German mould, with an added touch of agrarian suspicion and hostility towards (English?) capital."

However, a minimal common ideological denominator also characterizes the ruling Nationalist Party. It is no longer held together by shared principles. Its binding cement lies mainly in patronage and the spoils of office. It is therefore vulnerable to splits and defections. Herein lies the long-term chance of the democratic forces. With the Democratic Party no longer having the image of an English–Jewish–anti-Afrikaner–capitalist group, many current Nationalists could join an Afrikaner-dominated antiapartheid party. The surprisingly high vote for the more open-minded Minister of Finance Barend du Plessis in the succession race for P. W. Botha (61 caucus votes against 69 for F. W. de Klerk, Botha's likely successor) clearly shows a divided house. If some technocrats around du Plessis and the popular Pik Botha were to break away and join the opposition in a post-P. W. Botha era, it would mean the demise of the Nationalist Party as the ruling group in Pretoria. A vastly strengthened ultraconservative bloc would then face perhaps an even stronger antiapartheid grouping. Perhaps even a temporary alliance between the ruling nationalists and liberal democrats can be envisaged in the post-Botha era, once apartheid proves too costly for multinationals and a growing Afrikaner bourgeois alike.

The force in power would certainly enter negotiations about majority rule. Its problem would be to make a controversial compromise stick with the ultra-right. In the absence of a South African de Gaulle, a democratic government would totter at the brink of civil war with the die-hard racists, very much as the Afrikaner fascists battled the Smuts government decision to enter World War II on the side of the allies. So far the democratic opposition has ignored, belittled, or minimized the threat from the ultra-right. It is time to consider realistic options for neutralizing this bloc, which would otherwise force a nonracial government to become as authoritarian as its predecessor in suppressing its right-wing opposition.

Since the NP is paralyzed by the threat from the ultra-right, a case can be made that the ascent of the right to political power would actually facilitate fundamental change. Such an assumption would not have to be based on the false theory "that worse is better" or "that reform is the enemy of revolution." A conservative party in power would be confronted with the same economic imperatives, demographic changes, and objective conditions that it promises to arrest. Therefore, objective trends outside government control eventually force even a right-wing government to recognize reality, just as the wavering Nationalist Party was pushed into half-hearted "reform."

It may be argued that the ultra-right in power would have two decisive advantages for a negotiated settlement, if that route rather than civil war and economic deterioration is to be pursued:

1. A conservative party can legitimize a settlement better than a liberal or center party that is being perceived as soft on white interests. The right wing would make a controversial compromise stick without eliciting insurmountable opposition. Only a trusted conservative can neutralize a potentially dangerous backlash from an indoctrinated armed segment that a center/liberal party would have great difficulty controlling.

2. The rise of the CP to political power would further increase the alienation of South Africa's western allies to a point that decisive action could hardly be postponed any longer. By giving the lie to sham reform, the outside pressure on Pretoria would double. This in turn would spur the remaining business inside South Africa into action to use its influence with government in a much more structured and forceful way, since its survival is directly threatened by such polarization.

The crucial question, of course, concerns the costs of open white supremacy to the majority population. It is a facile suggestion by those who do not bear the brunt that it does not make much difference whether an NP or CP government sets the agenda of black repression. Those on the left who advocate polarization as a way to speed up change tend to understate the price to be paid and to overestimate the stimuli for resistance, which a totally ruthless despotism can stifle for a long time.

CONTAINMENT VERSUS POLITICAL SOLUTIONS

In a South African legitimation crisis, the Nationalist Party relies increasingly on the security establishment and justifies its role in terms of maintaining law and order rather than offering moral claims or visions of an alternative.

The military and security apparatus has not replaced politicians but has increasingly assumed a veto power over crucial policies. Imaginatively and insidiously, the generals have inspired a parallel military-controlled bureaucracy in the form of joint management committees at central, regional, and local levels. At the national level, the State Security Council (SSC) is a shadow cabinet. By being able to redefine any administrative problem as a security issue, from garbage removal to rent control, the local management committees bypass the regular channels. The committees give directives to local authorities without reference to normal committee or debating procedures of the councils. Fed by an intricate network of informers on the ground, the regular meetings of a few selected civil servants, local traders, managers, and police under security auspices identify potential unrest and grievances before they arise. In the name of the priorities of "security issues," key townships such as Alexandra, Mamelodi, and New Brighton are upgraded, coupled with harsh restrictions aimed at lowering expectations. The proactive instead of the usual reactive response, efficiently implemented and coordinated by a hierarchical command structure, is the essence of the "total strategy" against a "total onslaught." In the view of winning "the hearts and minds," there is little that has no security implications. Thus, the military has taken upon itself to make the counterrevolutionary strategy succeed, where the cumbersome state bureaucracy has failed. General Malan, for example, announced that he has identified certain townships and "taken responsibility" for them. "I want to see to what extent I can better the living conditions of the people, to what extent I can get the people to accept the government so that they don't break with the authorities and drift into the hands of terrorists."[8] A total psychological warfare is waged, based on material improvements, which the sole focus on the military repression is missing. Even several PFP councillors are participating in these improvement programs and feel good about doing something "constructive." Business participation is considered essential in the effort to pacify the townships.

CONCLUSION

The often-diagnosed crisis has not yet arrived in the perception of the majority of whites, despite a simmering civil war. Few politicians and privileged voters anticipate the long-term costs of a delegitimated state with a siege economy but, instead, rely on the short-term boom of import substitution and inflation. The growing structural unemployment and soaring crime rate have hardly yet made life intolerable in the secluded white enclaves of affluence. Unfortunately, it will worsen before it gets better in South Africa. Only when a shared perception of stalemate exists will both sides negotiate in good faith. As long as each side feels in the ascendancy, the violence without victory will continue.

The often-predicted revolution in South Africa has yet again been stalled. With the antiapartheid forces in retreat during heightened repression, the euphoria about a seizure of power has given way to a more realistic assessment of the power equation. The South African state can be eroded, but not overthrown in the foreseeable future. Activists like Zwelakhe Sisulu therefore contrast what they see as the impossible transfer of power with a possible shift in power. Continuing empowerment of the opposition and steady disempowerment of the government is a realistic strategy. Instead of waiting for liberation, the foundations of the postapartheid society are laid now.

NOTES

1. See Heribert Adam and Kogila Moodley, *South Africa Without Apartheid* (Berkeley: University of California Press, 1986) for a further discussion of many of these issues.

2. Leo Kuper, *An African Bourgeoisie* (New Haven: Yale University Press, 1965).

3. Merle Lipton, *Capitalism and Apartheid* (Aldershot: Gower, 1985).

4. *Financial Mail*, January 8, 1988.

5. Anthony Sampson, *Black and Gold* (London: Hodder and Stoughton, 1987).

6. *Financial Mail*, November 27, 1987.

7. *Ibid.*

8. *Cape Times*, March 30, 1987.

PART III
South Africa and the International Political Environment

8

SADCC as a Counter-Dependency Strategy: How Much Collective Clout?

RICHARD F. WEISFELDER

COPING WITH VULNERABILITY

The controversial contention that the SADCC states[1] have gained greater capacities through their collective efforts requires rigorous and serious evaluation. It can be substantiated by evidence that SADCC has become a meaningful regional actor able to influence outcomes regardless of South African hegemony or Western co-optation. Guy Arnold contends that SADCC offers only "a mirage of progress." He sees a fundamental contradiction in SADCC's use of Western aid to achieve greater self-reliance and to reduce dependence upon South Africa. "SADCC," he alleges, "makes it easier for the major Western donors to continue doing nothing about South Africa."[2] Thus their support for SADCC is merely a "charade" to buy domestic and international respectability—as demonstrated by their "quiescence" when South Africa's destabilization of SADCC states renders that aid ineffectual.

Most observers would agree with Arnold that South Africa has destabilized its neighbors and has the power to undertake extensive "countersanctions" against them.[3] Indeed, President P. W. Botha and other top-ranking officials have threatened reprisals against SADCC states, should international sanctions begin to exact an unacceptable price upon South Africa.[4] Thus Pretoria has introduced a frightening new dimension to regional transactions, holding these weak black-ruled states hostage to the behavior of the major Western powers as well as SADCC's own actions. Despite calling for comprehensive international sanctions, Zimbabwe and Zambia have refrained from imposing sanctions against South Africa, because these would be foolhardy without prior concerted action by the major Western powers. More vulnerable SADCC states such as Botswana and Lesotho have regularly delineated the damages that international sanctions against Pretoria exact upon their economies and have called for compensatory external assistance.

But many observers *would* question Arnold's assumption that Western action could be decisive in bringing Pretoria to heel. Scholars studying the regional subsystem have portrayed entrenched patterns of structural dependence, which affect communications, culture, education, and politics as well as the more obvious economic and military sectors.[5] Evaluation of Pretoria's frequent use of transnational terror has revealed an incredible diversity of coercive techniques, including coercive diplomacy, covert operations, surrogates, economic blockades, and, of course, direct military action. Heribert Adam has pessimistically predicted a process of satellization or recolonization that would destroy SADCC.[6] Some commentators argue that the Western nations imposing sanctions would be their own unintended victims, because lack of access to strategic resources of South Africa could exact a greater toll upon the United States, the EEC, and Japan than their selective measures would impose upon the Republic.

SADCC states themselves concur with Arnold that concerted international economic sanctions can succeed by exploiting underrated elements of South African vulnerability. But while agreeing that great powers must do more, they reject his view that Western aid has become a placebo preventing SADCC from lessening dependency.[7] They also deny assertions that SADCC is rendered irrelevant by the grim reality of South Africa's overwhelming power. SADCC sees itself as a process by which short-run augmentation or diversification of dependency provides the long-term basis for reducing subservience. To many Western observers, such optimistic prognoses may seem adventurism, naïveté, or cynical propaganda aimed solely at rallying mass support.

This chapter reviews the objectives, organization, operation, leadership, and policies of SADCC since its founding in 1979. I will examine the game of "underdog" as a methodological tool for evaluating the options of unequal adversaries engaged in threatening interactions. Johan Galtung's structural approach to imperialism provides the format for reviewing factors that have accentuated SADCC's underdog status. I then examine whether SADCC's collective endeavors have produced a wider range of external options or more sophisticated forms of dependency, and consider what new factors might deter South African countersanctions against SADCC. The chapter concludes with an evaluation of whether SADCC has genuinely altered regional outcomes.

SADCC'S BASIC CHARACTERISTICS[8]

For students of regional integration, SADCC offered an innovative approach deserving careful attention. The 1980 Lusaka Declaration sought to define an agenda of nonviolent economic liberation that would be distinct from the more militant political goals of the Front Line States.[9] To achieve these limited objectives, SADCC avoided the pretentious charter and bureaucratic framework characteristic of many regional groupings. Instead, SADCC emphasized coordination of existing national development strategies and decentralization of responsibilities for specific sectoral activities, such as transportation or energy, to each of the member states. The organization remained open to outside advice and assistance, and established mechanisms for regular consultation with external donors, both individually and collectively.

Though many observers questioned whether such an ideologically, economically, and politically diverse grouping of states could achieve anything without first confronting the great issues of development strategy, the founders of SADCC believed that pragmatism and incrementalism, much more than ideology, would be necessary if the new organization were to survive the inevitable South African reaction. Their approach rested on building ever-larger capabilities from small successes meaningful to the citizens of each member state. A sense of limits rooted in keen awareness of the failures of prior grandiose schemes for federations and common markets pervaded each aspect of the new format. As President Quett Masire of Botswana explained, "This deliberately business-like approach, in which institutions will follow achievement, surely promises greater dynamism than a system in which member governments merely react to proposals put forward by technocrats lodged in a centralised bureaucracy."[10]

All nine member states had experienced the perils of withstanding South African pressures in isolation; there was recognition that the price of overreaching the capabilities of the organization would be a devastating setback for regional cooperation. Neither turnover among the participant heads of state and government nor the stressful sequence of events in Southern Africa since 1979 have shaken the consensus supporting this approach. Even the civil servants staffing the small SADCC Secretariat in Gaborone remain atypically committed to the concepts of decentralization and minimal bureaucracy![11]

UNDERDOG: WHERE SADCC LEVERAGE
AGAINST SOUTH AFRICA ORIGINATES

Karl Deutsch, when examining asymmetrical games, where the players have unequal capabilities, notes that short-term rationality presupposes the weaker party or "underdog" will adopt compliant behavior to avoid substantial and immediate losses. However, he observes that the disadvantaged participant may engage in apparently risky and irrational behavior, which entails great cost for itself, but exacts a real—if smaller—price from the stronger party or "top dog." Deutsch argues that this behavior results from the discovery of "a new long-term rationality" where the underdog's acceptance of short-term costs may compel the stronger protagonist to concede more favorable arrangements. Three conditions must be fulfilled for disadvantaged states to benefit from a threatening strategy: first there must be a positive payoff within the system that can be shared among the contending parties; second, the favored side or actor must retain a sufficient share of this payoff to make it worthwhile to agree to a concession to the underdog; third, the costs of the threats and conflicts to the underdog must not be greater than that player can bear, nor greater than what that player can expect to gain over a longer period if the threat and struggle should be successful.[12]

How does this model apply to Southern Africa? Two intertwined dimensions need to be considered, namely, Pretoria's interactions with more powerful external powers, which impose or threaten sanctions, and its relationships also with the vulnerable SADCC states.

Despite its substantial military and economic power, South Africa remains an underdog with respect to the great powers, especially if they act in concert. Pretoria can exact a high price for Western initiatives by denying access to strategic minerals or imposing countersanctions upon the SADCC states. But, in accordance with the underdog model, South Africa would bear the more immediate risks of declining revenues, shortages of foreign exchange, losses of markets, and expanding regional chaos. Embarking on this potentially self-destructive strategy could make sense only if there were some prospect of concessions from the external top dogs. But as long as Pretoria remains unyielding in perpetuating white supremacy, no great powers can risk normalization of relationships. They would be deterred by public aversion to apartheid at home and abroad, and by vulnerability to reprisals of economic and strategic assets elsewhere. Otherwise, the Western powers and South Africa could reap the joint rewards from restoration of normal transactions that make an underdog strategy viable.

But the focus of this chapter is South Africa's role as regional top dog and the options available to the underdog SADCC states. Whether SADCC presently possesses or can develop the ability to play the underdog game successfully is the central question. It is not difficult to identify positive payoffs for South Africa in avoiding or ending interactions where the SADCC states play desperate underdog roles. However, it will be harder to show that SADCC can bear even short-term costs engendered by resistance to South African pressures—much less any additional risks from generating its own threatening initiatives. Certainly none of the individual member states has the capacity to do so individually. Whether the new and diverse SADCC group can utilize such a strategy collectively becomes the crucial evaluative issue.

FACTORS ACCENTUATING SADCC'S UNDERDOG STATUS

Long-Term Elements

Whether or not one embraces his Marxist idiom, Johan Galtung has provided a thought-provoking analysis of the structural components of contemporary imperialism.[13] He demonstrates that persistent dependency relationships involve a complex interplay of the traditional military and economic elements with communications, cultural, and political patterns. The overlap and spill-over among the five factors make core–periphery bonds extraordinarily difficult to fracture.

Galtung's typology can be applied to relations between South Africa and the SADCC states, but only with caution. He assumes that dependency relationships are bilateral because of the vertical ties that the dominant metropolitan center imposes upon peripheral states. SADCC epitomizes diversification or "defeudalization" of interactions among dependent states, which Galtung advocates as the appropriate means of shattering the bonds of imperialism. However, his analysis remains germane because of the enormous residual differential between the collective capacities of SADCC states and the might of Pretoria.

The necessity for what Galtung calls "horizontalization" of relationships has been recognized by the "peripheral states" composing SADCC. At the 1986 Non-Aligned Movement Conference, and in other international venues, Zimbabwean Prime Minister Mugabe and the majority of SADCC leaders sought broader Third World financial and military support for SADCC security programs. Such discussions raise the (admittedly remote) threat that Indian or Nigerian troops could join Zimbabwean and Tanzanian forces in defending the Beira corridor network against marauding South African surrogates. African leaders also emphasize "SADCC's growing participation in South/South cooperation," demonstrated by the attendance of Algeria, Argentina, Brazil, Egypt, India, and Nigeria at the 1986 SADCC Consultative Conference.[14] Through what Deutsch calls "side bets" with third parties, SADCC underdogs could alter the balance of risks and benefits from destabilization and countersanctions, thereby complicating Pretoria's strategic calculations.

Galtung argues that the generalized conflict of interest between dominant and dependent states conceals a more intricate harmony of interests between elites from both, as well as fundamental conflict between the subordinate classes. For the SADCC states the situation is murkier. Elites are loath to engage in confrontational actions that would induce South Africa to disrupt further their fragile economies and tenuous stability. Such compliant behavior conveniently protects the professional tenure, living standards, and other class interests of ruling elites. As an editorial in *M megi*, an independent Botswana newspaper, phrased it,

> We may be forgiven for thinking that what is paramount is the desire to protect and guarantee unimpeded imports and to ensure that the good life enjoyed by a minority goes on in the face of impending crises relating to railway operations, counter-sanctions or whatever.[15]

Whether toleration of the status quo represents a considered assessment à la Deutsch about the unacceptable risks of playing the underdog game or a rationalization of class interests à la Galtung is impossible to determine. Nevertheless, the apartheid system represents a constant affront to these elites, rendering regular collaboration with the rulers of South Africa psychologically debilitating and politically dangerous.

Conflicting interests between the subordinate classes of the SADCC states and the Republic are muted by the common impact of apartheid. The specialized concerns of migrants, subsistence farmers, and urban workers transcend state boundaries instead of differentiating citizens of the various states. For example, the active involvement of migrant workers from Lesotho in strike actions by the National Union of Mineworkers demonstrates that playing foreign workers off against black South Africans has not forestalled labor solidarity. SADCC leaders realize that their organization will have to resolve clashes spawned by structural dependency after majority rule comes to South Africa. Indeed, latent conflicting interests between South African and SADCC underclasses could be expected to intensify once economic rather than political and racial distinctions become paramount.

Using Galtung's approach, a good case can be made that SADCC is more vulnerable presently than at its inception in 1979. The long-term structural factors characterized by Galtung continue to work primarily to the advantage of Pretoria at the expense of the black-ruled neighbors. Moreover, most white South Africans believe this patron–client relationship to be wholly natural rather than deliberately designed to perpetuate white hegemony. Efforts by black states to alter the situation are perceived in Pretoria as part of an aggressive Soviet-inspired "total onslaught" against the Republic. As *Rapport* editorialized, "this onslaught and the way in which it is co-ordinated must not be underestimated."[16] Despite SADCC's focus on development coordination, South Africa treats the grouping as an implacable enemy whose destabilization can be rationalized as a necessary, preemptive method of self-defense.[17]

Application of either Deutsch's underdog game or Galtung's structural model is complicated by variation in the degree and types of dependency within SADCC. Its members are ideologically and politically diverse, reflecting their different colonial heritages, routes to independence, administrative patterns, leadership styles, economic systems, and linkages with external powers. Not all are equally ensnared economically, though none can escape South African military coercion. Lesotho is vulnerable in all respects, as proved by the South African embargo and resultant military coup.[18] By contrast, Angola and Tanzania lie beyond the immediate sphere of South African economic dominance. President Banda's maverick strategies, not a lack of alternatives, explain Malawi's economic linkages with Pretoria.

Galtung's analysis of dependency via communications, cultural, and political forms of structural imperialism exposes the more subtle dimensions of South African regional hegemony. SADCC states are fully aware of propaganda inserted in South African mass media, educational materials, and scholarly publications. However, perceptions and behavior in the regional periphery are still skewed by the intrusion of South African cultural, communications, and political networks.

The demise of colonialism in the region promoted an exodus to South Africa of white settlers unwilling to adjust to majority rule and of blacks tainted by collaboration or defeated in struggles for power. Disgruntled expatriate elements remaining in newly independent states often held important positions, which provided optimal vantage points for spying, sabotage, and other forms of subversion. Judicial proceedings in Botswana and Zimbabwe have provided persuasive evidence that such individuals have engaged in major acts of sabotage and facilitated incursions by South African security personnel.[19] Even without collaboration, the porous frontiers and the presence of English- and Afrikaans-speaking white citizens in SADCC states makes detection of South African infiltrators difficult. Needless to say, some disaffected black ethnic, religious, or ideological groups within SADCC states such as Angola, Mozambique, Zambia, and Zimbabwe have become surrogates, using South African support to pursue their goals. Botswana, Lesotho, and Swaziland (BLS) each have ethnic irredenta more numerous than their own populations in the corresponding South African "homelands," namely, Bophuthatswana, Qwaqwa, and KaNgwane. Lesotho and especially Swaziland have proved vulnerable to South African diplomatic manipulation because of their desire to reunite these lost territories and populations within their states.[20] By using the supposedly "independent" homeland government to close the border unless Botswana railway personnel acquired Bophuthatswana visas, Pretoria sought to compel Botswana to extend de facto recognition to that *bantustan*.[21] This action threatened economic catastrophe for Botswana, but also had unexpected political consequences. The Botswana government came under pressure from angry citizens denied access to their favorite shopping centers and prevented from visiting families or fulfilling other obligations across the border. Pretoria can also use ethnically identical black South African agents to commit destabilizing acts conveniently blamed on the alleged deficiencies of BLS governments.

Because of their common colonial heritage as British High Commission Territories compelled to be labor reserves for the Republic, Botswana, Lesotho, and Swaziland retain the most comprehensive network of dependency relationships with Pretoria. Membership in the Southern African Customs Union (SACU) and Rand Monetary Area were colonial diplomatic commitments that proved difficult to break. The BLS legal systems, utilizing elements of South African Roman-Dutch law and judicial precedents, epitomize Galtung's concept of political dependence. In some instances, their internal security legislation bears an uncanny resemblance to draconian measures on the South African statute books.[22] Indeed, during the initial years of Lesotho's independence, key government policies were drafted, implemented, and enforced by Afrikaner legal and judicial personnel on loan from Pretoria. All three BLS states have numerous South African expatriates working in important private sector roles, where they all too frequently replicate racist values and behavioral styles. BLS citizens utilize South African mass media, educational institutions, and labor recruiting organizations to gain access to information and services.[23] Such multifaceted dependency is not the result of voluntary choice, but is structurally entrenched, as Galtung postulates.

These encumbrances explain SADCC's passion to lessen dependency upon South Africa. To achieve their objective, SADCC members are rapidly expanding commitments to external powers and organizations ranging from former colonial rulers to the International Monetary Fund. A question beyond the scope of this essay is whether these external commitments by SADCC members reflect new forms of structural imperialism with the South African "semiperipheral" intermediary merely pushed aside.

Short-Term Elements

Five factors have temporarily accentuated SADCC dependency upon South Africa. These are global recession, deterioration of the South African economy, sustained drought, destabilization, and delays in implementing SADCC projects.[24] The most noteworthy consequences for SADCC states include balance of payments deficits, foreign exchange shortages, skyrocketing debt, inflation, and sharply reduced private investment. These problems have been compounded by sharp declines in the value of the rand currency because of South Africa's continuing political unrest. The result has been "the virtual doubling of loan commitments and non-rand denominated import bills of member states whose currencies are closely linked to the rand, notably Botswana, Lesotho and Swaziland."[25] To be sure, the devalued rand provided a short-term bonus for SADCC consumers of cheaper South African goods, but at the expense of greater dependence upon their producers. All states in the region have suffered from economic uncertainty, which deterred potential investors from new commitments and made budgetary projection unusually hazardous. Other costs have included the diversion of time and resources to caring for the unending flow of refugees from the Republic.

During 1982–1984 environmental forces of drought combined with human-induced catastrophe to intensify SADCC's economic plight. Over $2 billion of crops and livestock were lost.[26] Foreign exchange and scarce resources, which might otherwise have been expended on development programs, had to be diverted to purchasing food or transporting relief supplies. Utilization of South African ports and transport facilities increased.

Revitalization of production will be especially costly for states such as Botswana, where drought persisted through 1987. Drought relief from foreign donors partially offset these losses, although some of this aid may have been reallocated from funds otherwise available for development projects. Zimbabwe's ability to sell surpluses to drought-stricken South Africa was the only positive note, offering hope that SADCC can eventually achieve its goal of regional food security.[27]

Despite the importance of international economic conditions and natural disaster, purposive acts of the South African government aimed at keeping the region in thrall have been most devastating to SADCC. Joseph Hanlon explains the contorted logic that has rationalized Pretoria's depredations. He perceives "a particularly vicious circle."

> By blowing up railways and a variety of other actions, South Africa forces the neighbors to be dependent upon it. This permits South Africa to argue that because the neighbors are dependent, they will be hurt by sanctions. Thus destabilization creates the dependence which allows South Africa to argue against using sanctions to end destabilization.[28]

The SADCC Secretariat has estimated that damages caused by destabilization between 1980 and 1984 cost member states $10 billion. Extrapolating through 1986, Hanlon put the total at $18.7 billion. SADCC's estimate through 1988 is $30 billion, almost the annual gross domestic product of the entire SADCC region! The tangible components include direct war damage, extra defense expenditure, higher transport and energy costs, reduced production, lost exports and tourism, added costs of imports, lost investments and economic growth, and costs of caring for refugees.[29] The intangible human costs cannot be quantified.

While emphasizing the impact of these external factors, SADCC has been candid about deficiencies in its own performance that have perpetuated and augmented dependency. Indeed, the identification of recurrent problems led to preparation of a self-analysis, the *Macro-Economic Survey: 1986*. The following six weaknesses were pinpointed:

1. In the appraisal of projects, the objective of reducing dependence does not appear always to have been observed;
2. Data gathering and preparatory studies have tended to dominate some of the sectoral programs at the expense of concrete project implementation;
3. Insufficient attention has been paid to the role of directly productive and commercial enterprises and institutions;
4. There has been inadequate emphasis on the mobilization of SADCC's own resources—financial and human—and an excessive emphasis on attracting external funding and personnel;

5. Though the approved list of SADCC projects is already lengthy, and the implementation rate is still under half, new projects continue to be added at a rate which, if unchecked, could eventually undermine the credibility of the whole program;

6. Planning and programming of activities have tended to lack a long-term perspective.[30]

It will take strong leadership to remedy the most significant flaw, namely, a shopping list approach to development funding. Weak states under pressure find it difficult to reject questionable assistance. However, failure to assert SADCC objectives means that donors may be determining regional priorities by default.

The *Macro-Economic Survey* is itself an indication of the SADCC Secretariat's improved managerial capabilities since Simba Makoni became secretary-general. Nevertheless, the six professional staff members in that deliberately small body are not intended or able to set the organizational agenda for development. They are hard pressed to assemble the working papers and complete the other staff work necessary for the orderly conduct of SADCC's regular schedule of conferences.

Responsibilities for planning and implementing SADCC projects have been assigned to the sectoral coordinating units. Each state has assumed responsibility for at least one sectoral program, including arranging the meetings and preparing the reports required. Unfortunately, the quality of leadership and administrative accountability in the decentralized units has been uneven. A "lack of clarity on the responsibilities and functions of these units" has hindered both formulation and implementation of programs.[31] Often the personnel carrying out these functions are not explicitly differentiated from the ministries and civil service of the host state; distinguishing national objectives from sectoral responsibilities can become well nigh impossible. Poor execution of these duties has prompted sharp criticism from other members and the resulting embarrassment has served as an incentive to improve. What remains arguable is whether these are teething problems normal for a new organization or inevitable consequences of SADCC's very decentralized operating pattern.

Carrot-and-stick pressures from South Africa regularly play SADCC states against each other, complicate resolution of organizational difficulties, and accentuate internecine conflicts. Substantive coordination of foreign and development policies lapses under stress, when members make bilateral arrangements contradicting SADCC objectives, or remains empty rhetoric, when SADCC decisions are not implemented.[32]

President Samora Machel's unilateral signing of the Nkomati Accord with South Africa demonstrated that even Front Line States were not always able to coordinate fundamental foreign policy strategies. Swaziland's secret nonaggression pact with South Africa to regain lost territory was the sort of accommodation with Pretoria's homeland concept that SADCC sought to preclude. Moreover, Prince Bhekimpi Dlamini's opening address to the 1985 SADCC Annual Conference in Mbabane actually flaunted Swaziland's collaborationist relationships with South Africa.[33] Lesotho's Highlands Water Project and Botswana's Sua Pan Soda Ash Project are based upon agreements with Pretoria that accentuate dependence to promote development. Despite their firm commitment to SADCC, Botswana and Zimbabwe have had divisive exchanges over access to each other's markets. Similarly, joint Zimbabwean and Mozambican operations against MNR insurgents led to quarrels about the poor performance and political unreliability of FRELIMO troops.[34]

SADCC's most serious altercation stemmed from joint efforts by Mozambique, Zambia, and Zimbabwe to compel President Banda of Malawi to stop sheltering the South African–backed Mozambique National Resistance (MNR) guerrillas.[35] Suspicions emerged within SADCC that Pretoria had engineered President Machel's fatal airplane crash to counter threats against Malawi. Moveover, the Malawian president compounded the controversy by charging Front Line and other African leaders with hypocrisy. In his words, "We go to South Africa in the daytime, not like Nicodemus going to Jesus Christ at night. We deal with South Africa openly."[36] However, subsequent interactions within SADCC facilitated the establishment of a bilateral Malawi-Mozambique Joint Commission and "mended fences" sufficiently to permit Malawian troops to join in guarding Mozambique's Nacala railway against MNR insurgents.[37]

A final complicating factor is the emergence of a potentially competitive regional organization, the Preferential Trade Area for Eastern and Southern African States (PTA).[38] PTA covers a more extensive geographical area than SADCC, embodies more formal organizational concepts, includes a larger central administrative apparatus, and has strong backing from the Economic Commission for Africa. Both Anglin and Hanlon contend that PTA can "complement" or coexist in "creative tension" with SADCC.[39] Botswana's decision not to join PTA reflected concern that members might overextend their capacities to the detriment of SADCC. On the other hand, PTA enthusiasts question whether special preferences for the BLS states in SACU compromise the establishment of wider links with black Africa.[40] PTA's problematic role is exposed in articles decrying weak membership commitment and describing it as synonymous with "Plenty to Talk About."[41]

HOW SADCC LEVERAGE HAS BEEN AUGMENTED

The Basics

With so many liabilities, SADCC's survival for almost a decade is remarkable. The organization has promoted a regular sequence of meetings among heads of state, foreign ministers, and specialized governmental personnel as well as consultative sessions with external donors. Through sustained service as conference chairman, Botswana's Vice-President Peter Mmusi has provided a crucial element of continuity.

For most SADCC states, involvement has gone beyond mere attendance at meetings. Observers comment upon the remarkable degree to which a "SADCC mentality" has emerged and SADCC activities have become part of common parlance.[42] Leaders of most member states appear to think, talk, and not infrequently act as if SADCC were a significant component of their development and foreign policy calculations. Critics debate the depth of this commitment and note that SADCC has not dealt with issues of "participation, empowerment and social justice" or become a focus of mass mobilization.[43] However, several student, labor, professional, and women's associations have augmented development coordination by voluntarily organizing their own regional groupings as satellites to the SADCC core.

Under SADCC's aegis, member states have established bilateral linkages with each other. The joint commissions created have dealt with the gamut of political and economic issues specific to each set of participants.[44] In the case of Botswana and Zimbabwe, bilateral mechanisms have been crucial for preserving civility when sharp differences on Zimbabwean refugees and Botswanan textiles emerged. These regularized channels also promoted agreements on the joint marketing of beef to the European Community and on the transfer of the Ramatlabama-Plumtree railway from Zimbabwe's to Botswana's management. Membership in a multilateral organization is not sufficient to break what Galtung describes as the vertical feudal interaction pattern with a dominant power. Congruent with the decentralization of development tasks to members, SADCC promotes the emergence of diverse horizontal linkages among members through nongovernmental contacts and bilateral diplomacy.

The $3 billion of external aid pledged or delivered to SADCC since its inception falls short of the optimum, but is more extensive than early pessimists had predicted. Bilateral aid to member states has also risen sharply. Thus there are externally funded projects under way in every member state that might not have been implemented as swiftly—on so large a scale or at all—without SADCC. Such tangible gains are necessary if elite enthusiasm is to be translated into grassroots resolve to withstand South African countermeasures.

The Locus of International Involvement

Together with its Front Line States alter ego, SADCC has become a regular clearing house for diplomatic, economic, and political transactions linking the outside world to Southern Africa. Its consultative conferences are the medium where members annually join with aid donors in evaluating progress toward the goal of economic liberation. Although the United States and Great Britain have urged separation of political criticism of South Africa's destabilizing actions from SADCC's economic agenda, these two dimensions have become inextricably intertwined. The Nordic states and many Western European parliamentarians have joined SADCC members in linking security and development priorities and in denouncing South African tactics, which destroy, damage, or otherwise incapacitate projects.[45]

Aid to SADCC comes with many restrictive conditions. For example, the United States prefers bilateral channels and prevents funds from benefiting members deemed unsuitable. The International Monetary Fund (IMF) does not assist nonmembers. The European Community restricts aid to signatories of the Lomé Convention. But SADCC is not dependent upon any single source of financing and can compensate for these constraints. Aid from donors who impose few conditions can be channeled to the project components within countries excluded by the others. Multilateral development coordination sustains regional objectives.

Regional action through SADCC has received the strongest backing from what Hanlon calls a "like-minded" group of states including Australia, Austria, Belgium, Canada, Denmark, Finland, France, Ireland, Italy, the Netherlands, Norway, and Sweden.[46] The African Development Bank and the Commonwealth have also been strongly supportive. However, the real test of SADCC's mettle is whether its policies and programs have altered the behavior of sympathizers and skeptics.

The Nordic states provide strong affirmative evidence. Speaking for this group at the 1985 Mbabane Conference, Gösta Edgren of Sweden said:

> I would also like to point out that your association within SADCC has influenced us in getting together to exchange information and experience from development assistance and to pool resources in order to render support from our region to your region more effective. The fact that I am speaking today on behalf of four delegations from Denmark, Finland, Norway and Sweden is but one small illustration of this "region to region" cooperation which has been created through SADCC.[47]

SADCC's decentralized operational pattern has suggested new ways for these Scandinavian states to structure their relationships with each other and the Third World. They perceive their relationships with the SADCC group to be a prototype for a functional New International Economic Order.[48] To maximize their impact, they have made SADCC a priority area for collective development assistance. This partnership permits straightforward but nonthreatening criticism of SADCC policies and performance. Since SADCC has acted positively upon constructive suggestions, the Nordic states have offered an "initiative," which will provide considerable new funding in agricultural, trade, manpower, legal assistance, administrative, and security spheres. Proportionate to population and resources, the Nordic contribution to SADCC dwarfs all others.

Administrative practices in other states have also been adjusted to accommodate SADCC's regional role. Hanlon observes that the Canadians and European Community have organized SADCC desks within their foreign assistance bureaucracies; the Germans have apparently followed suit.[49] If more states and international institutions modify their structures in this manner, the tendency of organizational processes to condition foreign policy behavior will further enhance SADCC's impact.

Great Britain and the United States view SADCC's statist strategy of jointly planned and coordinated national development programs as contrary to free market mechanisms and their goal of "privatization."[50] They have shown little enthusiasm for SADCC's breaking what they believe to be "inevitable" linkages with South Africa. In spite of their reservations, the amount of U.S. and British assistance to SADCC has been substantial from the outset. Together with other potential donors, both were full participants in the 1979 Arusha Conference where the Front Line States proposed the SADCC concept. Militant commentators allege that Western donors succeeded in depoliticizing the organization and disabling "the region from embarking on the politically urgent and challenging developmental and distributional issues."[51] Therefore the Thatcher and Reagan administrations were able to overcome their distaste for SADCC's statist multilateralism and use the organization's need for "constructive engagement" against apartheid without confronting Pretoria.[52]

U.S. policy certainly falls short of this Machiavellian shrewdness, but its schizophrenic quality does draw sharp criticism from SADCC leaders. The Nordic states encourage SADCC to define the primary objectives of their partnership. By contrast, the United States uses a strategic equation full of East–West variables in calculating regional aid. Only UNITA insurgents in Angola get assistance. Radical rhetoric from Zimbabwe reduces U.S. aid to a trickle. Even such conservatives as President Banda have criticized this purposely divisive "discriminatory funding."[53] To be sure, some restraints have been imposed by Congress over executive objections. Nevertheless, SADCC leaders have been particularly offended by politically motivated legislation which made aid conditional upon their preventing cross-border violence and condemning necklacing.[54] U.S. preoccupation with its own agenda carries over to such minutiae as locating its SADCC mission in Harare rather than near the Secretariat in Gaborone.

What ultimately gives the United States and other Western donors little alternative to working with SADCC is the firm commitment of pragmatic friends such as Botswana to the organization. Western diplomats in Gaborone become immersed in a context and routine that promotes involvement with regional objectives. Futhermore, the smaller scale of external missions leads to more extensive interactions among their personnel, encourages shared perceptions of the regional situation, and promotes greater consensus on policy among their respective governments. Those viewing Gaborone or other SADCC capitals as provincial backwaters overlook the extent, diversity, and significance of this diplomatic activity.

Ironically, East–West calculations could swiftly enhance U.S. interest in SADCC. The long-standing presence of Chinese, Cuban, Libyan, and Russian embassies in capitals like Gaborone has compelled U.S. officials to compete for access to those wielding power. However, the socialist states had emphasized bilateral relations and kept SADCC at arm's length because of its close links with Western-oriented political and economic institutions. Now they have begun to take greater cognizance of the grouping. At Mbabane, the delegate of the German Democratic Republic stressed "the readiness of my country to participate in multilateral co-ordinated projects of SADCC."[55] Reflecting the more open Gorbachev policies, the Soviet delegation at the 1988 Arusha Conference revealed that during the period 1981–1986 the Soviet Union had provided $2.2 billion in economic assistance to SADCC states, not including its substantial military commitment.[56] Should negotiations for Namibian independence and Cuban withdrawal from Angola succeed, the Soviet Union and its allies might heed the pleas of their Southern African friends to become more involved with SADCC. Then, the United States could less well afford to slight the regional agenda.

The vigor of SADCC foreign relations, and especially of the Front Line States, is highlighted by the steady flow of visiting foreign diplomats, politicians, clergy, journalists, academics, and other notables concerned about Southern African issues. Whatever their specific objectives, representatives of Eastern, Western, and Third World governments, intergovernmental organizations such as the IMF and UNDP, and nongovernmental entities including churches, universities, trade unions, and transnational corporations regularly interact with counterparts in the SADCC states. Before 1980 South Africa would have been a mandatory transfer point on their journeys. Now their flights and telecommunications among the SADCC capitals can bypass the Republic. Moreover, consultation with SADCC has become mandatory for the success of any external initiatives regarding the future of the region.

Institutionalization of the Regional Role

Given many points of vulnerability, it would be premature to describe SADCC processes and structures as institutionalized. The organization remains prone to intermittent shocks certain to occur as states pursue expedients essential for survival—imagine the consequences that replacement of FRELIMO by a hostile MNR regime would have for the Beira corridor transportation project, SADCC's foremost economic security venture! On the other hand, prior setbacks have proved less decisive than initially feared. Consider also the new options opened if Namibian independence were achieved or the Angolan civil war ended!

South Africa's destabilization campaign and repression of internal dissent has not produced abject compliance, but greater vigilance and community of interests. Sporadic military raids and bombings have often spawned defiance and the will to resist. Botswana is no longer so relaxed as in the past. Botswana Defence Force (BDF) roadblocks and searches have made citizens alert to the danger of infiltration. The court-martial of a soldier for cowardice demonstrates that Masire's government will not tolerate BDF passivity. The capture of South African Defence Force infiltrators by Botswana and Zimbabwe permits no further doubt about Pretoria's role and raises the ante by precluding risk-free reconnoitering. Even compliant Swaziland could not ignore kidnappings perpetrated within its borders by South African police.

Pretoria's diplomatic threats, economic sabotage, and use of surrogate insurgents have led to innovation rather than surrender. Cloaked in secrecy, security planning has been added to the SADCC agenda. Military assistance from Zimbabwe, Tanzania, and Malawi, and concrete railway ties produced by Botswana have been committed to maintenance of Beira corridor transportation facilities. Refurbishing of this vital network has progressed rapidly with major funding from external donors and innovative implementation by an amalgam of private and public bodies. These include "the International Beira Group, a private company registered in Oslo, Norway; the Beira Corridor Authority, a public Mozambican company; and the Beira Corridor Group, a private Zimbabwean company owned by Tabex and Standard Chartered Merchant Bank."[57] Shares in the Zimbabwean corporation were purchased by approximately 250 private and parastatal firms desiring secure transport options, such as the Botswana Meat Commission and Zambia's Consolidated Copper Mines.

Unfortunately, the Beira corridor has not received optimum use since businessmen have preferred proven South African routes to the risks of port congestion, construction delays, low productivity, and sabotage. Economic returns have hardly matched the enormous increases in military expenditure required to secure the route. Nevertheless, small gains in volume have been sufficient to encourage SADCC and donors to begin diversification of transportation options through similar initiatives in Mozambique's Limpopo and Angola's Benguela corridors. Anticipating change in Namibia, Botswana has already placed development of a trans-Kalahari corridor on the SADCC agenda.[58] In the transportation sector, pressure upon SADCC has promoted the regularization and intensification of internal cooperation and external support.

SADCC recognized that the physical infrastructure being created would be purposeless unless production and intraregional trade grew apace.[59] To promote this "enterprise sector," SADCC invited representatives of the business communities from donor and member states to participate in the 1987 and 1988 Consultative Conferences. Although the initiative was well received, Executive Secretary Simba Makoni admitted that after several additional conferences there was "not necessarily much to show in the way of new investment."[60] Makoni noted that SADCC was moving to make necessary changes in credit facilities, foreign exchange policies, immigration regulations, and other matters worrisome to businessmen. The establishment of a seed capital fund with Nordic support was the sort of confidence-building measure required for slow but steady progress. Thus structural creativity and development, not disintegration and decay, have emerged from a climate of economic adversity.

Institutional consolidation has also occurred in the diplomatic sector. Ambassadors of SADCC states accredited to major powers or international organizations frequently approach their hosts collectively on matters of regional concern. Speaking with a single voice provides access for less visible small states and minimizes the risk of their being played off against each other. At least two efforts have been productive. SADCC diplomats jointly developed close working relationships with Nancy Kassebaum and other conservative U.S. senators who provided access to the Reagan administration and some input into the sanctions debate. Collective diplomatic pressure was instrumental in discouraging the Belgian government from receiving P. W. Botha during his European trip.[61] Useful information about SADCC origins, problems, prospects, and plans, distributed by the SADCC Liaison Committee in London and the Secretariat has helped to foster greater international awareness of the SADCC regional role. Nevertheless, the ignorance of SADCC's objectives demonstrated by the U.S. Congress has prompted calls for more formalized SADCC lobbying in Washington.[62]

Despite these achievements, by no means all officials or citizens of SADCC states are sanguine that South African pressures can be resisted. President Quett Masire warned the 1988 SADCC Summit Meeting that the economic woes of the region were "turning into a nightmare" that "threatens to seriously compromise our sovereign right to formulate policies of national development and management."[63] Domestic critics have alleged that Mugabe's and Kaunda's penchant for threatening sanctions against South Africa is "suicidal."[64] Are they correct? Whether SADCC has developed sufficient assets to have a reasonable probability of success in playing the risky underdog game remains the crucial evaluative question.

PLAYING THE UNDERDOG GAME:
HOW SADCC HAS ALTERED REGIONAL OUTCOMES

SADCC states are in a classic underdog situation. As the South Africans eagerly point out, they could save substantially in the short term by working within the current system and purchasing goods and services through established channels. However, acceptance of the dominance of the regional power will, in accordance with Galtung's views, shortchange them presently and stifle their potential. Taking risks now to gain positive payoffs in the future may be necessary to alter the pattern. Within Southern Africa, only a unified consortium of independent black states can play this underdog game with any hope of success.

The effectiveness of SADCC strategies depends more on elements of South African vulnerability than on some brilliant tactical insight. Members give lip service to participating in international sanctions. But like the proverbial tortoise, their task demands continuing stolidly on the course initiated within SADCC. All realize that direct threats to Pretoria's military or economic security would be foolhardy.

South Africa's rulers perceive the SADCC decision to disengage economically to be a serious challenge to the ironclad control over the region long taken for granted. Providing logistic support to the ANC or embracing regional revolutions would redouble Pretoria's rage at having its hegemony challenged. South Africa's "tit for tat" mentality is no idle threat, but a proven reality, making aggressive responses to confrontational behavior or rhetoric inevitable. Is there any hope that the regional underdogs can find means of altering this pattern?

A partial answer lies in the multidimensional international games involving South Africa, especially in its own underdog role vis-à-vis the Western world. Arnold argues that "South Africa's capacity to threaten and harm her neighbors depends on Western quiescence, which is always forthcoming."[65] But has this "quiescence" no limits? Would Western governments remain complacent if South African rulers took comprehensive economic or military action against several of the SADCC states? Do military setbacks in Angola, resistance to conscription at home, and internecine strife within Afrikaner ranks not limit South Africa's ability to conduct sustained regional operations without jeopardizing domestic order? Could Pretoria risk escalating instability in its backyard while simultaneously fending off international sanctions?

On the other hand, selective actions against individual SADCC states permit the others time to adopt countermeasures. Use of surrogates is costly, creates commitments not easily ended, and precipitates third party intervention, as by the Cubans in Angola or the Zimbabweans in Mozambique. Hence, South Africa has good reason to rely upon proven low profile tactics of destabilization, including repatriation of migrant workers, slowdowns of road and rail traffic, and economic embargoes, supplemented by surgical military strikes that present the world with a fait accompli.

The problem of the South African government is that these punitive actions impose serious costs on South Africa, even though the SADCC underdogs pay a higher price. Despite their brief duration, the Lesotho blockade and the stoppage of Botswana traffic into Mafikeng prompted complaints from South African merchants whose businesses were being disrupted. On a larger scale this pattern applies to all of South Africa. Trade in goods and services with SADCC states generates $1.5 billion in annual revenues, provides extensive employment opportunities within the transportation system, and brings in a considerable amount of foreign exchange. Could the Pretoria government sacrifice these beneficial transactions when its economy is under duress? Moreover, the migrant mineworkers imported from SADCC states are highly skilled. Could South Africa swiftly repatriate them when the strategic minerals they produce are the primary means of thwarting sanctions? If countersanctions should fail to bring SADCC underdogs to heel, could Pretoria could ever hope to regain the lost business?

Contrary to common belief, a series of confrontations between the SADCC underdogs and the South African top dog would have strongly negative payoffs for *both* participants. Two parallel elements have restrained the ferocity of interactions to date. The first is SADCC pragmatism in the face of constant provocation from Pretoria. SADCC leaders have resolved to begin the slow process of building the internal economic strength and external support required to play the underdog game more successfully. They have resisted adventurist options that could inflict greater disabilities upon their peoples without improving the odds that their sacrifices would be vindicated. Second, South African behavior, though extreme and bent on the reprehensible goal of preserving white domination, is also constrained by complex rational calculations of cost and benefit.

SADCC has proved far more resilient and innovative than its strongest proponents would have thought possible at the beginning of the 1980s. It has provided a psychological and substantive safety net, enabling its members to persevere despite great adversity. SADCC has altered the perspectives and behavior of the Nordic states, "the like-minded group," and, to a lesser degree, the great powers regarding the Southern African region.

What are the prospects that SADCC's gentle counterpressures will persuade Pretoria to abandon its unilateralist top dog mentality? SADCC's program of action will have marginal impact unless it remains part of a growing network of global pressures upon the white redoubt. If governments led by P. W. Botha or F. W. de Klerk, or even a more conservative successor regime under A. P. Treurnicht, persist in ignoring the certain negative payoffs of recalcitrant policies, Southern Africa and SADCC will face a holocaust of enormous proportions. SADCC, like any underdog, must hope that South Africa will ultimately tire of no-win, zero-sum strategies and seek the positive-sum, mutually beneficial outcomes possible for both participants.

NOTES

I am grateful to the University of Toledo Faculty Research and Fellowship Program for the 1986 summer grant that permitted me to do research in Botswana, Lesotho, and South Africa during August and September 1986. Essential support was also provided by the Faculty Development Program of the College of Arts and Sciences and the small grants program of the Graduate College. Without the willing cooperation of many scholars, public officials, and personal acquaintances in Southern Africa, this chapter could not have been possible. The full responsibility for these materials is mine, including any misstatements of fact or misinterpretations of evidence.

1. The members of SADCC are Angola, Botswana, Lesotho, Malawi, Mozambique, Swaziland, Tanzania, Zambia, and Zimbabwe.

2. Guy Arnold, "A Mirage of Progress," West Africa (London), June 20, 1988.

3. Discussions of destabilization appear in Deon Geldenhuys, "South Africa: A Stabilising or Destabilising Influence in Southern Africa?" in Calvin A. Woodward, ed., On The Razor's Edge: Prospects for Political Stability in Southern Africa (Pretoria: Africa Institute of South Africa, 1986), pp. 59–75; Joseph Hanlon, Beggar Your Neighbours: Apartheid Power in Southern Africa (Bloomington: Indiana University Press, 1986); Simon Jerkins, "Destabilisation in Southern Africa," The Economist 288, no. 7298 (July 16, 1983), pp. 19–28; Robert M. Price, "Pretoria's Southern Africa Strategy," African Affairs 83, no. 530 (January 1984), pp. 11–32; and Richard F. Weisfelder, "Peace Through the Barrel of a Gun: Nonaggression Pacts and State Terror in Southern Africa," in Michael Stohl and George A. Lopez, eds., Terrible Beyond Endurance: The Foreign Policy of State Terrorism (Westport, Conn.: Greenwood Press, 1988), pp. 446–495.

4. "SA War Dead Honoured at Delville Wood," South African Digest, week of November 21, 1986, p. 1064; and "SA Warns UN on Sanctions," South African Digest, week of February 20, 1987, p. 3.

5. The pioneering work was Larry W. Bowman, "The Subordinate State System of Southern Africa," International Studies Quarterly 12, no. 3 (September 1968), pp. 231–261. Seminal articles representative of the radical political economy approach to dependency can be found in Charles K. Wilber, ed., The Political Economy of Development and Underdevelopment (New York: Random House, 1973).

6. Heribert Adam, "Constitutional Engineering and Economic Recolonization in South Africa," Issue (1984), pp. 32–33.

7. "More Needed than Support for SADCC," The Herald (Harare), March 29, 1988, p. 2.

8. Detailed analyses of SADCC appear in Douglas G. Anglin, "Economic Liberation and Regional Cooperation in Southern Africa: SADCC and PTA," International Organization 37, no. 4 (Autumn 1983), pp. 681–711; Joseph Hanlon, SADCC: Progress, Projects and Prospects (London: Economist Intelligence Unit, 1985); Amon J. Nsekela, ed., Southern Africa: Toward Economic Liberation, papers presented at the Arusha and Lusaka Meetings of SADCC (London: Rex Collings, 1981); Arne

Tostensen, *Dependence and Collective Self-Reliance in Southern Africa: The Case of the Southern African Development Coordination Conference (SADCC)*, Research Report No. 62 (Uppsala: The Scandinavian Institute of African Studies, 1982); and Richard F. Weisfelder, "The Southern African Development Coordination Conference: A New Factor in the Liberation Process," in Thomas M. Callaghy, ed., *South Africa in Southern Africa: The Intensifying Vortex of Violence* (New York: Praeger Publishers, 1983), pp. 237–266.

9. The Front Line States are a consultative grouping of presidents originated to plan common strategy regarding Smith's Rhodesia and continuing with a similar purpose regarding Namibia and South Africa. The current members are Angola, Botswana, Mozambique, Tanzania, Zambia, and Zimbabwe. See Douglas G. Anglin, "The Frontline States and the Future of Southern Africa," unpublished paper presented at a conference on "The Indian Ocean: Perspectives on a Strategic Area," at Dalhousie University, October 14–16, 1982; and Carol B. Thompson, *Challenge to Imperialism: The Frontline States in the Liberation of Zimbabwe* (Harare: Zimbabwe Publishing House, 1985).

10. Q. K. J. Masire, "Opening Statement by the Chairman," Summit Meeting of the Southern African Development Coordination Conference, Salisbury, July 20, 1981 (typescript), p. 6.

11. Based on interviews with SADCC civil servants conducted in September 1986.

12. Karl W. Deutsch, *The Analysis of International Relations*, 2d ed. (Englewood Cliffs, N.J.: Prentice-Hall, 1978), pp. 148–150.

13. Johan Galtung, "A Structural Theory of Imperialism," reprinted in Richard A. Falk and Samuel S. Kim, eds., *The War System: An Interdisciplinary Approach* (Boulder, Colo., Westview Press, 1980), pp. 402–455. An application of Galtung's study to the Southern African scene appears in Arnold H. Issacs, *Dependence Relations Between Botswana, Lesotho, Swaziland and the Republic of South Africa: A Literature Study Based on Johan Galtung's Theory of Imperialism*, Research Report No. 15 (Leiden, Netherlands: African Studies Centre, 1982).

14. Southern African Development Coordination Conference (SADCC), *1985–1986 Annual Progress Report*, Luanda, August 1986 (typescript), p. 23.

15. "Mr. Mmusi Offers More of the Same," *Mmegi wa Dikgang (The Reporter)* 4, no. 7 (Serowe, Botswana), February 21, 1987, p. 12.

16. "That Onslaught," *Rapport* (Johannesburg), February 8, 1987, translated from Afrikaans and reprinted in *South African Digest* (Pretoria), week of February 13, 1987, p. 21 (italics included).

17. The "total strategy" is explained in Deon Geldenhuys, *Some Foreign Policy Implications of South Africa's "Total National Strategy"* (Braamfontein: The South African Institute for International Affairs, 1978). Its current applicability is discussed in Hanlon, *Beggar Your Neighbours*, pp. 10–26, especially pp. 20–21.

18. James Cobbe, "Lesotho: Economic Factors in and Implications of the Coup," unpublished paper presented at the African Studies Association

Meeting, Madison, Wisconsin, October 1986; and Hanlon, *Beggar Your Neighbours*, pp. 117–121.

19. Douglas Tsiako, "Arrest of Couple Suggests Extensive Network of Infiltrators Here," *Mmegi* 5, no. 26 (July 9–15, 1988), pp. 1, 3; and "Harare Jailbreak Bid Casts Suspicions on Ex-Rhodesians," *Ibid.*, pp. 1–2.

20. John Daniel, "The South African–Swazi State Relationship: Ideological Harmony and Structural Domination," unpublished paper presented to the Inaugural Congress and Workshop on Development and Destabilization in Southern Africa of the Southern African Development Research Association, National University of Lesotho, October 17–20, 1983, pp. 14–17; and Richard F. Weisfelder, "The Basotho Nation-State: What Legacy for the Future?" *The Journal of Modern African Studies* 19, no. 2 (1981), pp. 242–249.

21. Patrick Lawrence, "Rail Crisis: Crucial Meeting Today," *Weekly Mail* 3, no. 6 (Johannesburg), February 13–19, 1987, p. 3; and "Last Week's Talks on Railway Impasse: SA Officials Had Nothing Positive To Offer?" *Mmegi* 4, no. 7, February 21, 1987, pp. 1, 3.

22. Gabrielle Winai Ström, *Development and Dependence in Lesotho, The Enclave of South Africa* (Uppsala: The Scandinavian Institute of African Studies, 1978), pp. 87–90; and Richard F. Weisfelder, "The Decline of Human Rights in Lesotho: An Evaluation of Domestic and External Determinants," *Issue* 6, no. 4 (Winter 1976), pp. 26–27.

23. This point together with more comprehensive coverage of the cultural dimensions of BLS dependency on South Africa appears in Issacs, *Dependence Relations*, pp. 68–79.

24. The most thorough survey of the factors shaping SADCC's economic performance appears in Southern African Development Coordination Conference (SADCC), *Macro-Economic Survey: 1986* (Gaborone), pp. 5–38.

25. SADCC, *1985–1986 Annual*, p. 5.

26. SADCC, *Macro-Economic Survey*, p. 27.

27. Food security issues are discussed in Coralie Bryant, ed., *Poverty, Policy, and Food Security in Southern Africa* (Boulder, Colo.: Lynne Rienner Publishers, 1988).

28. Hanlon, *Beggar Your Neighbours*, p. 60.

29. SADCC, "The Cost of Destabilisation," memorandum presented by SADCC to the 1985 Summit of the Organisation of African Unity, reprinted in Hanlon, *Beggar Your Neighbours*, pp. 265–270; SADCC, *Macro-Economic Survey*, pp. 23–25; and Colin Legum, "SADCC Plans to Weather Sanctions Storm," *The Sunday Mail* (Harare), July 20, 1986, p. C 10.

30. SADCC, *Macro-Economic Survey*, pp. 3–4.

31. SADCC, *1985-1986 Annual*, pp. 24–25. My interviews revealed that this issue was one of the major problems troubling personnel in the SADCC Secretariat.

32. "SADCC Links Should Be Strengthened—Zamchiya," *Sunday Mail*, August 9, 1987, p. 6.

33. *SADCC 1985: Mbabane, Proceedings* of the Annual Southern African Development Coordination Conference, held in Mbabane on January 31 and

February 1, 1985, pp. 31–33. Hanlon claims that his impromptu remarks were more vitriolic. Hanlon, *Beggar Your Neighbours*, p. 91.

34. Peter Younghusband, "Marxist Allies Quarreling in Mozambique," *The Washington Times*, February 20, 1987.

35. "Machel Threatens to Blockade Malawi," *The Herald*, September 12, 1986.

36. "Banda Slams Neighbours," quoted in *South African Digest*, week ended February 6, 1987, p. 9.

37. "Mozambique and Malawi Sort Out Differences," *The Herald*, April 30, 1987, p. 8.

38. Anglin, "Economic Integration," pp. 682–711.

39. *Ibid.*, p. 709; and Hanlon, *SADCC*, pp. 74–77.

40. Whether or not SACU benefits the weaker participants has been debated at length, most recently in "Customs Union: Pros & Cons," *Mmegi 4*, no. 5 (February 6, 1987), pp. 6–7. A positive assessment appears in Derek J. Hudson, "Botswana's Membership of the Southern African Customs Union," in Charles Harvey, ed., *Papers on the Economy of Botswana* (London, Nairobi, Ibadan: Heinemann Educational Books, 1981), pp. 131–158. More negative views appear in Issacs, *Dependence Relations*, pp. 18–67, and Hanlon, *Beggar Your Neighbours*, pp. 81–90.

41. "Lack of Trade Co-Operation Threatens PTA Operations," *The Herald*, December 10, 1987, pp. C 1, 3; and "Making PTA Work," *The Herald*, March 23, 1988, p. 6.

42. This insight, based on interviews conducted in SADCC states during September 1987, confirms the views of Maurice Foley, a top European Community official, quoted in Hanlon, *SADCC*, p. 23.

43. Fantu Cheru, "Food Security and Institutional Development in SADCC," in Bryant, ed., *Poverty*, pp. 266–267; and "SADCC Links."

44. Their role is noted in Douglas G. Anglin, "SADCC after Nkomati," *African Affairs* 83, no. 335 (April 1985), p. 173.

45. "Regional Defence and Development 'Cannot Be Separated'," *The Herald*, March 31, 1988, p. 1; and George Nyembela, "Nordic States Assist Liberation Struggle in Southern Africa," *The Herald*, September 22, 1987, p. 8.

46. Hanlon, *SADCC*, p. 21.

47. *SADCC 1985*, p. 36 (italics included).

48. Thompson, "Regional Economic Policy," p. 26.

49. Hanlon, *SADCC*, p. 23; and interviews with diplomatic personnel from SADCC states.

50. Carol B. Thompson, *Regional Economic Policy under Crisis Conditions: The Case of the Southern African Development Coordination Conference (SADCC)*, Current African Issues No. 6 (Uppsala: The Scandinavian Institute of African Studies, 1986), pp. 5–8.

51. Cheru, "Food Security," p. 255.

52. Arnold, "A Mirage of Progress."

53. Hanlon, *SADCC*, pp. 20–21.

54. "U.S. 'Insult' in Aid Offer Slammed," *The Herald*, July 25, 1987, p. 1.

55. *SADCC-1985*, p. 84.

56. "SADCC Gets over Billion in Pledges," *The Herald*, January 30, 1988, p. 1.

57. "Beira Corridor Backers Meet Soon to Firm Up Pledges," *The Herald*, September 23, 1986.

58. "Trans-Kgalagadi Railway: Project Needs To Be Given Consideration," *Daily News* (Gaborone), January 15, 1988, p. 1.

59. SADCC, *1985-1986 Annual*, pp. 9-10, 26; and "Business Community Has Vital Role in SADCC Region—Makoni," *The Herald*, February 25, 1988, pp. 9-11.

60. "SADCC Moves To Cut Investment Barriers," *The Herald*, February 9, 1988, p. 9.

61. Interviews with diplomats from SADCC countries conducted in August and September 1986.

62. Lynda Loxton, "SADCC 'Needs Tough Lobby Campaign in US'," *The Herald*, June 11, 1977, pp. C 1, 3.

63. Paul Fauvet, "SADCC Ponders Its 'Economic Nightmare'," *Weekly Mail*, July 22-30, 1988, p. 23.

64. "Zambian MP Slams Sanctions," *South African Digest*, week of February 27, 1987, p. 6.

65. Arnold, "A Mirage of Progress."

9

The Effects of South Africa on Zambian Politics and Society: Overt and Systematic Destabilization

JAMES R. SCARRITT

The literature on South African regional policy indicates that Zambia is of secondary importance to South Africa and that it has been less a target of South African destabilization activities than have most of its neighbors. The literature on Zambian domestic and foreign policy suggests that increasing class formation among the bourgeoisie in that country is the main factor that has led to increased pressure for economic and political accommodation with South Africa. Ronald Libby states that reopening the Rhodesian border in 1978 and, by implication, acts of accommodation with South Africa, have bolstered state power in Zambia.[1] In this chapter I argue that all of these analytical viewpoints give inadequate emphasis to the pervasive, multifaceted destabilizing influence that the South African presence has had on Zambian politics and society.

In developing this argument, I will first summarize a theoretical framework that encompasses all of the factors relevant to the analysis of international and societal influences on political change. I will next review the literature on South African regional goals, strategies, and tactics in Southern Africa with an emphasis on Zambia, then describe the nature and extent of economic decline, class formation, and ideological cleavages in Zambia, paying special attention to South Africa's influence on these developments. Finally, I will describe in some detail the influence of both overt South African actions and Zambian actors' awareness of South African goals and tactics on major political change events in Zambia since the inauguration of the Second Republic at the beginning of 1973.

THEORETICAL FRAMEWORK

It is useful to conceive of African societies, including that of Zambia, as influenced by both the capitalist world economy and the international state system.[2] The former accepts Zambian exports and provides it with goods to import, investment capital, and various types of aid; however, at the same time it also constrains Zambia to produce primary products for export to developed capitalist countries, accept imports, investment, and aid on terms determined by those countries or by organizations based there, and participate in cycles of international inflation and recession rather than to develop in a self-reliant manner.

Although the world economy and the international state system are closely related, it is useful to analyze their influence separately, because the latter involves a greater number of conflicting forces. Although the Soviet Union, China, and other socialist countries remain tied to the capitalist world economy, they are free to oppose the major capitalist powers politically, and rivalries among the latter are by no means insignificant. South Africa has a semiperipheral status in the world economy and plays a subimperial role in Southern Africa, but it too is relatively free to pursue its own strategic and political goals in the region.[3]

Within a society it is useful to conceive of the interaction among four subsystems defined in terms of the functions they perform, with varying degrees of effectiveness, for the society as a whole. The economy's primary function is to produce goods and services. Zambia, like most African economies, primarily exemplifies the capitalist mode of production despite the existence of large state-owned enterprises. This is in large part due to that country's high level of dependence on the world economy. Without the energy provided to society by the economy, the other subsystems of society could not continue to function at all; they are severely constrained by a substantial reduction in the level of such energy, as has occurred in Zambia since 1975.

The stratification system distributes wealth, power, and influence among classes and groups and, more or less successfully, integrates the activities of these categories of the population. In the definition of *class* I use in this chapter, classes can be based on either production relations or power relations, or a combination of the two. Since the class structures of African societies, including Zambia, are not fully formed, fractions (types of economic or political roles within a class) and/or organized groups are often more significant determinants of behavior than are classes. Many patterns of alliance and conflict among classes, fractions, and groups are possible, and both class structure and alliance/conflict patterns can change rapidly.

The cultural system perpetuates and changes (by means of lifelong socialization) the values, norms, identities, beliefs, and ideologies constituting the society's culture. This culture is never completely homogeneous; rather it is characterized by a wide variety of inconsistencies among its various elements. Such inconsistencies are numerous and extensive in most African societies, including Zambia, and most are manifested in ideological cleavages among fractions of the emerging dominant class. Culture is the primary source of regulative information in the society, on which the other subsystems are as dependent as they are on the energy provided by the economy.

The primary function performed to some degree by the polity is to make and ensure compliance with decisions and policies that are applicable to the whole society, but usually result in the attainment of goals desired by only some of its members. Thus, the polity must allocate the rewards and costs flowing from decisions and policies among various classes of citizens and must attempt to resolve the conflicts generated in this process. Like the stratification system, the polity is the source of both energy and information. It uses energy to maintain or change culture, meet the demands of certain classes and groups, and, in the longer term, contribute to class and group formation through policy implementation. It receives information in the form of definitions of reality and some degree of legitimacy from the culture, and in the form of support from certain classes and groups in the stratification system. The polity uses information to control the mode and level of economic production, more or less effectively, through the provision of regulations and receives from economic production some percentage of the energy necessary to its effective functioning. Most of these interchanges have operated at a relatively low level of effectiveness in Zambia in recent years because of economic decline, increasing class formation, continuing cultural heterogeneity, and negative international pressures.

Within the polity, mobilization of individuals and groups for political participation is the most important technique for gaining and demonstrating control of power, especially when class formation is incomplete. Participation can be formal or informal, peaceful or violent; in Zambia it takes all of these forms. Various class fractions and groups, which are to some extent mobilized, compete for the power that is inherent in control of government. In Zambia, this competition takes the form of elections to fill positions within the ruling United National Independence Party (UNIP) and the government, as well as informal competition for appointment, usually by the president, to other party and government positions. Some classes and groups, mainly those whose members are the least privileged people in the society, are left out of the mobilization and competition processes almost entirely. The organization of the party and its relationship to the government are major determinants of the outcomes of mobilization and competition.

Government structure, processes, and capacity are strongly affected by political mobilization and competition, as well as by inputs from the other subsystems of society. In Zambia, the most significant aspects of government are the structure and processes of central government institutions, relations between these institutions and local governments, and the interpretations that top leaders, particularly the president, place on their roles. Finally, all of the international and domestic social and political factors previously discussed, and the relationships among them, determine the content of public policies affecting the economy, the stratification system, the culture, and political mobilization and competition.[4]

SOUTH AFRICAN GOALS, STRATEGIES, AND TACTICS REGARDING SOUTHERN AFRICA AND ZAMBIA

Southern Africa is of vital importance, both politically (including strategically) and economically, to the "total strategy" for survival being pursued by the apartheid regime in South Africa. Robert M. Price analyzes South Africa's regional goals as long-term, medium-term, and short-term objectives; other writers concur with this categorization, if not with the details of which policies and actions belong in each category.[5] In the long term, South Africa's goal remains the creation of a "Constellation of States" in Southern Africa that will enhance its military security, further its economic development by becoming increasingly dependent on it, and legitimize a "reformed" version of apartheid. In this South African utopian vision, other states in the constellation would view their own security as closely linked to that of South Africa, so that all would eagerly collaborate in keeping "communists" bent on the violent overthrow of any or all of these regimes out of the Southern African region and totally repressing those who could not be kept out. Other states would also believe that their economic development would be maximized within a highly integrated regional economy in which South Africa would play the subimperial role as the main producer and exporter of manufactured goods, the main source of investment capital, and the hub of the regional transportation system. Finally, the other states would recognize the African homelands or *bantustans* (four of which have been given formal independence by South Africa but which are as yet unrecognized by any other country) and establish relationships with them (including, in three cases, annexation). The existence of such a mutually supportive Constellation of States would make it much easier for the West to maintain and enhance its "constructive engagement" with South Africa.

Although these long-term goals are far removed from present-day reality in a number of respects, most analysts believe that South African policymakers retain sufficient self-confidence to believe that such goals are potentially attainable. Thus, long-term goals exert a significant influence on strategy and tactics. They are being pursued concurrently with medium- and short-term goals, which are both generally compatible with them and more likely to be realized in the near future.

In the medium term, strategic and political goals include muting criticism of South Africa and eliminating hostile diplomatic action against the country by neighboring states, and, most importantly, prohibiting the African National Congress from establishing a presence in those states. Economic goals include maintenance of at least present levels of dependence on South Africa for imports, capital, expertise, and transportation, and non-participation in all types of sanctions against South Africa.

Contrary to the prevailing wisdom in U.S. governmental circles, Price believes that the major short-term regional objective of South African policy is to maintain the Soviet-Cuban presence in Southern Africa. This presence is needed to preserve the West's sense that its strategic interests in the region are at risk.

The South African government, often acting in collaboration with private firms and groups, has undertaken a number of strategic and tactical initiatives in pursuit of these goals since the loss of white-ruled buffer states with the independence of Angola and Mozambique in 1975. In the late 1970s, the Constellation of States was formally proposed, along with a Southern African Development Bank. When the response to these proposals was negative from virtually all of the countries in the region, and they founded the Southern African Development Coordination Conference as an alternative, South Africa turned to destabilization tactics. According to several authors, these efforts were directed selectively against the most vulnerable and most threatening states, which did not include Zambia.[6] They involved support for antigovernment movements, incursions of varying strength and duration by South African military forces, and several types of economic sanctions; they were directed toward either the overthrow of existing regimes or substantial changes in their policies toward South Africa.

Destabilization tactics brought to the surface the contradictions inherent in South African medium-term regional policies. Creating weak and disorganized states was not compatible with substantial expansion of South African economic activity in these states. Divisions appeared between those South African groups favoring one or the other of these alternatives: the military emphasized the security advantages of destabilization, while large-scale capital, and to a lesser extent foreign ministry professionals, emphasized the economic and long-term political advantages of friendly relations. These divisions persist, but their significance is difficult to ascertain, especially from the vantage point of Southern African countries whose leaders are so well aware of destabilization activities.

The significance of the Nkomati and Lusaka accords signed by South Africa with Mozambique and Angola, respectively, in 1984 (as well as a similar pact with Swaziland two years earlier) can only be appreciated in the context of the South African goals, previous strategies and tactics, and the internal divisions discussed earlier. These accords, especially Nkomati, represent both a change in South African medium-term strategy and a major but temporary achievement of that strategy. They were, or at least appeared to be, a change in the relationship between South Africa and two of the most radical regimes in the region, from one of destabilization to one of limited cooperation. They were initially regarded as a major achievement because they would substantially improve South African security by denying the ANC (and SWAPO of Namibia) access to vitally important territory, would dramatically improve the chances of increasing profitable economic relations with two major countries in the region at the expense of SADCC, and would, because they involved the most radical states in the region, rekindle progress toward the long-term political goal of a Constellation of States.[7]

This major achievement was temporary, however, because the accords have proved virtually impossible to enforce; this was due mainly to South African reluctance to give up support of antigovernment guerrillas in Angola and Mozambique, the reluctance of these groups and ANC to abide by treaties to which they were not parties, and South Africa's inability in a period of recession at home to deliver the economic benefits implied in the accords. The expected improvements in South Africa's relations with other countries in the region, including Zambia, did not follow. Finally, the continuous disturbances in South Africa's black townships, beginning a few months after the accords were signed and resulting in the declaration of a state of emergency, indicated very clearly that agreements with neighboring states were insufficient to stem or even slow the tide of demand for substantial change in South Africa.

As pointed out earlier, Zambia is usually viewed as a secondary target of South African regional policies. It is relatively distant from South Africa and does not share a common border with that country (though it does border on Namibia). Thus it can be permitted to host the regional headquarters of the ANC. Because President Kenneth Kaunda has advocated détente with South Africa on more than one occasion, many South African decisionmakers view his continuation in office as a political benefit rather than a threat, despite his outspoken criticism of apartheid and leadership of the Front Line States.[8] Economically, Zambia is important to South Africa, but the former has not been able to mount a serious, sustained effort to sever economic ties; until 1980 it needed South Africa to help it substantially reduce ties with Rhodesia, and its economic decline since 1975 has made it more vulnerable. Because of all of these factors, South Africa has apparently never felt the need for a dramatic change in its relations with Zambia of the type represented by the accords with Angola and Mozambique.

Because the data on which to base a systematic comparative evaluation of South Africa's overt destabilization tactics against Southern African countries have not been collected, it is not possible to challenge the assertion that Zambia has been less a target of these tactics than other countries have been. In absolute terms, however, there is no doubt that South Africa has taken many potentially destabilizing actions against Zambia. As Joseph Hanlon puts it, "there is a continuous thread running through all the stories [of Zambian–South African relations], namely that when Zambia is in difficulties, South Africa exploits those troubles."[9] Hanlon believes that elements of the South African military have taken the lead in destabilization tactics directed at Zambia, but the events I will describe later demonstrate that there has been much broader participation in them. Although Zambia's behavior has sometimes been compatible with South Africa's medium-term goals, and has even aided in their attainment, this behavior has been almost completely incompatible with South Africa's long-term goals, as is clearly recognized by the apartheid regime. Once South Africa realized that Rhodesia would have to become Zimbabwe, limited cooperation with Zambia toward the attainment of that end was possible, since Rhodesia was the top medium-term priority in Zambian foreign policy; however, both sides realized that this situation was very temporary.

Although South Africa's interest in Zambia goes back to the time of the latter's independence in 1964,[10] it is sufficient for the purposes of this chapter to summarize South African actions during the period since 1973. First, in the security sphere, there were reports of a number of military incursions by South African troops into Zambia during this period. Only a few of these reports were denied by the South Africans. Most of the incursions involved only a few soldiers and lasted for very short periods of time; but in 1980 and 1981–1982 there were battalion-sized invasions of southwestern Zambia, and some troops remained in that country for several months.[11] Dramatic raids in 1985 and 1986 indicated that South Africa had not abandoned military action against Zambia.

South African support for antigovernment groups in Zambia, involving both the security and political spheres, is more difficult to document, and there has undoubtedly been a tendency for UNIP and the Zambian government to tar their opponents with the brush of South African sponsorship in order to discredit them. Nevertheless, there are instances for which this charge appears to be amply justified. The Mushala Gang, which terrorized parts of the Western Province from the mid-1970s until the early 1980s, almost certainly received its initial training in South Africa. In 1980, a number of Zambian civilians—some of whom were prominent in politics or business—and military men were accused of participating in a South African–backed plot to overthrow the government. In 1981, allegations were made of another attempted coup, aimed in part at freeing those arrested the previous year. The dropping of charges against some of those initially accused, and the acquittal of most of the others following lengthy trials, indicate that the net of charges stemming from these alleged coup plots had been cast too widely. Yet, the 1980 plot investigation was initiated by a battle between Zambian police and armed men, as well as the discovery of an arms cache on the farm of a white Zambian with well-known South African connections, who fled to South Africa to avoid arrest. This was another example of South Africa's exploiting Zambia's troubles, though only a small number of Zambians were active collaborators.

Even during the period of tentative Zambian–South African cooperation over Rhodesia, political relations between the two countries were very strained. As indicated previously, the apartheid regime knew that Zambia remained firmly opposed to its long-term regional goals and its very existence, even while collaborating on medium-term goals. In their meetings with President Kaunda in 1975 and 1982, respectively, South African prime ministers John Vorster and P. W. Botha lectured him on the dangers of confrontation with South Africa and the advantages of supporting the Constellation of States or more informal long-term collaborative arrangements. Subsequently, both repeated these lectures in public speeches in response to Kaunda's failure to heed their private warnings.[12] After each peak of détente, there was a deterioration in relations between the two countries. The independence of Zimbabwe was the occasion for mutual lectures by South African and Zambian leaders, warning each other to keep hands off their newly independent neighbor.[13] More recently, the South African government has forced Zambia to ban ANC training within its borders and has expressed displeasure over Kaunda's efforts to arrange talks between that organization and white South African business and church leaders, students, and opposition politicians. Now that South Africa's post-Nkomati success in regional strategy has been shown to be short-lived, Zambia's long-term hostility has become more threatening.

Events from late 1986 through the end of 1988 indicate that South Africa continues to be interested in destabilizing Zambia. During that period, a number of Zambians and South Africans, as well as a New Zealander resident in South Africa, were charged in Zambia with spying for South Africa; a South African commando raid on Livingstone resulted in the deaths of four Zambians; a parcel bomb on a train from South Africa exploded in the Lusaka railway station; and three car bomb explosions, probably set by South African agents, went off in or near Lusaka and Livingstone. In early 1988, President Botha stated that the era of détente with neighboring states was at an end, and that South Africa would now get tough with those states that supported the ANC. He had earlier indicated that Zambia was becoming increasingly hostile to his country.

In the economic sphere, South Africa has taken a number of actions to maintain Zambia's economic ties to it, reinforcing pressures in this direction from the world economy and the emergent Zambian bourgeoisie. Since 1973, there have been a number of instances of economic espionage in Zambia by reputed South African agents. A number of road and railway bridges have been blown up in Zambia, Tanzania, Angola, and Mozambique in order to force Zambia to remain dependent on lines of transportation running through South Africa. These lines have been temporarily closed, and goods have been held up by the apartheid regime on several occasions to express its displeasure with actions of the Zambian government or just to demonstrate

Zambia's vulnerability. To cement economic dependency, the South African government and private sector have worked together to provide Zambia with goods—from maize to feed the general population to luxury consumer goods for the bourgeoisie—quickly, at relatively competitive prices, and on relatively generous credit terms in response to shortages produced by Zambia's economic decline and continuing transportation bottlenecks.

South African firms operating in Zambia, especially the Anglo-American Corporation, continue to have substantial leverage over the Zambian economy despite extensive nationalization. They utilize a variety of techniques to maximize economic ties with their mother country, including keeping control of research, technical management, sales, and accounting in expatriate hands; carefully socializing Zambian management employees to accept company subcultures and patronage relationships; and importing equipment and other goods from South Africa to the greatest possible extent.[14] As the result of these various South African actions, working in conjunction with other factors, Zambia's imports from South Africa increased fourfold between 1978 and 1982,[15] and have remained high since then. At the same time, South African companies have not hesitated to interfere with Zambian international trade in order to foster their own interests. The instance of such behavior that had the most devastating consequences for Zambia was Anglo-American's leading role in persuading the government of Zimbabwe to build a coal-fired power station at Hwange (using Anglo's coal) to replace electric power long imported from Zambia.[16]

ECONOMIC DECLINE, CLASS FORMATION, AND IDEOLOGICAL CLEAVAGE IN ZAMBIA: THE SOUTH AFRICAN FACTOR

To appreciate the systemic effects that South Africa's overt destabilizing and dependency-maintaining actions in pursuit of its long- and medium-term regional goals have had on Zambian politics, it is necessary to place these actions in the context of Zambia's economic decline since 1975, and the processes of class and fraction formation and ideological cleavage in that society since independence. This can be done briefly, noting the influence that South Africa has exercised on these trends.

Between 1973 and 1985, Zambia's real gross domestic product (at 1977 prices), adjusted for terms of trade (which declined by 74 percent), fell from 2,661.5 million Kwacha to 1,953 million.[17] Real per capita income (again at 1977 prices) fell from a high of 322.6 Kwacha in 1974 to 275.7 Kwacha in 1984, according to government statistics; these figures were probably actually much worse in reality. The consumer price index (1975 = 100) rose to 336.8 for high-income people and to 373.5 for low-income people in 1984. Paid employees fell from 30 percent of the labor force in 1974 and 8.2 percent of the population in 1973 to 19.8 percent of the labor force and 5.7

percent of the population in 1984, because of the loss of more than 20 thousand jobs and substantial increases in the labor force (over 600,000) and population (over 2 million people). Government expenditure in 1984 was reduced to less than one-half of what it had been in 1974, largely because the inability to make a profit from the sale of copper in most years reduced the contribution of mining to government revenue from 53 to 6 percent, having hit zero in four of the intervening years. Adequate infrastructure had not been developed to allow agriculture or manufacturing to make up the revenue lost from mining.

While the causes of this rapid and devastating decline are not found exclusively in Zambia's economic relationships with South Africa, those relationships are a significant causal factor. Zambia has not been able to break away from its dependence on copper revenues, in large part because of its economic ties to South Africa and the Southern African regional economy controlled by that country, in which Zambia is assigned the role of copper producer and importer of manufactured goods. This role is maintained through overt actions such as those already described. The support of core capitalist countries is, of course, crucial to the maintenance of the Southern African regional economy.

Data on income distribution in Zambia have not been collected on a regular basis, but those data that do exist reveal an extremely uneven distribution. The 1974 Household Budget Survey found that the top 20 percent of households in a national sample had 67.1 percent of the income, the top 10 percent had 45.6 percent, and the top 5 percent had 34.6 percent; the distribution of income has almost certainly grown more unequal since then. The 1974 figures reveal greater inequality than existed in 1959 when the country was dominated by a European colonial-settler ruling class.[18] Since Europeans and Asians together constitute less than 1 percent of the Zambian population, increasing income inequality must reflect increased class formation among Africans.

There is a widespread consensus among analysts of Zambian society that a potentially dominant class is forming, but there is less agreement on the base of this class (is it primarily economic or political?), on the nature of the fractions into which this class is divided and the relations among them, and on the extent of conflict and collaboration between this emergent class and others that are probably less fully formed.[19] It is neither possible nor necessary to resolve these issues here. It is sufficient to note that those who gained control of the Zambian polity at the time of independence and used that control to nationalize the "commanding heights" of the Zambian economy have thus acquired control over state wealth and, in many cases, have used this control to acquire private wealth using a variety of techniques. The private sector combines this national capital with multinational capital, which employs a number of Zambians in management positions. As we have seen, much of this multinational capital is South African, and it actively encourages class formation among its Zambian executives. Furthermore, Zambian leaders' fear and resentment of South Africa was one significant factor leading to the nationalizations, and thus indirectly to further class formation. The future of the relationship among political power, state wealth, and private wealth cannot be known at this time. There may well be an increasing concentration of all these factors in the hands of the same people, but there is also the potential for increasing populist resentment against both types of wealth or increasing conflict among those who control the two types.

In the absence of systematic data, statements about class consciousness within various fractions of the emergent bourgeoisie are bound to be somewhat speculative. However, there is some reasonably good evidence that both class consciousness and fractional cleavages have existed for a long time, and that they have increased in recent years. In a study of 120 top-level Zambian politicians and civil servants conducted shortly after independence, I found a general rejection of economic equality because it was thought to discourage talent. "The uneducated man—the laborer—cannot expect to be equal to the educated man holding a responsible position," it was widely agreed. But civil servants and politicians with business backgrounds were even less egalitarian than were other politicians.[20] The combination of increased class formation and severe economic decline since 1975 can be assumed to have threatened dominant class interests and thus heightened awareness of them.

Many of those accused of treason in 1980 eagerly agreed that they opposed government policy, even though they denied that such disagreements had led them to collaborate with South Africa. Most of these people were representatives of private wealth, and Carolyn Baylies and Morris Szeftel have documented the increasing political influence of representatives of such wealth, involving both political office-holding and organized interest-group activity. They show that members of this class constituted almost half of the nonincumbent candidates elected to the National Assembly in 1973 and have continued to maintain this proportion in subsequent elections; that they articulate political demands through the Zambia Federation of Employers, the Zambia Industrial and Commercial Association, the Zambia National Chamber of Commerce and Industry (for small businesses), and a number of other organizations; and that they have had a substantial influence on government policies.[21]

The proximity of an economically strong and politically hostile South Africa has contributed significantly to increasing cleavages among fractions of the emerging dominant class. Lengthy conversations with members of the fraction based on private wealth inevitably turn to the topic of South Africa, and a greater degree of accommodation with that country is almost always advocated. It is important to note that such accommodation almost never includes acceptance of apartheid or the Constellation of States. Rather, it focuses on reducing Zambia's sacrifices by accepting "natural" economic ties and on supporting the forces for genuine political reform in South Africa.[22] It is recognized that fractional and class interests would benefit most from such a change in Zambian policy, but it is also claimed that national interests (and thus those of other classes) would benefit substantially. The fraction of the emerging dominant class based in the occupancy of party and government roles has maintained a more consistently hostile and fearful attitude toward South Africa and tends to question the patriotism of those who do not share this attitude. Conflicting sets of norms and beliefs, generated by energy from the economic and stratification subsystems but now possessing a partially independent cultural existence, have developed around this issue. This cultural complex provides information that reinforces class formation and fractional conflict.

The most fully formed and politically articulate class or fraction outside of the emerging dominant class is the working class or unionized labor. Although it claims to represent the entire working class, it is probably more accurate to designate the trade union movement and its umbrella organization, the Zambia Congress of Trade Unions (ZCTU), as a fraction. There is debate about the extent to which this fraction participated in an alliance with the emergent bourgeoisie in the early years of independence, but there is no doubt that economic decline has destroyed any alliance that may have existed. This has been replaced with intense conflict, accompanied by increased class consciousness on the part of unionized workers.[23] The unions have lost power in this conflict, and some of them have also lost members. In their desperation to reverse these trends by halting economic decline, they too have begun to advocate greater accommodation with South Africa. Their position on this issue is sufficiently ambivalent that it is unlikely to form a basis for forming or reconstituting an alliance with the bourgeoisie; yet, it creates one more basis for conflict between the unions and government.

THE SYSTEMIC DESTABILIZING EFFECTS OF SOUTH AFRICA ON ZAMBIAN POLITICS

South Africa's overt destabilizing and dependency-maintaining actions against Zambia have occurred at a time of economic decline and increasing class formation and conflict, and at a time when Zambia's political and cultural institutions are still struggling to cope with the effects of earlier conflicts. Therefore, these actions have had broad systemic destabilizing effects on Zambian politics that have not received adequate attention in previous analyses. Following the theoretical framework outlined earlier in this chapter, these systemic effects will be analyzed in terms of: (1) political mobilization and competition (including political party organization); (2) government structure, processes, and capacity; and (3) policies affecting all subsystems of society.

In briefly summarizing the effects of the South African presence on class formation and conflict in Zambia, I have already touched on its effects on political mobilization. It provides an additional issue around which bourgeois groups can mobilize politically and thus increases their formation. More recently, it has also provided an additional issue for the political mobilization of trade union members against the government. Because the South African presence has no effect on the political mobilization of peasants or the unorganized urban poor, it increases disparities in the level of mobilization between the most and least mobilized classes and fractions in Zambian society.

The systemic effects of South African actions on political competition are considerably greater; in fact, they are probably the most important systemic effects of such actions in the political realm. Competition has long been pervasive in Zambian politics. UNIP originated from competition for leadership within the original nationalist movement in colonial Northern Rhodesia—the African National Congress—and competition between these two parties continued from the time of their split, in 1959, until the creation of a one-party system in 1973. Competition within UNIP came into the open at party elections in 1967 and remained intense for at least the next five years. Two parties—the United Party (UP) and the United Peoples' Party (UPP)—broke away from UNIP during this period, and competition between the latter splinter party and UNIP was particularly intense. Studies of local-level politics have revealed numerous instances of more informal competition for party and government offices.[24] The one-party system was instituted by top political leaders to mitigate competition and channel it in what were considered to be constructive directions.

During the period of interparty competition it became well known in Zambia, in large part through the progovernment South African press, that the South African government preferred any or all of the opposition parties to UNIP. The ANC had been considered more "moderate" all along, and the UP and UPP were considered worthy of support because they kept Kaunda and UNIP preoccupied with Zambian internal conflicts, rather than with the struggle against apartheid. Furthermore, all of these parties advocated greater accommodation with South Africa (and Rhodesia), using the same arguments now employed by the emergent bourgeoisie, most of whom are at least nominal members of UNIP. There is no evidence that opposition parties received material support from South Africa, but UNIP was deeply concerned that this might occur.

While the implementation of the one-party system shifted the emphasis in National Assembly elections from national to local-level competition, it by no means drove the former type of competition from its prominent place in the minds and behavior of political activists.[25] Former members and leaders of opposition parties were hindered in their efforts to gain power within the one-party system by a number of factors, one of which was their position on accommodation with South Africa (and, until 1980, Rhodesia). South Africa's continued exercise of economic and military pressure—even during periods of détente—reinforced by economic decline and increasing class formation, greatly heightened the importance of this factor. Because greater accommodation was seen as a way to relieve the painful consequences of economic decline and halt military incursions, as well as a way to further the interests of the politically influential emergent bourgeoisie, former opposition politicians continued their advocacy of this policy. They were joined by other politicians who had been in UNIP all along. Accommodation may have been especially popular in areas that formerly gave strong support to opposition parties, because both military incursions and many of the worst effects of economic decline occurred there.

The inclusion of the South African issue in intraparty competition within UNIP increased the insecurity felt by top party leaders because of this competition. They were well aware of the short-run appeal of the accommodationist position, but President Kaunda and some others were determined not to give in to it. Their fear that competition would lead to greater South African involvement in Zambian politics on behalf of its political favorites continued and probably increased in periods of the most intense Zambian–South African conflict. Their increased insecurity led them to change the rules of competition in ways that they hoped would reduce the level of competition. Some of these changes had the opposite effect, however. The charges of treason made against more people than actually participated in the 1980 and 1981 coup plots, as described earlier, were symptomatic of the leaders' insecurity when political opposition appeared to be supported by South Africa.

A brief description of the major political competition events that constituted the process discussed in the preceding paragraphs will demonstrate the accuracy of the general characterization of competition presented here.[26] In June 1973, Kaunda and the former leader of the ANC signed a pact declaring that former ANC members (including UPP members, since that party had merged with ANC) would join UNIP. Disagreement soon arose, however, over whether they would join UNIP branches as individuals, or whether former ANC branches would become UNIP branches. Since competition with UPP had been especially intense immediately before the one-party system was declared, former UPP members could join UNIP only with the approval of the Central Committee. The electoral process that year, the first under the one-party system, began with primary elections within UNIP. Twenty-six of the winners were rejected by the Central Committee, who wanted to give its favored candidates a good chance of winning in the general elections. Voter turnout in those elections was the lowest in Zambian history, dropping to less than half of what it had been in the previous general elections in 1968. Voters in former ANC strongholds, who could not vote for their former leaders, defeated three ministers and eight junior ministers.

In September 1976, a confrontation over economic policy, including economic relations with South Africa, took place in the broadly representative National Council of UNIP. Factions were identified with specific ideologies more explicitly than had previously been the case. In September 1977, former UPP leaders were finally allowed to rejoin UNIP. Shortly thereafter, members of the National Assembly called for the abolition of the UNIP Central Committee as an independent body, and its reconstitution as the cabinet, with members wearing party rather than government hats. Instead, at Kaunda's insistence, the Central Committee's powers were increased. These events raised tension about the 1978 general elections, especially when the former leaders of both the ANC and UPP announced that they planned to challenge Kaunda for the presidency, campaigning on platforms that included greater accommodation with South Africa. Party rules were quickly changed to prevent them from running. The Central Committee rejected more primary election winners than it had rejected five years earlier. Turnout for the general elections increased over 1973, but more voters rejected Kaunda (though 80 percent still supported him), and more incumbent National Assembly members were ousted.

In 1982 and early 1983, primary elections were abolished on the grounds that they were too divisive, and the Central Committee was given the power to approve all candidates before they could stand; it used this power extensively in the 1983 general elections. Turnout in these elections was about the same as in 1978, and about the same number of incumbents were ousted, but nobody challenged Kaunda, and his vote increased substantially. The following year, prior party membership requirements for future candidates were increased. Overt political competition was somewhat more effectively channeled according to the top leaders' wishes in 1983 than it had been in 1973 or 1978, mainly through tighter central controls. But it is also interesting to note that accommodation with South Africa was less an issue, at least in part because this was one of the peak periods of détente. In the 1988 elections, conducted under the same rules as the 1983 elections, Kaunda increased his percentage of the vote slightly, but turnout decreased substantially.

Government's continuing fear of South African–inspired opposition involving members of former opposition parties, the private sector fraction of the bourgeoisie, and the unions is illustrated by a number of events that occurred in 1987. President Kaunda accused unnamed rich business leaders— some of whom formerly held government positions—of plotting with South Africa to instigate a military coup, and a short while later 100 business leaders had their passports withdrawn. Kaunda also linked South Africa with the spate of wildcat strikes that took place in the early part of the year, and postponed a trip to Ghana because of what he said was a planned sabotage campaign. Finally, a former UPP leader was arrested for trying to start up that party again as a guerrilla movement in alliance with UNITA, the South African–sponsored opposition movement in Angola.[27]

Centralized control over political competition has been paralleled by centralization of power in government. Within the central government, by far the most significant trend is centralization in the hands of the president.[28] He appoints the top officials in the civil service and the parastatal corporations, as well as the UNIP Central Committee and a majority of the National Council. He has great legal powers, enhanced by Zambia's permanent, officially declared state of emergency, and he is the initiator of most important legislation. He has acquired and maintained this power because many other political leaders feel that he is better able than any other possible president to deal with the combined crises of economic decline, class conflict, continued political competition, and external threats. Even those who oppose his policies fear the intense competition that would follow his departure from office. Kaunda's style of leadership tends to be authoritarian only when he feels that he is opposed by a majority of powerful leaders and/or a number of organized groups on issues that are of central concern to him. Relations with South Africa fit these conditions very well, and the South African presence almost certainly increases his authoritarianism directly, aside from being a part of the general crisis that led to centralization of power in his hands. Ending apartheid is at least as important to Kaunda as it is to any Front Line State leader; no matter how much tactical flexibility he has evidenced, racially based minority rule is totally abhorrent to him as a matter of principle. Because of his central role in Zambian politics, he is more aware than is anyone else of the extent to which economic decline and class formation have increased pressures for accommodation with South Africa. Thus, he is determined to accumulate the power necessary to have his own way on this issue.

In the realm of central-local government relations, centralization of power has taken the form of a group of related changes ironically labeled decentralization. These changes have abolished urban local governments and placed all local government in the hands of district councils, whose members are elected only by UNIP members in the district rather than by all citizens, and whose leaders are appointed by the president. The new system was opposed by the unions and many members of the emergent bourgeoisie, so its introduction increased political conflict, at least temporarily. No evidence is available to link this conflict directly to South African actions, but it is a part of the general Zambian crisis described previously.

Finally, South African overt destabilization and dependency-maintaining actions, together with the systemic effects of the South African presence on political mobilization, centralization of power, and especially political competition, have greatly decreased the Zambian government's capacity to implement policies that would effectively combat economic decline, class formation, and cultural inconsistencies, or policies that would contribute significantly to bringing about change in South Africa. Many policies relating to the first of these goals have been formulated, including the elaboration of the ideology of Zambian humanism; enactment of a leadership code that officially restricts the participation of a wide variety of political leaders in private economic activities; nationalization or indigenization of wholesale and retail trade, mining, manufacturing, newspapers, and some financial institutions, and the placement of the larger of these operations into parastatal corporations; introduction of works councils into larger firms, accompanied by intensified control of trade unions; increased government control over land; attempts to increase and redistribute wealth in the rural areas, avoid food imports, and earn additional foreign exchange from exports through several comprehensive rural development programs; creation of a National Service obligation for most citizens; and far-reaching proposals for educational reform.

None of these policies has been implemented in ways that have effectively counteracted economic decline or class formation. There is a continuing struggle over the definition of humanism; the leadership code has not been effectively enforced; nationalization has led to state capitalism because of the incorporation of the parastatals into the world economy; indigenization of smaller businesses has greatly accelerated class formation; works councils, where they have been implemented, have been less effective than have unions in protecting workers' interests; the long leases now in effect on land have not yet proved to be different in practice from the freehold tenure they replaced; rural development programs have failed to cope with Zambia's colossal problems of agricultural marketing; the National Service has been virtually discontinued for lack of funds; and the original education reform proposals were watered down considerably before implementation.[29]

CONCLUSION

Because of South African pressures, a degree of incoherence exists in Zambian policies toward that country. Rhetoric based on the long-term goal of ending apartheid often accompanies actions that reflect short-term tactical flexibility, making the former appear empty. Recent examples of this are the ambiguous "partial military mobilization" declared in response to the 1986 South African raid, and Zambia's role in the abortive campaign by some Commonwealth members to institute new sanctions against South Africa in the face of opposition from Great Britain in 1986–1987.[30]

The systemic policy effects of the South African presence reinforce its effects on the economy, class structure, and political competition, already discussed. The South African presence provides numerous disincentives for breaking away from the world economy and putting more emphasis on agriculture. The inability of Zambia to enhance its self-reliance through participation in a development-oriented regional market drove it more fully into the arms of the IMF, which gave aid only under conditions that led to greater political instability in 1986 and 1987. In response to this popular protest, Kaunda rejected the IMF conditions and embarked upon a difficult New Economic Recovery Program, which is by no means certain to improve the economy. The South African presence also encourages the emergent bourgeoisie to resist the implementation of many of the policies described earlier by providing them with "easy" alternatives that are more compatible with their short-run interests. The accommodationist theme in bourgeois political culture is closely tied to the rejection of humanism, which is becoming a dominant feature of that culture. All of these developments are likely to increase fear of political opposition, either mobilized or covert. South Africa is likely to foster such opposition and will be perceived by UNIP and the Zambian government as supporting any opposition that arises, whether it is actually doing so or not. This fear of South African destabilization on the part of key Zambian actors leads them to take actions that are themselves destabilizing. This is the essence of systemic destabilization, which undermines state power.

NOTES

1. The former literature is cited in notes 5 and 6. In addition, it is worth noting that one volume on South African regional policy that contains chapters on eight countries does not have a chapter on Zambia. See Thomas M. Callaghy, ed., *South Africa in Southern Africa: The Intensifying Vortex of Violence* (New York: Praeger, 1983). The literature on Zambian foreign policy that takes this point of view includes Douglas G. Anglin and Timothy M. Shaw, *Zambia's Foreign Policy* (Boulder, Colo.: Westview Press, 1979); Marcia Burdette, "Zambia," in Timothy M. Shaw and Olajide Aluko, eds., *The Political Economy of African Foreign Policy* (New York: St. Martin's Press, 1984); Karen Eriksen (pseud. for Carolyn Baylies), "Zambia: Class Formation and Détente," *Review of African Political Economy* 9 (May–August 1978), pp. 4–26; and Timothy M. Shaw and Agrippah T. Mugomba, "The Political Economy of Regional Détente: Zambia and Southern Africa," *Journal of African Studies* 4 (Winter 1977), pp. 392–413. Libby's argument is found in Ronald T. Libby, *The Politics of Economic Power in Southern Africa* (Princeton: Princeton University Press, 1987), pp. 229–245. A more balanced view of Zambian–South African relations is found in Marcia Burdette, *Zambia: Between Two Worlds* (Boulder, Colo.: Westview Press, 1988), pp. 143–145.

2. This framework is presented in greater detail in James R. Scarritt,

"The Explanation of African Politics and Society: Toward a Synthesis of Approaches," *Journal of African Studies* 13 (Fall 1986), pp. 85–93.

3. This framework combines regional subsystems and subimperial complex analysis, which are contrasted in the Southern African context in Roger J. Southall, "Southern Africa: Regional Sub-System or Sub-Imperial Complex?" *The African Review* 9, no. 2 (1982), pp. 36–61.

4. These factors also determine the content of foreign policy, but that will not be analyzed in this paper because I have not collected systematic data on it.

5. Robert M. Price, "Creating New Political Realities: Pretoria's Drive for Regional Hegemony," in Gerald J. Bender, James S. Coleman, and Richard L. Sklar, eds., *African Crisis Areas and U.S. Foreign Policy* (Berkeley: University of California Press, 1985), pp. 64–88. See also Price, "Pretoria's Southern African Strategy," *African Affairs* 83 (January 1984), pp. 11–32; Robert Davies and Dan O'Meara, "Total Strategy in Southern Africa: An Analysis of South African Regional Policy Since 1978," *Journal of Southern African Studies* 11 (April 1985), pp. 183–211; Davies and O'Meara, "The State of Analysis of the Southern African Region: Issues Raised by South African Strategy," *Review of African Political Economy* 29 (1984), pp. 64–76; Joseph Hanlon, *Beggar Your Neighbours: Apartheid Power in Southern Africa* (Bloomington: Indiana University Press, 1986), pp. 27–43, 57–65; and Steve Kibble and Ray Bush, "Reform of Apartheid and Continued Destabilisation in Southern Africa," *Journal of Modern African Studies* 24 (June 1986), pp. 203–227.

6. Davies and O'Meara, "Total Strategy in Southern Africa," pp. 199–206; Hanlon, *Beggar Your Neighbours*, pp. 27–32; Richard Leonard, *South Africa at War* (Westport, Conn.: Lawrence Hill, 1983), pp. 72–95; Price, "Pretoria's Southern African Strategy," pp. 18–19; Robert I. Rotberg, "Introduction: South Africa in Its Region—Hegemony and Vulnerability," in Robert I. Rotberg et al., *South Africa and Its Neighbors* (Lexington, Mass.: Lexington Books, 1986), p. 6.

7. This analysis is taken from Davies and O'Meara, "Total Strategy in Southern Africa," pp. 207–210; Price, "Creating New Political Realities," pp. 80–86; and Rotberg, "South Africa in Its Region," pp. 1–4.

8. Hanlon, *Beggar Your Neighbours*, p. 243.

9. *Ibid.*, p. 244. Hanlon is a partial exception to the lack of emphasis on Zambia in the literature on South African regional policy; he has a very good chapter (pp. 243–254) on overt destabilization and dependency maintenance in that country, in which he discusses the role of the emergent bourgeoisie, but he does not deal with what I call systemic destabilization. Kenneth Good, "Zambia and the Liberation of South Africa," *Journal of Modern African Studies* 25 (September 1987), p. 514, disagrees forcefully with the statement by Hanlon just cited, arguing that because of South Africa's recognition that Zambia's policies against it are half-hearted, based on misperceptions, and ineffective, "South Africa usually does not exploit Zambia's many and frequent difficulties, and . . . it is not obviously in Pretoria's interests to want to do so." Aside from this statement, his analysis focuses on Zambian actions and policies and has very little to say about South

African actions, policies, or goals. He recognizes neither the long-term incompatibility of the two countries' goals nor the systemic destabilizing effects of South Africa's actions toward Zambia.

10. On South African interest in and action toward Zambia between 1964 and 1972, see Anglin and Shaw, *Zambia's Foreign Policy*, pp. 276–290; Kenneth W. Grundy, *Confrontation and Accommodation in Southern Africa* (Berkeley: University of California Press, 1973), pp. 32–59, 83–96, 131, 169, 207–211, 235, 274, 298; Richard Hall, *The High Price of Principles* (London: Hodder and Stoughton, 1969), pp. 178–188; B. V. Mtshali, "South Africa and Zambia's 1968 Election," *Kroniek van Afrika* 2 (1970), pp. 126–135; and Jan Pettman, *Zambia: Security and Conflict* (Lewes, England: Julian Friedmann, 1974), pp. 157–164.

11. Hanlon, *Beggar Your Neighbours*, pp. 244–245; *Africa Contemporary Record* 13 (1980–1981), p. B905; 14 (1981–1982), p. B850.

12. *Africa Research Bulletin*, Political, Social, and Cultural Series 13 (April 1976), p. 4003; 19 (May 1982), p. 6455.

13. *Ibid.*, 17 (February 1980), p. 5889. President Kaunda's annual address to the National Assembly in January 1980 contained more references to South Africa than has any other address delivered between 1973 and 1983 (Scarritt data). The context of virtually all of these references was warning South Africa to keep its hands off independent Zimbabwe.

14. Hanlon, *Beggar Your Neighbours*, pp. 248–252, presents a good analysis of these techniques.

15. Republic of Zambia, *Monthly Digest of Statistics* (Lusaka: Central Statistical Office, 1986) 21, no. 8/9 (August–September 1985), p. 22.

16. Hanlon, *Beggar Your Neighbours*, pp. 210–212.

17. These data were compiled by the author from various Zambian government documents, including various issues of *Monthly Digest of Statistics*; Republic of Zambia, National Commission for Development Planning, *Economic Review and Annual Plan 1986* (Lusaka: Government Printer, 1986); and Republic of Zambia, Office of the President, National Commission for Development Planning, *Economic Report 1984* (Lusaka: Government Printer, 1985). They are similar to data presented in Theodore R. Valentine, "Income Distribution Issues in a Structurally Dependent Economy: An Analysis of Growing Income Inequality in Zambia," in International Development Research Centre, *The Zambian Economy: Problems and Prospects* (Lusaka, 1985), pp. 209–236. Mimeo.

18. Republic of Zambia, Central Statistical Office, *Housing Budget Survey 1974–75 Preliminary Report* (Lusaka: Central Statistical Office, 1980). Hanlon, *Beggar Your Neighbours*, p. 253n, cites an unpublished 1983 study showing that inequality has increased since 1974, and Valentine, "Income Distribution Issues," cites several types of data pointing in the same direction. The Gini coefficient for the 1959 data was .48, while that for the 1974 data was .59.

19. Conflict and consensus among analysts on these issues are described in James R. Scarritt, "The Analysis of Social Class, Political Participation, and Public Policy in Zambia," *Africa Today* 30, no. 3 (1983), pp. 5–22.

20. James R. Scarritt, "Elite Values, Ideology and Power in Post-Independence Zambia," *African Studies Review* 14 (April 1971), pp. 42–43.

21. Carolyn L. Baylies and Morris Szeftel, "The Rise of a Zambian Capitalist Class in the 1970s," *Journal of Southern African Studies* 8 (April 1982), pp. 187–213; Baylies and Szeftel, "The Rise to Political Prominence of the Zambian Business Class," in Carolyn Baylies and Morris Szeftel, *The Dynamics of the One-Party State in Zambia*, ed. Cherry Gertzel (Manchester: Manchester University Press, 1984), pp. 58–78.

22. Hanlon, *Beggar Your Neighbours*, pp. 253–254.

23. Changing relations between the Zambian government and the unions are discussed in Jane L. Parpart and Timothy M. Shaw, "Contradiction and Coalition: Class Formation in Zambia, 1964–1984," *Africa Today* 30, no. 3 (1983), pp. 23–50.

24. National-level political competition in Zambia between 1964 and 1972 is described in Pettman, *Zambia: Security and Conflict*, pp. 51–69; Thomas Rasmussen, "Political Competition and One-Party Dominance in Zambia," *Journal of Modern African Studies* 7, no. 3 (1969), pp. 407–424; and William Tordoff, ed., *Politics in Zambia* (Berkeley: University of California Press, 1974), pp. 62–196. Sources on local-level competition are listed in James R. Scarritt, "The Decline of Political Legitimacy in Zambia: An Explanation Based on Incomplete Data," *African Studies Review* 22 (September 1979), pp. 28–32, 36–38.

25. Carolyn Baylies and Morris Szeftel, "Elections in the One-Party State," in Baylies and Szeftel, *The Dynamics of the One-Party State in Zambia*, pp. 46–49.

26. These events and those reported in subsequent sections of this paper are part of a systematic events data set for the period 1973–1985 compiled by the author and his research assistants from a number of news sources. At the present time, expert judges are scaling these events in terms of the amount of various types of change involved in them. This will provide more meaningful measures of the importance of various events. The selection of events for inclusion in this paper was made on the basis of the author's own perceptions and the rankings of those judges who have completed their questionnaires.

27. *Africa Research Bulletin*, Political Series 24 (1987), pp. 8842, 8518, 8547, 8647.

28. This trend is described in Cherry Gertzel, "Dissent and Authority in the Zambian One-Party State, 1973–80," in Baylies and Szeftel, *The Dynamics of the One-Party State in Zambia*, pp. 102–106; and Burdette, *Zambia*, pp. 75–77, 106–110. Earlier discussions of Kaunda's presidency are found in John Hatch, *Two African Statesmen: Kaunda of Zambia, Nyerere of Tanzania* (Chicago: Henry Regnery, 1976); Pettman, *Zambia: Security and Conflict*, pp. 31–45; and Tordoff, *Politics in Zambia*, pp. 11–39, 363–401.

29. Citations to the literature on the implementation of these policies are found in Scarritt, "The Analysis of Social Class, Political Participation, and Public Policy in Zambia," pp. 21–22.

30. Good, "Zambia and the Liberation of South Africa," pp. 511–523, 538–539.

10

Southern Africa in Conflict: Problems Enough to Share

JOHN SULLIVAN

The analysis of interstate relations in Southern Africa is dominated by discussion of South Africa's policy of apartheid and East–West rivalry. Both of these are important factors in understanding the situation in this area of the world and in appreciating the interest or disinterest that foreign capitals have shown for events in the region. This chapter will concern itself only with the former, as it is central to understanding Southern Africa. We will also look at the interaction of the governmental and nongovernmental actors in the region.

Apartheid, the forcible continuation of white predominance in South Africa, and the struggle to overcome that situation, is the central problem for Pretoria and its neighbors. The difficulties among these national actors, however, are also symptomatic of relations between weak and more powerful states, especially when those states share so many common interests. Because of South Africa's key role in the region's transportation network, its strong industrial infrastructure, and modern military establishment, almost any of its actions will have repercussions for at least one of its neighbors and could infringe on another's national sovereignty. Institutionalized racism, however, complicates an already difficult situation for Pretoria's neighbors.

Dealing with South Africa is a matter of morality and economics. Unfortunately, in many capitals it has become common to emphasize the former while frequently trying to benefit from the latter. For the states of Southern Africa, Pretoria is not thousands of miles away, and dealing with their neighbor is not something those states can take or leave as they please.[1] Even if they wished to, they cannot ignore their ties with the white-ruled regime. But neither are they insensitive to how people of color are treated within the borders of the republic.[2]

How does the internal situation in South Africa influence events in the region? Is Pretoria alone to blame for the cycle of violence or are there other contributing factors? How have the black-ruled states handled their relations with their larger neighbor and with the insurgent groups seeking to overthrow white rule? Finally, can we expect the current situation to continue? I will answer these questions by discussing recent events in the region and bilateral relations between South Africa and its neighbors, as represented by Botswana, Lesotho, Mozambique, and Zimbabwe. I have chosen these countries because of their close economic and geographic ties to Pretoria, their interest in the elimination of apartheid in South Africa, and because each has different ties to Pretoria and South African opposition groups. Each has been accused by Pretoria, accurately or not, of supporting insurgent groups seeking to overthrow that government.

Blainey reminds us that war occurs when diplomacy fails, and when war fails, diplomacy ensues.[3] Therefore, this chapter is about the failure of diplomacy and the use of force in Southern African politics. Why has this happened? Is there an alternative to the cycle of violence that occurs as insurgents seek to replace the minority government in Pretoria, and as white security forces strike out to preempt the guerrillas?

Pretoria's strategy over the past twelve years has been to mobilize internal support for its policies by claiming that South Africa is the target of a "total onslaught," that is, a concerted attack controlled from Moscow against the people of the region. There is some debate whether this campaign continues or whether there ever was any reason to believe it was Soviet policy, but it has been the hallmark of Pretoria's regional policy since the end of Portuguese rule in Angola and Mozambique.[4] Even before General Magnus Malan set out the principles of this policy, the government and its military forces had been preparing to defeat their enemies. The government sought to acquire modern military equipment for the South African Defence Force (SADF) and to give it the capability "to conduct large-scale preemptive and punitive raids against guerrilla bases in neighboring countries."[5] The external policies have included a number of measures. Best known is the frequent use of military force against suspected insurgent facilities in neighboring states, which has the effect of increasing domestic support for the white government, a phenomenon not limited to South Africa.[6] Pretoria has also provided aid to guerrilla movements in at least two of the neighboring states and physically occupied Namibia and parts of southern Angola.[7]

The actions of the SADF have been aimed at persuading the governments of neighboring states to prevent South African insurgents—primarily the African National Congress, but also the Pan-Africanist Congress—from using those countries to stage attacks against Pretoria. The goal of Pretoria's cross-border operations is to force behavior acceptable to the South African government. The questions are whether the neighboring states have been deterred, and, if they have, why do the attacks continue?

In 1975, South Africa's military forces became involved in the civil war in Angola, backing the losing side. This behavior was, however, atypical.

With the exception of an area in southern Angola that Pretoria's forces seized in 1983–1984, and continuing South African military activity in southern Angola in support of UNITA guerrillas or against SWAPO insurgents, conventional SADF units have not attempted to occupy the territory of neighboring countries. Rather, they have adopted a practice of supporting insurgent groups in Mozambique and Angola and striking at suspected ANC and SWAPO camps and facilities throughout Southern Africa. No country in the region has been immune from SADF cross-border raids; Angola, Botswana, Lesotho, Mozambique, Swaziland, Zambia, and Zimbabwe have all been struck with varying military reprisals for real or imagined assistance to South African insurgents.

South Africa also uses its economic power against its neighbors. The more notable instances, such as the blockading of Lesotho's borders in early 1985, are well known to most observers, but the practice can also be handled more subtly. President Chissano of Mozambique noted in early 1987 that the volume of South African traffic going through Maputo harbor had dropped to less than one-tenth the volume in 1980. Although not necessarily an overtly aggressive act, this was certainly an effective way to tell Maputo that South Africa is unhappy with its policies.

Pretoria tried to develop better relations with its neighbors in the early 1970s,[8] but that policy failed with the incursion into Angola in support of pro-Western insurgents in 1975.

REGIONAL OVERVIEW

Much more than in any other area of Africa, the southern states are tied together by economic linkages.[9] South Africa remains the regional hegemon, with the largest and best-trained population, the most developed infrastructure and industrial plant, and a highly efficient transportation system that serves the entire region. The same rail lines that carry South African coal to Richards Bay on the Indian Ocean carry minerals from the interior states as far north as Zaire. In addition to the railbeds, South Africa provides neighboring countries with additional rolling stock and locomotives when needed.[10] This relationship is far from one-sided. The other states send thousands of workers to toil in the mines and on the farms of the republic, even while black unemployment in South Africa remains high. The remittances of these migrant workers are a vital source of foreign exchange for their home countries (it is estimated that one-third of Mozambique's foreign exchange earnings are related to remittances and port fees);[11] remittances are later spent on imports from South Africa.

For opposition groups struggling to overthrow white minority rule in South Africa, relations with the black-ruled states are difficult. For individuals who have decided not to live under apartheid, or those fleeing from Pretoria's security forces, the black-ruled states provide a refuge and safe haven. This is especially important to those who do not want to leave Southern Africa—and for the ANC. Since 1960 the ANC has been forced to operate from exile, and in 1962 it formed a military wing to work for the end of white rule. The military wing, known as UmKhonto we Sizwe or MK, has failed to establish itself within South Africa, except for isolated individuals, and must try to strike at Pretoria from abroad. The headquarters for the ANC is in Lusaka, Zambia, but most of its military camps have been located in Angola.[12] The states between those camps and the republic serve as an escape route for potential ANC members and other refugees going in one direction, and as an infiltration route for ANC guerrillas headed in the other.

These countries are then caught between the insurgents, who want to use their territory as launch sites for attacks against South Africa and as bases to return to after operations in the republic, and Pretoria, which sees the neighboring states as a buffer from the dissidents.

In the mid-1970s, Pretoria's appreciation of its problems changed greatly. Before 1975, controlling South African dissidents was easily accomplished, as neighboring states were ruled by minority white regimes that formed a barrier between white-ruled South Africa and the newly independent black-ruled states of central and northern Africa; these white-ruled states had no reason to sympathize with the insurgents. After 1975, as the Portuguese empire fell apart and majority rule came to Zimbabwe, black-led states served to show South Africa's blacks that they too might take over the seats of government.

For the greater part, it is outside the borders of South Africa that the struggle is waged between the ANC and the security forces of the white government. Since 1985 the state of emergency and internal unrest continue with little if any connection to the activities of the insurgents, though the use of mines and other acts of sabotage increased in 1988. The reduction in violence within South Africa, from its peak in 1986, is due largely to the efforts of the government to disrupt the internal opposition. Yet, Pretoria appears to view the external battle as necessary to solve its internal problems. The regional politics of the Southern African states are but a highly visible sideshow to the real story—how to achieve justice in South Africa without destroying the people and the land. The burden of the external struggle rests to a large degree not on the insurgents or their protagonists, but on the nations where this external battle is fought. If the ANC held territory in South Africa, the fighting would be different; but it does not. Instead, it fights from outside and therein lies the problem.[13]

THE VIEW FROM PRETORIA

The attitude of the government in Pretoria toward internal dissidence has generally been one of denial. There would not be a problem—as Pretoria sees it—if the outside world would just leave South Africans alone to work out their differences and permit them to develop in their own way. The world, most white South Africans think, is seeking to overthrow white rule and replace it with revolutionaries and communists opposed to the West and Western values—the "total onslaught." In order to prevent this from happening, the government of South Africa has adopted a policy of military retaliation and deterrence. If the insurgents are going to strike at Pretoria from neighboring states, then the insurgents must be attacked in those countries. This policy denies insurgent forces sanctuary and signals neighboring capitals not to permit hostile activity by antiapartheid groups against South Africa. Outside of South Africa, many would argue that Pretoria has no right to do this, emphasizing that the sovereignty of the neighboring states must be respected.

Many observers, both within South Africa and in the world at large, argue further that the ANC's struggle is justified. If the blacks were permitted full political rights in South Africa there would be no need for foreign bases and an armed struggle. Few countries, however, subscribe to the notion that when their own interests are under attack, their foreign-based opponents are immune from retaliation. From the South African government's point of view, the world has different standards for Pretoria's behavior.

Southern Africa's problems with South Africa are not centered solely on economic domination. Pretoria is already the dominant actor in Southern Africa. Its economy, infrastructure, large and well-educated population, natural wealth, and command of regional transportation networks ensure that any government in South Africa will exercise tremendous influence throughout the region. Rather, at the forefront of Pretoria's interests and difficulties is its desire to continue apartheid—white predominance even as petty racial discrimination is curtailed—and its campaign to deny the ANC access to neighboring countries. Since its internal difficulties are viewed as the result of foreign interference, maintaining a buffer zone around its borders reduces outside access to the country and protects Pretoria from the ANC military capabilities. Furthermore, South Africa can rationalize that it is contributing to its own internal stability by striking at ANC camps in neighboring countries. The target of the SADF is often suspected ANC offices or sympathizers in the adjacent states of Botswana, Zimbabwe, Swaziland, Mozambique, or Lesotho, and not the organization's headquarters in Lusaka or camps in Angola or Tanzania. Although this may seem a less than efficient means of dealing with the insurgents, Pretoria appears to recognize that it cannot eliminate the ANC through military means, but, by using its coercive ability against weaker states, it can prompt those governments to reduce the ability of the ANC to operate throughout Southern Africa. Insurgents isolated in camps in Tanzania are little threat to white rule in South Africa, but if those same opponents could establish camps along Pretoria's northern border, their military campaign might take on additional importance.

A series of early-morning raids by the SADF against targets in Botswana, Zambia, and Zimbabwe in May 1986 are typical of the actions the world decries.[14] The blatant use of force over the past decade has been intended to intimidate the weaker states in the area and to silence South African citizens who have fled into exile. While few observers would deny that the armed opposition to Pretoria uses facilities in Southern African states to launch military attacks against South Africa, when the SADF strikes out against its armed opponents many of the victims are innocent bystanders.

Pretoria views the collateral damage caused in neighboring countries and the deaths of citizens of those states as a result of the unwillingness of their governments to take the necessary steps to control South African insurgent groups. If neighboring states sign agreements (such as the 1984 Nkomati Accord with Mozambique) preventing the ANC from using their territory to launch attacks against the republic, cross-border raids by the SADF, it is argued, would not be necessary. Furthermore, Pretoria points out that the insurgents themselves are responsible for placing their facilities in residential and business districts, which results in the deaths of noncombatants and encourages international condemnation of Pretoria for acting in what it sees as self-defense.

Southern African states have all denounced apartheid, but each state has attempted to deal with the regional hegemon in its own way. The approach favored by Pretoria is modeled on the agreements signed with Mozambique and Swaziland. Other regional governments have managed to avoid such agreements, but nonetheless they must make their own peace with Pretoria and deal with the insurgents at the same time. The difficulties in trying to reconcile two such opposite policies are obvious.

MOZAMBIQUE AND THE ANC

Portuguese colonialism in Mozambique and Angola ended in 1975, but South Africa adopted different policies for each country. In Angola, Pretoria became involved in the civil war and, along with other African and Western countries, supported Jonas Savimbi's UNITA forces, as well as Holden Roberto's National Front for the Liberation of Angola (FNLA). In its dealings with Maputo, however, Pretoria continued to maintain good economic relations, even paying the Mozambican government in gold for migrant laborers who worked in South African mines. The exchange rate was artificially set, so that Maputo realized a substantial profit when it transferred the workers' earnings to the local currency.[15]

Pretoria, however, was unable to buy Maputo's allegiance. The late Samora Machel closed his borders with white-ruled Rhodesia, welcomed Robert Mugabe's insurgents to Mozambique, and developed close ties to the ANC.[16] ANC military cadres were using Mozambique to infiltrate into

Swaziland and then into South Africa. This infiltration route was closed, at least temporarily, with the signing of the Nkomati Accord.

The Nkomati Accord, signed in 1984 and named after the river on whose banks it was signed, called on both Maputo and Pretoria to end any support they may have been providing to insurgent groups operating against the other. For Mozambique this meant ceasing support for the ANC, and South Africa had to cease giving aid to RENAMO, an anti-FRELIMO guerrilla organization.

RENAMO was formed in the late 1970s with the assistance of the white minority government of Rhodesia.[17] When black majority rule was achieved in Rhodesia and the country became Zimbabwe, the Mozambican insurgents found new supporters south of the Limpopo River. Contrary to many expectations at the time, RENAMO did not evaporate following the severing of its relations with Rhodesia but instead flourished in the early 1980s. This occurred despite several military victories by Maputo forces in uncovering and occupying guerrilla bases in central Mozambique. The depressed economy (attenuated by regional drought), the flight of Portuguese technical expertise after independence in 1975, and mismanagement by the FRELIMO government, provided a medium for the growth of the opposition movement.[18] At the same time, Pretoria apparently decided to broaden its support to the insurgents, providing military training and equipment. This significantly destabilized the economy and put pressure on Maputo to end its backing of the ANC. The goal was achieved with the Nkomati Accord, as Maputo did halt ANC operations against South Africa from Mozambican territory. Before the accord was signed, Maputo had served as a convenient way station for ANC guerrillas on their way from the camps in Angola to South Africa.[19]

For a while the accord seemed to benefit both countries, as once again observers believed RENAMO would dissipate without South African assistance. Other African states, and supposedly the Soviet Union, were opposed to the accord, seeing it as a defeat for the liberation movement in South Africa. Mozambican President Machel, however, saw the accord as an expedient means of ending the internal insurgency situation in his own country. In much the same way that Lenin had defended "Socialism in One Country"—the Soviet Union after World War I—at the expense of supporting revolution in other European countries, Machel appears to have seen the need to prevent Mozambique from coming under the control of RENAMO as more critical for Maputo in 1984 than giving limited assistance to the ANC's military campaign. The ANC had little chance of overthrowing white rule in South Africa in the short term, while RENAMO was a real and present threat to the FRELIMO government.

In retrospect, it is now possible to argue that with that agreement Pretoria received the better of the deal. RENAMO is now an even greater threat to the FRELIMO government than it was in 1984, while ANC attacks originating from Maputo appear to have been greatly reduced.[20] Although neither Mozambique nor South Africa seems to support the accord fully, neither is willing to end the agreement entirely.[21]

In South Africa, the unrest that has racked the country since September 1984 is unrelated to efforts by the ANC to incite a rebellion against white rule. It is unclear if that situation might have been different had the ANC had more direct access to the population centers of South Africa during this crucial period. At the same time, the ANC's continuing need for foreign bases of operation and its small number of trained military personnel suggest that, among South Africa's majority population, support for a military solution to the country's internal problems is not as widespread nor as deep as many observers might believe.[22]

There is little doubt, however, that Pretoria views the Nkomati Accord as a foreign policy success. Pressure continues to be brought on other states, especially Botswana, to sign a similar agreement, but with no success. The only other such treaty is a nonaggression pact signed with Swaziland in 1982.[23] Pushing the ANC away from its frontiers remains one of Pretoria's prime objectives. As the ANC found itself without a base of operations in the eastern areas of Southern Africa, pressure mounted on Botswana and Lesotho to cooperate with the SADF.[24] Both states managed to avoid making such commitments, but the result has been to subject them to economic and military retaliation. Pretoria wants these independent countries to help control ANC activities, and it has stepped up efforts to halt insurgent infiltrators before they can reach South Africa.

LESOTHO: INDEPENDENT NUGGET

On December 9, 1982, South African security forces struck at suspected ANC facilities in Maseru, Lesotho, killing about forty South African refugees, including an unknown number of ANC members. Pretoria claimed that its target was the headquarters for ANC "terrorism" in the Orange Free State, the Transkei, and Ciskei. The government of Prime Minister Leabua Jonathan and the Security Council of the United Nations condemned Pretoria's actions, but neither was able to alter Lesotho's relationship with South Africa. In 1983 Pretoria flexed its economic muscle and instituted a customs slowdown at the border-crossing points with Lesotho to demonstrate its displeasure with Jonathan's relations with antiapartheid groups.

Lesotho is totally dependent on South Africa for its imports and for employing hundreds of thousands of its citizens, as well as for providing a majority of the government's revenues through the South African Customs Union. Prime Minister Leabua Jonathan had been on good terms with Pretoria when he came to power in 1966 but increasingly came to espouse more radical causes; he allowed the Soviet Union, China, and North Korea to open embassies in Maseru and welcomed South African refugees associated with the ANC into Lesotho.[25] In late 1985, the border-crossing points with South Africa were effectively closed. Customs officials instituted delays that caused many trucks to turn around to prevent their cargos from spoiling. As the action continued, the military lost patience with Jonathan's handling of the situation and on January 20, 1986, removed his government from power in a coup d'état. The border controls were lifted immediately. This was followed by the deportation of hundreds of South African refugees, not to South Africa but to Mozambique and Tanzania.

Although there is no evidence of South African direction of the coup, the border restrictions were seen as instrumental in the military's decision to oust Jonathan. The military was said to be concerned with the increasing power and radicalization of the youth wing of Jonathan's ruling Basotho National Party, which was reportedly being trained by North Korean advisers. Then, when Jonathan publicly threatened to seek aid from the Soviet Union to circumvent the South African border restrictions, the military decided to act.[26] Whether or not Pretoria actually participated in the demise of the Jonathan regime, his departure served South African interests and deprived the ANC of an infiltration route.

Maseru's new, more stringent policies toward suspected ANC presence in Lesotho were rewarded in September 1986, when an agreement was signed for the Lesotho Highlands Water Project. Although the water will be used in South Africa, doubling the resources of the Vaal River, the construction of six major dams and 112 kilometers of tunnels will provide over 3,000 jobs in Lesotho.[27]

BOTSWANA: NEXT DOOR TO THE LION

Although Botswana is approximately 10 percent larger than France, its small population and lightly armed defense force make it extremely difficult for the government even to hope to control its own borders against incursions by the military forces of its stronger neighbors, or by refugees and insurgents as they transit the region. To deal with these conditions, the Batswana have tried to maintain a careful balance between their internal needs and the regional powers. On the one hand, Botswana is a member of the South African Customs Union and derives a major portion of its budget from trade with or through South Africa.[28] In addition, South African firms are active in Botswana, most notably the De Beers involvement with diamond mining at Orapa. The Botswanan government adopted a policy of noninterference in the internal affairs of its neighbors, and condemned the use of force in settling disputes.[29] On the other hand, Botswana is one of the Front Line States, a member of SADCC (and home of that organization's secretariat), and has not established official diplomatic relations with Pretoria.

The proximity of Botswana to areas of potential conflict has made it a safe haven for refugees for hundreds of years, and in the last two decades the fighting in Rhodesia, and now South Africa, has brought people fleeing their problems into Botswana. Thousands of Zimbabweans fled to Botswana from Rhodesia during that country's independence struggle, placing a great strain on Gaborone's ability to provide for their welfare and safety. The Botswana government, seeking to manage this influx by offering assistance, erected a refugee camp at Dukwe in eastern Botswana but did not permit the nation to be used as a staging site for attacks against Rhodesia. Today, most of the residents at Dukwe are South African, and Gaborone exercises the same controls over their actions that it exercised over the Zimbabweans. Nevertheless, the refugees are a target for SADF raids.

Cross-border raids by Pretoria's security forces serve to heighten the sense of vulnerability in Gaborone,[30] but they are not the only tool used against Botswana. In November 1987, following statements by a member of the ANC that the organization was planning to increase its military activity inside South Africa, Pretoria accused Gaborone of assisting the ANC in infiltrating insurgents into South Africa. The charges were rejected by the government of Botswana as slanderous.[31] Subsequently, South African police began extensive searches of cars and trucks waiting to cross the border between Botswana and South Africa, apparently trying to uncover ANC infiltrators.[32] Pretoria did not report finding any insurgents during these searches, and no major military activity occurred in South Africa before the end of 1987. In 1988, ANC and PAC infiltration increased significantly.

Although there is no evidence that the government of Botswana actively assists the ANC, it does appear that Botswana is a major route used by the insurgents for infiltration into South Africa, and for exfiltration as well.[33] For the Batswana, this situation is likely to continue. As a multiracial democracy, the country offers sanctuary to the refugees, but at the same time the rebel groups want to use Botswana in their own struggle to change the internal situation in South Africa. The government in Gaborone has refused military support to insurgent groups, though not because it supports apartheid or does not approve of the aims of the ANC. Rather, it wished to dissuade first Rhodesia and then South Africa from using their extensive military force in Botswana. The evidence continues to mount, however, that neither insurgents nor their governments respect Gaborone's desires to remain apart from the military conflict in Southern Africa.[34]

ZIMBABWE: MODEL FOR SOUTH AFRICA?

Relations between Harare and Pretoria are both similar and dissimilar to those between other regional states and the last white-ruled government in Southern Africa. Like its economically weaker neighbors, Zimbabwe is highly dependent on South African transportation links to provide access to foreign markets. In 1984, 74 percent of Harare's exports transited South Africa.[35] This was not always the case.

Before 1976, most Rhodesian trade was sent the shorter and less expensive route to the Indian Ocean through Mozambique and the ports of Beira and Lourenço Marques—now Maputo. After FRELIMO came to power, however, the border with Rhodesia was closed. This resulted in a shift of Rhodesian traffic to South African rails and ports. In the former Portuguese colony the lack of use and regular maintenance led to the deterioration of the transportation network, and in Beira the harbor filled with silt because of an absence of dredging.[36] These reversals, coupled with the antiregime attacks by RENAMO on the transportation network, continue to tie the new majority government in Harare tightly to Pretoria. The Mugabe government would like to decrease its dependence on the South African transportation system, but the lack of secure alternatives has made this difficult. In addition, Pretoria supplies the Zimbabwe Railroad with needed rolling stock and, in early 1987, sold Harare 34,000 tons of fuel when the Beira oil pipeline was damaged by sabotage.[37]

The links between the two states are not one-sided. While 16 percent of Zimbabwe's exports are sold to South Africa, 19 percent of its imports come from that republic.[38] If these ties were cut, Zimbabwean industry would be forced to pay higher prices for European goods and face problems importing these items if available, and South Africa would lose an important customer. Pretoria is also one of the largest investors in Zimbabwe.[39] Tourism is extensive, with South African Airways being one of the most important users of Harare Airport.

Unlike many of the other regional states, Zimbabwe does possess an efficient army, which could pose a limited deterrent to South African incursions. While the defense forces of Botswana and Lesotho, on the other hand, might wish to oppose such aggression, their limited manpower and light arms prevent a meaningful defense. Even the Zimbabwe National Army (ZNA) is not capable of preventing cross-border operations, as was evidenced by the events of May 1986, when South African forces raided suspected ANC offices and facilities in Harare without opposition from the ZNA.[40]

This mixture of dependency and self-reliance places Harare in a difficult position. As one of the newly independent states of Southern Africa, it has been described as a potential model for South Africa under majority rule; and indeed when Mugabe came to power there was rejoicing in the black townships of its southern neighbor. With a strong military and an outspoken president, the country was seen as the natural sanctuary that the ANC needed to wage a guerrilla war against Pretoria.[41]

This has not yet come to pass, even though the occasional land mine incident near Beitbridge suggests that insurgents do operate through

Zimbabwe to reach South Africa. In July 1986, then–Prime Minister Mugabe called for an Organization of African Unity military force to protect the Front Line States[42] from the SADF and to overthrow the Pretoria government. This indicates that he does not see Zimbabwe as capable of taking on South Africa by itself.[43] The reasons for Mugabe's reluctance are manifold: the military disparity between the two states, their strong economic ties, and the damage Zimbabwe would suffer if Pretoria took action to cut off the country from its ports are sufficient in themselves to prompt caution. There may also be an ideological difference between Mugabe, the ruling Zimbabwe African National Union (ZANU), and the major South African insurgent group, the ANC.

During its independence struggle ZANU competed with the Zimbabwe African People's Union (ZAPU) for the leadership of the black majority. Before independence ZAPU was backed by the Soviet Union, and ZANU was aided by China.[44] This mirrored the split between the ANC and the PAC and their backers. In the end, the ZANU party, with its backing among the largest ethnic groups in the country, was able to come to power. But it did not forget those who had supported its rival. ZANU established closer ties with the PAC than with the ANC, and the unwillingness of the Mugabe government to embrace the ANC's military struggle may have its roots in its preindependence relations with the two insurgent groups and in Mugabe's distrust of the Soviet Union. If the PAC were a more capable insurgent group and posed a real threat to Pretoria, it might be able to call on Zimbabwe for assistance, but those same ties do not appear to exist between the ANC and Mugabe. This might change as the PAC and ANC come to grips with their own differences, or as the PAC fails to evidence any real military capability. In 1987, however, Zimbabwe did not seem to be an active supporter of military action against South Africa.

It is also possible that the major rationale for Harare's lack of support for the ANC or PAC is its own economic interests. If the transportation links through Mozambique can be rehabilitated—an unlikely occurrence until the current civil war is brought to an end—Harare may feel that it can provide more assistance to the liberation struggle in South Africa. Even if that occurs, the SADF remains capable of striking at guerrilla facilities anywhere in Zimbabwe, making such a move by Mugabe potentially very costly.

CONCLUSIONS

Rhetoric, of course, is cheap while action is not. States more distant from South Africa, with fewer economic ties to Pretoria and greater security from military reprisals, are more willing to combine words with deeds. Even for these countries, however, there are limits to what can be accomplished. Insurgent bases in Angola and refugee camps in Tanzania are out of easy reach of the SADF. Close relations between the government in Luanda and the Soviet Union facilitate providing military assistance to the ANC, assistance that Zimbabwe or Botswana must refuse to give to the insurgents.

However, this same remoteness, which offers some measure of security from attack, also causes a major problem for the insurgents: how to get back to South Africa? If the countries being crossed simply permit or facilitate such activity, they are subject to military retaliation from Pretoria. If they try to control the insurgents, they are seen as supportive of Pretoria. In addition, the need to travel these long distances makes it more expensive for the ANC to finance its operations and more difficult to ensure security. Strangers passing through remote villages easily arouse suspicions, not just of insurgents but of drug traffickers and poachers.

Relations among the states in Southern Africa, a struggle between a number of weak states and the regional hegemon, are overshadowed by apartheid. Social and political justice in South Africa would largely eliminate the need for the ANC's military struggle and Pretoria's projection of coercive power beyond its borders. Short of this end, however, the present situation is likely to continue for the indefinite future. Whether they like it or not, the states near South Africa are not permitted simply to pass and let the belligerent parties settle their differences themselves. The sovereignty of these states is not respected by any of the antagonists. National leaders committed to ending apartheid must recognize that the achievement of that goal may come at the expense of economic and social development within their own territories.

One possible solution is international backing for regional transportation and economic development schemes, such as has happened through SADCC. This effort is of questionable value, however, and will remain subject to military action by Pretoria or its allies if it is seen that this independence permits the regional players to increase their support to the ANC or other antiapartheid military groups.

A state that denies sovereign rights to another state, for whatever reason, cannot expect that same state to then accord it such rights. This is not to argue that the situation in South Africa should be accepted by the international community. Rather, it suggests that the to-ing and fro-ing over sovereignty and which side is at fault is not really the issue. The black-ruled states in Southern Africa have clearly stated their opposition to apartheid and have rejected Pretoria's insistence that they deal with the white minority government and not interfere in South Africa's internal situation. At the same time, it would be foolish to expect any government to respect the sovereignty of another when it believes its survival is in danger. The question is how to bring racial harmony to South Africa. When that problem is addressed, the other issues will fall by the wayside, and the states of the region can concentrate on the justice or injustice of their almost certain economic domination by Pretoria under a majority government.

It remains to be seen if any program for change in South Africa can avoid a bloody and debilitating civil conflict, but the current struggle between the SADF and the insurgents trying to move from camps in Angola through the territory of reluctant allies and into South Africa apparently, at this point, has little relevance to forcefully bringing about change in that republic.

The ANC, in the short term, does not expect to overthrow the regime in Pretoria with military force. Indeed, Joe Modise, in an interview in the *New York Times* of January 13, 1987, said: "We do not foresee a situation now where we can mount military action that will defeat the enemy. Obviously the enemy is strong. In terms of weapons they have the most sophisticated weapons."[45] Why then, we must ask, is the ANC waging this campaign? According to Modise, it is to take the war to the white South Africans; however, that has not happened. Despite an increase in "terrorist" attacks in South Africa, the victims are often black. When a hand grenade is thrown in a black township, it is most likely to injure a resident of that township. When bombs go off in city centers, it is again blacks who are likely to be involved, though the use in 1988 of limpet bombs in predominantly white restaurants and sports facilities may change this picture. How then is this taking the war to the white community? Through publicity, both the ANC and the National Party seek to broaden their basis for support by claiming to operate militarily, when the actions that occur are of little significance to anyone other than the few individuals involved and the occasional innocent bystander.

For Pretoria, a highly visible raid on an ANC propaganda office in Gaborone is not going to end the insurgent threat. It will, however, signal the white electorate that the government is doing what is necessary to wipe out the external threat. To be convincing, the white audience must believe that the raid was connected to numerous terrorist attacks and that Moscow and the neighboring states were involved as well. That the problem continues is simply evidence of the need for greater vigilance and even more cross-border raids. For the black audience, such raids are a signal that they cannot expect assistance to come from outside South Africa's borders.

To justify the buildup of arms and the frequent call-ups to military service, the SADF must be shown to be providing a service to the community. In reality the problems are internal, but Pretoria has shown little interest in addressing those issues in a meaningful manner. It is simply more readily accepted by the white electorate that shooting the opposition is the solution. Many in South Africa would argue that the cost to the whites in political and economic power would be greater if they tried to share the country's wealth than if they emphasize keeping what they already have. The use of force allows them to follow such a narrow path, seemingly oblivious to the continuing danger their country faces internally as the roots of the actual problem are ignored.

From the ruling National Party's perspective, however, their choices are rational and understandable.[46] Observers removed from the scene may disagree with Pretoria's values, but since those values are well known, it should come as no surprise that change does not occur easily or readily in South Africa. As long as there are foreign-based insurgents, Pretoria will accuse them or their supporters of creating the problems that over 400 years of history have generated.

That said, it is also important to look at the role of the insurgents. If they recognize the futility of their struggle, why does it continue as it does? That is, why is so much effort placed on the military struggle, when that is not the way to power in Pretoria? Unfortunately, the same line of reasoning applies to the insurgents as to the government. As the ANC claims to wage an armed struggle, the passions of the youth of South Africa can be brought to side with the insurgents and not with those who renounce violence in their efforts to overcome apartheid. Young blacks in the various townships are understandably impatient. They seek a quick end to a system that has oppressed them and their countrymen since birth. Held out in front of them is the use of guns and bombs, the examples of Soviet backing for the anticolonial struggles in Angola and Mozambique, and the successful bid for independence by Zimbabwe's majority. This, they believe, is the path for South Africa. Unfortunately, the analogies are weak, though the emotions may be strong. The end of Portuguese colonialism in Angola and Mozambique came as a result of war-weariness in Lisbon over a foreign entanglement. It was not by the force of insurgent arms alone that those countries won their freedom. The small minority of whites, most with British passports and little history in Rhodesia, should not be confused with a larger, better-armed white minority with strong emotional ties to South Africa and few options for retreat. White South Africans are protecting *their country*, which they feel—albeit with great selectivity of facts—they have built through *their own efforts*. The extremes to which they are willing to go to protect what they believe they have built do not allow for easy comparisons with other African experiences.

It might be interesting to compare the situation of the French settlers in Algeria with that of the whites of South Africa. It was not a military defeat, but rather the political will of the French government in Paris that brought independence to Algeria. The comparison is important for two reasons: (1) it is possible to defeat an insurgency if you are willing to take whatever steps are needed and use whatever means are called for to accomplish that task; and (2) political will is as important as military might, if not more so. There is no reason to believe that the white population of South Africa is lacking in either of these areas. Barring a dramatic, unforeseen event, military struggle will take years to wear down the white minority government, though it could contribute to the deterioration of white resolve. Even the latter is unlikely to occur in the short term, and it would seem more efficient to seek majority rule through peaceful means. Additionally, the development of black political and economic power through vehicles such as the unions is more likely to bring about success than are the military efforts of the ANC, even though this is largely dependent on the cooperation of the white leadership.

The ANC leaders seem unwilling to end their military struggle, because they, like the government, see the need for arms to attract support and are fearful that without the gun they will not come to power. Furthermore, there is the probability that a split will arise between exile members of the ANC and those who remain in South Africa. If power is achieved through the barrel of a gun, the exiled elements will be situated to take over the government. If, on the other hand, internal reform can be made to work, and political power is gained through the combined efforts of internal groups such as unions, the United Democratic Front, and organizations such as the Zulu cultural group Inkatha, where does that leave the exiles? Can they legitimately claim to represent the people when the people have selected their own government? Although it is likely that the majority of South Africans support the ANC, it should not be assumed that support would represent victory in open elections when the issue will no longer be apartheid.

It is inevitable that South Africa will achieve majority rule. But while the military campaign of the ANC addresses black aspiration, it also increases white fears and resistance to majority rule. At the same time, there is little reason to believe that a guerrilla campaign will be effective in ending apartheid. The killings continue, the play goes on, but victory remains an elusive goal.

Where, then, does this leave South Africa's neighbors? A new element has been added in the Southern African equation. For the first time, the black-ruled states of the region, especially Zambia and Zimbabwe, have threatened to take unilateral action to cut their ties with Pretoria. They have discussed denying landing rights to South African Airways and ending all economic and trade ties.[47] This has so far failed to materialize, but, however improbable, if it should come to pass it will turn the tables on South African deterrence and could introduce compellance.

Compellance, as used by Schelling, is described as taking a step that, though it causes harm to both the initiator of the action and the recipient, forces the second party to take steps to end the discomfort.[48] In this case, Zimbabwe would suffer potentially great economic loss by cutting ties to South Africa, but so would Pretoria. To reestablish those ties, Pretoria would have to take steps to eliminate or greatly modify apartheid, rather than simply use military force to retaliate against Zimbabwe. It is possible that striking back would be the reaction, but Harare (in this scenario) would have already accepted the economic dislocation it imposed on itself. It would face a loss of respect among other African nations if it reopened ties to Pretoria without some evidence of change on the part of South Africa.

It is unlikely, however, that South Africa's neighbors can take such steps on their own. If other countries can be persuaded to increase their economic assistance to Southern African states to alleviate the losses suffered from cutting ties to Pretoria, some states may be encouraged to step forward; however, this has yet to occur. For the countries of Southern Africa the issue of apartheid is not something new. It is part of their past and influences their relations with the rest of the world. They do not support apartheid, but neither can they ignore it. They will continue to walk a fine line, trying to assist antiapartheid movements but not forgetting the welfare of their own citizens.

NOTES

The opinions expressed in this paper are those of the author and do not necessarily reflect those of the Department of Defense or the United States government.

1. According to the Southern African Development Coordination Conference, Pretoria's military and other aggressive actions have cost the nations of the region $10 billion between 1980 and 1984. Joseph Hanlon, *Beggar Your Neighbours: Apartheid Power in Southern Africa* (Bloomington: Indiana University Press, 1986), p. 1.

2. See Colin Legum, "Southern Africa in South Africa: The Impact of Regional Events on Domestic Politics," in Thomas M. Callaghy, ed., *South Africa in Southern Africa: The Intensifying Vortex of Violence* (New York: Praeger, 1983), pp. 153–161.

3. Gregory Blainey, *The Causes of War* (New York: The Free Press, 1973), p. 245.

4. Hanlon makes this argument in *Beggar Your Neighbours*, pp. 7–8.

5. John E. Spence, "South Africa's Policies and Military Operations in Southern Africa," (unpublished paper, 1986), p. 9.

6. John E. Spanier and Eric M. Usianer, *How American Foreign Policy Is Made* (New York: Praeger, 1976), pp. 25–26.

7. Robert I. Rotberg et al., *South Africa and Its Neighbors* (Lexington, Mass.: Lexington Books, 1985), p. 7.

8. Legum, "Southern Africa in South Africa," pp. 156–157.

9. Rotberg's *South Africa and Its Neighbors* provides numerous instances of these linkages.

10. Kent H. Butts and Paul R. Thomas, *The Geopolitics of Southern Africa* (Boulder, Colo.: Westview Press, 1986), p. 26.

11. John de St. Jorre, "South Africa Embattled," *Foreign Affairs* 65, no. 3 (1987), p. 554.

12. The Namibia agreement of spring 1989 calls for their removal. The ANC also maintains educational facilities in Tanzania. See S. M. Davis,

Apartheid's Rebels: Inside South Africa's Hidden War (New Haven: Yale University Press, 1987), pp. 61–65.

13. *Ibid.*, pp. 66–72.

14. Washington called its ambassador home from Pretoria to demonstrate its opposition to the widening conflict in Southern Africa, and most European states withdrew some diplomatic personnel from Pretoria.

15. Hanlon, *Beggar Your Neighbours*, p. 134.

16. Davis, *Apartheid's Rebels*, pp. 128–129.

17. The Rhodesian Security Forces organized various Mozambican dissidents—including blacks who had fought for the Protuguese and even former members of FRELIMO—into a fifth column to attack Zimbabwean insurgents in Mozambique and to provide a cover for Rhodesian activity in Mozambique. Hanlon, *Beggar Your Neighbours*, pp. 139–140.

18. It is undeniable that RENAMO attacks on economic and development targets worsened the country's plight, but much of the damage was self-inflicted. See Gavin G. Maasdorp, "Squaring Up to Economic Dominance: Regional Patterns," in Rotberg, *South Africa and Its Neighbors*, pp. 100–101; see also Butts and Thomas, *Geopolitics*, pp. 82–86.

19. Butts and Thomas, *Geopolitics*, pp. 82–86.

20. Davis, *Apartheid's Rebels*, p. 129, attributes increased ANC activity in Natal after 1985 to a gradual resumption of infiltration from Mozambique, especially as Maputo blames Pretoria for assisting RENAMO.

21. De St. Jorre, "South Africa Embattled," p. 554.

22. See Davis' discussion of the ANC's reaction to the unrest in South Africa, *Apartheid's Rebels*, pp. 131–135. He argues that the exiled organization was not prepared to exploit the situation and faced severe problems trying to establish an internal military organization.

23. Umtata Radio, April 1, 1984.

24. Hanlon, *Beggar Your Neighbours*, pp. 224–225, 228, notes claims that South Africa provided funding for internal opposition in Botswana in exchange for support of a nonagression pact.

25. *Ibid.*, pp. 112–113. Hanlon notes that Pretoria's concern with the flow of refugees began during the 1970s. While the number of individuals fleeing South Africa through Lesotho would fluctuate with the domestic situation, it was the potential for supporting the ANC that South African officials found objectionable.

26. *New York Times*, January 21, 1986, p. A3.

27. South African Press Agency, October 1, 1986.

28. *New York Times*, March 6, 1987, p. A6.

29. J. Parson, *Botswana: Liberal Democracy and the Labor Reserve in Southern Africa* (Boulder, Colo.: Westview Press, 1984), pp. 106–111.

30. Hanlon, *Beggar Your Neighbours*, pp. 221–224.

31. Gaborone Domestic Radio Service, November 27, 1987.

32. South African Press Association, Johannesburg, December 2, 1987.

33. See Davis, *Apartheid's Rebels*, pp. 125–126.

34. During the first seven months of 1986, forty aliens with weapons and

ammunition were arrested in Botswana. Gaborone Domestic Radio Service, August 8, 1986.

35. *New York Times*, July 6, 1986, Sec. 4, p. 3.

36. Butts and Thomas, *Geopolitics*, pp. 20–21, discuss the decline of both Beira and Maputo ports and the country's transportaion network in general.

37. South African Press Agency, January 19, 1987.

38. *New York Times*, July 6, 1986, Sec. 4, p. 3.

39. Larry Bowman, et al., in Callaghy, *South Africa in Southern Africa*, p. 340.

40. *Ibid.*, pp. 344–345.

41. *Ibid.*, p. 336.

42. Angola, Botswana, Mozambique, Tanzania, Zambia, and Zimbabwe.

43. Reuters News Service, Harare, June 15, 1986.

44. Robert Legvold, "The Soviet Threat to Southern Africa," in Rotberg, *South Africa and Its Neighbors*, p. 35.

45. Commander of the ANC's military wing, UmKhonto we Sizwe.

46. The most common demand is for majority rule, but that is viewed as political suicide. It is unreasonable, therefore, to expect whites to accept total surrender. Rotberg puts forth a similar proposition for why the Luanda government refuses to negotiate with UNITA. Rotberg, *South Africa and Its Neighbors*, pp. 6–8.

47. *New York Times*, March 6, 1986, p. A6.

48. Thomas C. Schelling, *The Strategy of Conflict* (London: Oxford University Press, 1973), pp. 195–199.

Beyond Constructive Engagement: U.S. Foreign Policy Toward Southern Africa into the 1990s

LOUIS A. PICARD & ROBERT GROELSMA

"Occasionally," during reviews of U.S. foreign policy in the Nixon presidency, according to Robert Jackson, "in National Security Council meetings, Africa was . . . treated as a comedy." For example, Alexander Haig, then serving as staff assistant to Kissinger, "would pound his fists on the table 'jungle drumbeat style' whenever the NSC would undertake discussions of African affairs."[1] According to R. W. Johnson, "Kissinger's attitude to independent Africa reinforced Nixon's predispositions: it was poor, dependent, laughably irresponsible, and violent, and in general not worthy of much consideration."[2] Perhaps at least in part as a consequence of these attitudes, U.S. policy in Southern Africa was caught up short after the 1974 military coup in Portugal.

This chapter examines the evolution of U.S. foreign policy toward Southern Africa after World War II, places the Reagan administration's policy of "constructive engagement" in historical perspective, and speculates on the nature of U.S. foreign policy toward Southern Africa during the post-Reagan years.

South Africa as a U.S. *domestic* politics issue can be dated to the November 1984 demonstrations in front of the South African embassy in Washington. U.S. *foreign* policy toward Southern Africa has had two main tendencies since 1945. First, prior to 1974, the United States had little direct and consistent involvement with the region. After 1974, U.S. interest in the region was overshadowed by events in other parts of the world. Occasional action, such as involvement in the Congo during the 1960s, was characterized by the search for the quick fix. Otherwise, the United States either deferred to NATO allies or came to the conclusion that the region offered few strategic or political interests. Second, especially after 1974, the United States has seen developments within Southern Africa through the lens of East–West confrontation. With occasional exceptions, policymakers did not place primary emphasis on national and regional politics.

This evolution of U.S. foreign policy has taken place against the backdrop of changing racial perceptions in the United States and around the world. Policymakers can certainly be influenced by cultural or racial stereotyping.[3] It is an intriguing question whether U.S. leaders have allowed such stereotyping to affect them in the past or in the present—in particular, whether U.S. officials relied on colonial empires or on the South African government because they were white, while conversely downplaying the importance of various opposition movements because they were black.[4]

A LEGACY OF NEGLECT

U.S. foreign policy toward Africa generally, and Southern Africa more specifically, has been characterized variously as "benign neglect," "minimal engagement," and "weak and nonreactive."[5] Both before and after decolonization, the United States assumed that Africa was primarily the responsibility of the former colonial powers. In the words of an assistant secretary of state for African affairs in 1959: "We support African political aspirations when they are moderate, nonviolent and constructive and take into account their obligations to and interdependence with the world community. We also support the principle of continued African ties with Western Europe."[6]

South Africa itself continued to be seen as an informal extension of NATO. Washington saw South Africa largely as South African elites saw themselves. Nagorski commented: "South Africa's ruling classes saw themselves, and were largely seen by others until the 1950s, as a snug Western enclave at the tip of Africa. Faithfully Christian, they staunchly opposed communism and governed themselves according to a Westminster model of parliamentary democracy."[7] Both Truman and Eisenhower maintained good relationships with all of the minority governments of Southern Africa. Department of State spokespersons periodically expressed U.S. abhorrence of racism, apartheid, and colonialism. The U.S. occasionally voted for mild UN resolutions condemning apartheid. South Africa's racial laws, however, were seen largely as a matter of domestic jurisdiction.

After 1961, President Kennedy projected a new foreign policy image by beginning a two-track policy toward Africa that included action as well as rhetoric. Kennedy and his advisers (particularly Chester Bowles, G. Mennen Williams, and Adlai Stevenson) made a conscious effort to identify with African aspirations and maintained a dialogue with most African leaders—including some perceived as "radical." Kennedy met with a number of African leaders (usually shortly after a country's independence), and Mennen Williams, Kennedy's assistant secretary of state for African affairs, traveled widely throughout the continent.

Kennedy's rhetorical efforts were largely successful. The effort cost little politically, and as a result "the Kennedy administration was generally regarded as representing the most pro-African presidency and period."[8] Despite the lack of substance to the Kennedy policy, there can be little doubt of its success. Within Africa, Kennedy's public image of concern influenced a whole generation of African school children and secondary school students. Until the exploits of Muhammad Ali, Kennedy was the most widely known U.S. citizen in Africa. Long past his death, portraits of the late president, Kennedy clubs, sweatshirts, and even Kennedy bars could be found in the remotest rural villages.

Kennedy's rhetoric may have had some effect on colonial policymakers as well. According to one former colonial governor, the president's rhetoric was almost as important as Macmillan's "Winds of Change" speech in determining the fate of Britain's colonial dependencies. He says, "We sensed that there was a changing environment after Macmillan's speech in Cape Town. Then Soapy Williams came floating in talking all about 'Africa for the Africans.' All of this was bound to affect our decisions."[9] One European view in the early 1960s was that the United States was fomenting colonial revolts in order to replace European predominance in the region.[10]

The minority-ruled states in Southern Africa were largely excluded from the rhetoric about majority rule, though lip service was given to criticism of South Africa's racial policies. The United States did support a UN arms embargo against the republic and voted in favor of a number of UN antiapartheid resolutions.

But Washington did little to discourage investments in Rhodesia or South Africa. Both policymakers and academics continued to view South Africa as separate from sub-Saharan Africa and as a part of the European community. Rupert Emerson spoke for many of that period when he argued that "the Republic of South Africa . . . despite its strong African majority . . . is for present purposes a predominantly European country."[11]

It was in action rather than rhetoric, of course, that Kennedy had the greatest impact upon U.S. foreign policy. The rhetoric suggested African political developments stemmed primarily from regional and national events. U.S. action in the Congo crisis, however, began a pattern of perceiving crucial African conflicts primarily in terms of East–West confrontation. This action was replicated later in a number of other African and Third World crises. Jackson labels this "the Congo syndrome," a "practice by which the United States intervenes in an African nation, especially in its moment of internal crisis, to support a moderate or pro-Western elite struggling for power against local opponents, who may be socialists and recipients of Soviet bloc assistance."[12] While direct and overt U.S. intervention in Africa remained rare in the 1960s, the pattern of U.S. involvement in the Congo (later Zaire) was an important model for much U.S. activity in the Third World for the next twenty years.

President Lyndon Johnson continued Kennedy's policy of publicly criticizing South Africa, placing it within the context of his commitment to civil rights in the United States. But U.S. investment in Southern Africa, particularly in South Africa, continued to increase throughout the decade. Major loans and credit arrangements were encouraged by Department of Commerce officials.

When Ian Smith declared unilateral independence in Rhodesia in 1965, the United States, following the British position, saw the issue as a British problem that did not affect U.S. foreign policy interests. The Johnson administration saw Portuguese policy in its Southern African territories within the context of the Salazar regime's strategic importance to NATO. Only on the issue of South-West Africa (Namibia) did the United States take a pro-majority rule position, arguing that Pretoria had no right to occupy the territory in defiance of UN resolutions. In 1966, the United States called for the United Nations to supervise self-determination for the territory.

Johnson and his aides placed less emphasis on Africa because of mounting U.S. involvement in crises in Latin America, the Middle East, and particularly Vietnam. Johnson policymakers did show a marked tendency to favor more "moderate" political leadership among African leaders and remained conscious of the global dimensions of East–West conflict.[13] But, "South Africa as a concern of American foreign policy was at a near nadir because there appeared to be stability in that country and dangerous instability elsewhere, particularly in the Middle East and southeast Asia."[14]

FROM TAR BABY TO SHUTTLE DIPLOMACY

In the Joel Chandler Harris fable, Brer Rabbit becomes entangled in the Tar Baby when he misperceives the nature of its substance. Department of State critics of the Nixon administration's Southern Africa policy (located mainly within its African bureau) used the term *Tar Baby Option* because they felt it paralleled the fable. Like Brer Rabbit, the United States would become stuck in an association with the region's white regimes from which it could not disentangle itself, if and when minority governments collapsed. Events between 1968 and 1976 proved the critics right, and the U.S. government, not "born and bred" in the Southern African briar patch, gravely miscalculated events in an increasingly volatile Southern Africa.

Shortly after Richard Nixon took office, his national security adviser, Henry Kissinger, ordered a major review of U.S.–Southern African policy. But the administration remained preoccupied with Vietnam and the Middle East. Also, both domestic politics (the Nixon southern strategy) and globalist assumptions about the nature of East–West conflict, presaged a shift to a status quo emphasis in Southern Africa.

The Nixon Doctrine worldwide called for a strengthening of regional forces that would cooperate and collaborate with the United States to contain communist and communist-assisted insurgencies. This would allow the U.S. government to pursue its foreign policy interests without large-scale military involvement of the kind characterized by the Vietnam war. In Southern Africa only the white minority-ruled states, and especially South Africa itself, could perform this function.

National Security study memorandum number 39 (NSCM 39) was completed by August 15, 1969 and approved by the National Security Council in January 1970. The favored option called for a partial relaxation of U.S. measures against minority regimes; increased aid for black African states in the region, such as Botswana and Zambia; and a series of diplomatic efforts to resolve tensions between the white governments and their black neighbors. This option concluded:

> The Whites [in Southern Africa] are here to stay and the only way that constructive change can come about is through them. There is no hope for the blacks to gain the political rights they seek through violence, which will only lead to chaos and increased opportunities for the communists.[15]

U.S. policy to 1974 was based on the major tenets of NSCM 39. Strategists assumed that Southern Africa did not contain any vital strategic or political interests for the United States, though the region, and particularly South Africa, held important business interests. Southern Africa was a zone of political stability controlled by pro-Western regimes in South Africa, South-West Africa/Namibia, Rhodesia, Mozambique, and Angola. Because of these regimes, Southern Africa fell outside the East–West conflict area. The United States could maintain a low profile in the region.

Why did the U.S. government miscalculate so badly before 1974 in terms of its assumptions about the long-term stability of minority-rule regimes in Southern Africa? "The dominant concern of U.S. policy in the twenty-five years after World War II was containment of the Soviet Union, and thus in that period the status quo in Southern Africa was consistent with the goal of containment policy."[16] This globalist view misled policymakers about the nature of the regional forces that would make fundamental change inevitable. There is little doubt, either, that cultural and racial stereotypes carried by senior policymakers led them to the conclusion that the white regimes were impregnable to African challenge. Ferguson and Cotter, in an article in the influential journal *Foreign Affairs*, noted:

> A related constraining force on policy options is that imposed by racism. It is sometimes useful to remind ourselves that there are Americans who sympathetically identify with the architects of apartheid in South Africa. Many more would vigorously deny such identification but nonetheless assert that the outside world has no

right to judge the exigencies of a system developed by the Whites for their own survival.[17]

The 1974 military coup in Portugal fundamentally changed the nature of political conflict in Southern Africa. The war-weary Portuguese military government began immediately to withdraw from its colonies in Mozambique and Angola. Forces were set in motion after 1974 that would ultimately result in majority rule in Zimbabwe and Namibia.

In Southern Africa, there was increasing unrest in South Africa, increased guerrilla activity in Namibia, and deadlock in the talks between the Smith regime and the African nationalists in Rhodesia. In June 1975, a Socialist government (FRELIMO) came to power in Mozambique, and Angola collapsed into a three-sided civil war. "Dormant fears came to a head: fears of radicalization, major revolutionary violence, and deepening Soviet involvement."[18]

By August 1976, the former chief of the Central Intelligence Agency task force for Angola reported:

We were mounting a major covert action to support two Angolan liberation movements about which we had little reliable intelligence. Most of what we knew about the FNLA came from [Holden] Roberto, the chief recipient of our largesse, and it was obvious that he was exaggerating and distorting the facts in order to keep our support. We knew even less about Savimbi and UNITA.[19]

U.S. covert assistance to the FNLA and UNITA was no match for overt Soviet assistance and Cuban combat involvement on the side of the People's Movement for the Liberation of Angola (MPLA).[20] In only a matter of weeks the MPLA, backed by over 12,000 Cuban troops, was able to secure effective control of the country. By February 1976, the war was over. The abortive U.S. involvement in Angola had a significant impact both in the United States and in South Africa.

The U.S. government stood without a foreign policy in Southern Africa in the wake of the Angola debacle. That this should be so is not surprising given the basic misconceptions that the Kissinger policy of containment carried into the conflict. For Kissinger, "Angola might be far away but . . . it was a test case of the super-power relationship [and] the Kremlin [was] seeking unilateral advantage from the general relaxation of tensions."[21] A new policy for the region would have to take into greater account the domestic and regional origins of a conflict.

The post-Angola Kissinger policy had several goals. It assumed that the Soviets, having "imposed their solution on Angola," would entrench their forces there and look for new opportunities to expand their influence. The United States could preempt this by seeking an overall reduction in tensions in the region and by searching for a peaceful settlement to the conflicts in

Rhodesia and Namibia. Kissinger hoped to ensure that when majority rule did come in Southern Africa, moderate African leaders would come to power.

In the spring of 1976, Kissinger began what would be his last effort at shuttle diplomacy, a widely publicized series of meetings with both the Front Line States and South African and Rhodesian leaders, in a search for a peaceful settlement to the civil war in Zimbabwe. The U.S. approach to Southern Africa shifted from direct confrontation to crisis management.

The Kissinger mission achieved one major breakthrough when the United States, with the cooperation of South Africa, pressed Rhodesian leader Ian Smith to agree to a two-year timetable for instituting majority rule. However, the shuttle, which was aborted by Ford's loss of the presidency in November, failed in its ultimate goal to end the conflict and construct a constitutional agreement. The Kissinger plan was rejected by both the Zimbabwe nationalist leaders and the Front Line States, because they felt too much power would remain in European hands during the transition.

The Ford/Kissinger period saw a new era of active involvement in the Southern African region. There would be no return to the benign neglect of the earlier period. After 1976, U.S. diplomats, following Kissinger's lead, would assume the role of mediator between the Front Line States and the African nationalists on the one hand and minority-ruled regimes on the other. While Carter's approach might provide a sharp break from the past in terms of public rhetoric, the new administration would inherit many of the assumptions and techniques of the last two years of the Kissinger period.

THE CARTER YEARS: GLOBALISM VERSUS REGIONALISM

The Carter administration presented a new policy style on Southern Africa. In a December 1977 interview, President Carter put it this way:

> We . . . believe that our overall conduct of foreign relations will be strengthened by the moral premise inherent in our stance on [Southern Africa] questions. . . . We made it very clear that we oppose apartheid. We think that because the South African system is unjust, it may well lead to increasing violence over the years.[22]

The new rhetoric was somewhat moralistic in tone and more pro-African than that of any administration to that point. For many of Carter's advisers, including Andrew Young, who was most identified with this faction, the conflict and unrest in the region was caused not by Soviet and Cuban agitation, but by the inherent injustice of the apartheid system itself. The issue was not the minority regimes in Namibia and Rhodesia, but the South African government that propped them up. Hence the Carter/Young approach "tended to apply a single regional solution to the problem of white-minority dominance."[23] The solution was to identify openly with the aspirations of black Africa and other Third World states against South Africa.

The May 1977 meeting between Vice President Mondale and South African Prime Minister Vorster pinpointed the new approach. At that meeting Mondale called not only for majority rule in Rhodesia and Namibia but for a "progressive transformation of South Africa's society to the same end [and for] full participation by all the citizens of South Africa—equal participation in the election of its national government and its political affairs."[24] As a result, "the strategic bond between South Africa and the U.S. . . . snapped in 1977."[25]

Beyond the rhetoric, however, the substance of the Carter approach showed a remarkable continuity with the Kissinger approach after Angola. Washington's efforts continued to focus on Rhodesia in an effort to contain the escalating violence and find a settlement to the crisis acceptable to all parties. Hence, the "newly elected Carter administration . . . adopted the essentials of the Kissinger policy, now modified into the Anglo-American Plan for Zimbabwe."[26]

Young, along with British Foreign Secretary David Owen, continued the Kissinger policy of using South Africa as a conduit to bring about changes in Namibia and Rhodesia, and, like Kissinger, they approached each problem separately. The Carter people stressed the tactical nature of their contacts with Pretoria and reiterated that they were not meant to downplay the need for change in South Africa.

The United States continued to use the Front Line States and Nigeria as intermediaries in negotiations with the Namibian and Zimbabwean nationalists. Indeed, under Carter the Front Line States' leaders[27] played a more active and initiating role. Carter and his advisers continued the Kissinger search for moderate elements among the contending forces in the region. Carter used what Rothchild calls "an accommodative policy style":

> Accommodation utilized a broadly similar game plan in all three conflict situations: to come to terms, so far as possible, with moderate elements in advance of radical turnover. What was desired was to establish regimes satisfactory to leaders in the independent African states that would be linked to the international economic order through Western capital, skills, and technology. It was in part a conscious application of the "Kenya model" to Rhodesia and Namibia in the immediate future, and, possibly in altered form to the South African situation at a later date.[28]

Carter's commitment to an open trading system in Southern Africa followed from the accommodation policy. All the major Carter advisers saw U.S. investment as a positive force in South Africa and the region. U.S. business, by following the so-called Sullivan Principles,[29] would effectively moderate the harshest elements of the South African system.

Carter and his staff expended a great deal of effort to negotiate a peaceful settlement in the Rhodesian and Namibian conflicts. Young and Owen took over the Kissinger shuttle diplomacy role. From 1977 to 1978, they made an effort to get both sides to accept the Anglo-American plan for Rhodesia. The plan included a transitional arrangement for the country, an end to the illegal status of the regime, an interim UN force during the transition, and free elections on the basis of universal adult suffrage.

Andrew Young's face-to-face, direct negotiating style in South Africa was blunt and, for some, unsettling. The 1978 Malta talks on Zimbabwe illustrate this pattern; Arthur Gavshon recaptures the tone:

> Young chose the hotel where Patriotic Front leaders were living. He arrived near midnight on the eve of the conference, dropped his bags and all protocol in his hotel room, descended to the bar, introduced himself to some of the black guerrilla leaders, ordered a round of beer and immediately got down to listening, talking, arguing, agreeing, into the small hours.[30]

In Namibia, the United States encouraged the development of a "Western contact group."[31] Much of the effort to negotiate a Namibia settlement lay with Young's deputy and successor, Donald McHenry. Proximity negotiations were held in 1978 between the two sides and an agreement was reached on a number of the issues relating to the establishment of a UN authority, a cease-fire, and UN-supervised elections. South Africa then abruptly broke off the talks, and further negotiations in Angola in July 1978 were inconclusive. By 1979, the South Africans had begun to draw back from the negotiations. As the 1980 election year approached, they began to anticipate the possibility of a Carter defeat.

Carter administration efforts in Rhodesia had little more success. The Anglo-American plan was rejected by the Smith regime in 1978, and Smith established an internal transitional government ultimately headed by Bishop Abel Muzorewa. Two more years of war and the efforts of the Thatcher administration (without direct U.S. involvement) would lead to an independent Zimbabwe in April 1980.[32]

By the end of 1978, both the Rhodesian and Namibian talks had stalled. In South Africa, the death of black nationalist leader Steven Biko in September 1977 was followed by a massive clampdown against critics of the regime in October. In September 1978, P. W. Botha replaced Vorster as prime minister. Botha spent the greater part of 1979 consolidating his position, and there was little progress on regional negotiations.

The year 1979 marks a turning point in Carter policy toward Southern Africa. Throughout the Carter years there was an internal conflict between the regionalists, who saw internal factors in Southern Africa as the key to dealing with the problems of the region, and the globalists who felt the U.S. policy toward Africa had to be related to a general U.S. policy toward the

Soviet Union. Andrew Young and Zbigniew Brzezinski represented the two
ends of the policy spectrum. According to Gavshon, "The tussle between
Young and Brzezinski began almost as soon as the Carter team took office.
As Young freely acknowledged after resigning, the issue centered on the
Cuban role in Africa."[33]

A series of events signaled the ascendancy of the Brzezinski position.
Internationally, the fall of the shah of Iran in January 1979, the taking of
U.S. hostages in November of that year, and the Soviet invasion of
Afghanistan in December combined to traumatize the Carter presidency
during its last year. In Africa, Cuban involvement in Ethiopia became
pronounced by 1978. A revolt in the Shaba province of Zaire in the same
year had its origins among exiled Katangan soldiers living in Angola.
Department of State officials became convinced by January 1979 that the
Patriotic Front led by Robert Mugabe and Joshua Nkomo would come to
power in Zimbabwe,[34] possibly further strengthening the Soviet position in
Southern Africa.

By mid-1979, elements in the U.S. Senate were pressing for recognition
of the Smith-backed Muzorewa government. Young lost his position at the
UN. His departure signaled the return of U.S. policy to the globalist position
that "an increasingly assertive Soviet Union [was] the primary problem for
the United States in Africa and thus the proper target of policy."[35]

This shift in policy back toward globalism, while never complete,
provided a greater continuity with the incoming Reagan presidency than the
political rhetoric of the electoral campaign suggested. The Carter African
policy, which showed such promise in 1977, ended much the same as the rest
of his foreign policy efforts—confused, ambiguous, paralyzed by events in
South Asia, and guided by the paradigms of earlier administrations.

THE REAGAN ADMINISTRATION:
ALL CARROTS AND NO STICK?

The 1980 campaign suggested the possible main lines of a Reagan policy
toward Africa: under Reagan, there would be little concern for domestic and
regional issues. The view of the Southern African situation that emphasized
the elimination of injustice based on race was "a naive oversimplification":
"The basic issue is a power struggle between the United States and the Soviet
Union."[36]

For the first six months of the Reagan presidency there were no clearly
delineated policies toward Southern Africa other than an assumption of the
primacy of confrontation with the Soviet Union, and a positive view of the
South African government as a bastion against Soviet intervention. In a
March 4, 1981 CBS interview, Reagan said: "Can we abandon a country that
has stood beside us in every war we fought? A country that, strategically, is
essential to the free world in its production of minerals that we all must

have?"[37] Even the more regional policy thrust under Chester Crocker's leadership upheld the early view that Southern Africa was a testing ground for East–West domination and influence. That U.S. interests in the region should be equated first with keeping Moscow in check are reflected in Crocker's statement on U.S. policy toward Mozambique:

> The policy of the Reagan Administration has helped to bolster a conscious decision by the Government of Mozambique to reduce its dependence on Moscow and move toward genuine nonalignment and improved relations with the West. In so doing, we have reduced Soviet influence in southern Africa and advanced prospects for regional peace and stability. This successful course has the support of our allies and our African partners and has placed the Soviets squarely on the defensive.[38]

There were early indications that Reagan wanted to repeal the Clark Amendment of 1976 precluding U.S. assistance to opposition guerrilla movements in Angola. In Reagan's first year, for example, Secretary of State Alexander Haig petitioned the Congress repeatedly to pass such legislation. At the same time, the White House assured Congress that it had no intention of intervening there. The repeal effort in concert with the administration's strident anticommunist rhetoric fostered sympathy among certain archconservatives toward South Africa. Playing up the Soviet threat, they pressured the Democratic-controlled House into repealing the amendment in July 1985. In February 1986, following Savimbi's visit to Washington and a meeting with President Reagan on January 30, the administration announced that it would provide UNITA with $15 million in military aid.

Speculation also abounded about an official visit to the United States by South African Prime Minister P. W. Botha. In March 1981, the Department of State was embarrassed by a visit made to the United States by five senior South African military officers, despite a long-standing ban on official military visits.

Many concerned U.S. citizens and the leaders of the Front Line States considered these and other related decisions as violations of the administration's self-proclaimed neutrality role in the region.[39] U.S. actions that resulted from some of these early policy decisions were selling South Africa cattle prods for riot control; allowing South Africa easier access to U.S. military technology; approving a major IMF loan to the South African government; and failing to join the United Nations Security Council in condemning the South African raid into Angola in search of SWAPO guerrillas. Apparently the administration also authorized $28.3 million in sales of computers and nonmilitary industrial equipment, which, in the hands of the South African police, could be used to crack down on internal opposition.[40] When, finally, the Reagan administration formally linked independence for Namibia to the withdrawal of all Cuban troops from

Angola, hopes for an early implementation of the UN Security Council Resolution 435 were dashed. By the end of 1982, South Africa was successfully stalling for time while U.S. credibility in the region and official relations with the African continent reached their nadir.[41]

Within South Africa, reaction to the new administration was mixed. As one South African newspaper put it, the Reagan attitude was tantamount to "killing apartheid with kindness."[42] However, other accounts suggested that South African leaders were simply confused over the direction of the new administration. For the Johannesburg *Sunday Times*: "Anchorless, with key policymakers still not confirmed in their places, America's strongest figures cannot act, leaving the weaker ones blundering through, reacting to developments they have no hand in shaping."[43]

Most seriously, in light of the events of Reagan's first two years, the Pretoria government was interpreting U.S. policy as acceptance of the status quo rather than an effort to get movement on the Namibian question. R. F. Botha, the South African minister of foreign affairs, described the emerging U.S.–South African relationship:

> Our discussions on South West Africa, as well as the full range of problem areas in which we are both interested, have been conducted at an increased level of understanding on both sides in a way that would have seemed improbable a few years ago. Even when we have disagreed, there has always been a frank and fair communication of our differences and appreciation on both sides of the reasons. I do hope that this relationship continues to mature to the mutual benefit of both countries.[44]

One thing became clear to South African policymakers. The advent of the Reagan presidency meant the end of South Africa's "polecat status" and a return to membership in the "free world."[45]

IMPOSITION OF THE STICK

Reagan criticism of South Africa resulted from mounting public dissatisfaction with constructive engagement and what was perceived to be the administration's tacit alliance with the intransigent Botha regime. With nothing to show for its efforts in Namibia or in dismantling apartheid, the administration took exception to its policy of quiet diplomacy. In November 1982, Vice President George Bush fired the opening salvo during a trip to Nairobi: "Apartheid is wrong. It is legally entrenched racism—inimical to the fundamental ideas of the United States." Then in June 1983, Under Secretary of State Lawrence Eagleburger delivered the harshest administration criticism of apartheid to that date, including this implicit threat: "By one means or another, South Africa's domestic racial system will be changed." Even President Reagan—whose silence on apartheid had been conspicuously loud—found an occasion to proclaim his moral indignation over the high cost of apartheid to humanity.[46] The political pressure both from the public and within Congress succeeded in forcing the president to issue an executive order in September 1985 imposing limited trade and financial sanctions on South Africa, including the ban on importation of the Krugerrand and prohibition of most loans to the republic.

While the 1985 sanctions package may have diffused the issue for the 1986 congressional elections, they did not stop a bipartisan coalition in Congress from pushing through wider and tougher sanctions—over President Reagan's veto. Known as the Comprehensive Anti-Apartheid Act of 1986, these sanctions represented the culmination of a public foreign policy debate over South Africa that swept the country. Private citizens and antiapartheid groups demonstrated (and were arrested) almost daily outside the South African embassy in Washington, D.C. U.S. blacks in particular identified with the struggle as their own. At the forefront, the Free South Africa movement opposed constructive engagement because "it was soft on apartheid."[47] Representative Howard Wolpe termed the overwhelming bipartisan repudiation of a popular president's foreign policy "one of my proudest moments since I have been in Congress."[48]

Sanctions also signaled the muting of constructive engagement as the administration was forced to pursue a policy at odds with its own conception of progress for the region. At the same time, the policy drew fire from the right wing for its rapprochement with FRELIMO in Mozambique. Pleasing no one—with the possible exception of Pretoria—constructive engagement was chalked up as the "first major foreign policy defeat of Ronald Reagan's second term."[49]

Both the administration and its critics seemed to agree, however, that the 1986 act conveyed an important antiapartheid message to the South African government. Fewer agreed on the effectiveness of the act in bringing about meaningful reform within South Africa and in its regional policy. The package was a potpourri of some eighteen different kinds of sanctions ranging from trade restrictions, bans on loans and investments, and termination of U.S.–South Africa air travel, to authorization of an assistance program for apartheid victims. Policy assumptions such as U.S. dependence on strategic minerals were to be studied and reported on. The act called for U.S. multilateral sanctions in concert with the industrialized democracies. Persistent intransigence on Pretoria's part was to be met with still tougher sanctions.[50]

Not surprisingly, the administration's 1987 review of the act found that sanctions had not coerced Pretoria into dismantling apartheid:

> The report concludes that there has not been significant progress toward ending apartheid since October 1986, and that none of the goals outlined in Title I of the act—goals that are shared by the

Administration and the Congress—have been fulfilled. Moreover, the South African Government's response to the act over the past year gives little ground for hope that this trend will soon be reversed or that additional measures will produce better results.[51]

The impotency of the act, according to this evaluation, was apparent in the continued state of emergency and in the unabated political repression of black South Africans. Nelson Mandela and other key political prisoners were no closer to freedom than they had been a year before. The Botha regime had set no timetable for the repeal of the remaining apartheid laws. Violence both inside South Africa and in neighboring states had intensified. If anything, so claimed the report, the act had exacerbated an already stagnating economy and contributed to the increased misery of the population it was designed to aid by stripping them of jobs. Disinvestment had hurt fair labor programs and eliminated social-welfare programs that would have been funded by foreign investors. These findings, heralded in the text of the president's veto a year earlier, confirmed the administration bias against sanctions. Although he "vigorously" supported the purpose of the legislation—signaling the United States' categoric opposition to apartheid and firm commitment to its demise—still he claimed: "Black workers—the first victims of apartheid— would become the first victims of American sanctions."[52] The administration voiced its support of the goal but could not swallow the medicine.

As for the South Africans, they appeared to be interpreting the administration's signals—or at least those of Ronald Reagan—to mean that U.S.– South African relations could proceed on track with a fair degree of elasticity. Clough documents the pro-South African flavor of the president's one key policy speech of July 22, 1986: "'[T]he South African government is under no obligation to negotiate the future of the country with any organization [ANC] that proclaims a goal of creating a communist state and uses terrorist tactics to achieve it.'"[53] At least one analyst perceived in President Reagan a valuable friend and urged the republic to take advantage of his amity.[54]

GLOBALIST ASSUMPTIONS

U.S. policy under Reagan assumed that Southern Africa, and especially South Africa, was important strategically, economically, and politically. For this reason the area had increasingly become the scene of U.S.–Soviet confrontation since the early 1970s. Chester Crocker, in an article in *Foreign Affairs*, which had considerable impact upon Reagan administration thinking, put it this way: "The real choice we will face in Southern Africa in the 1980s concerns our readiness to compete with our global adversary in the politics of a changing region whose future depends on those who participate in shaping it."[55]

Security assumptions revolve around three concerns. First, the Cape route, always an important conduit between Europe and Asia, took on a new importance after the closing of the Suez Canal. Continued Western control of the Cape would be a major concern for U.S. policymakers. Second, and linked to the sea route argument, was concern over control of important South African ports and naval installations, such as the Simonstown complex on the eastern side of the Cape peninsula. For these to fall into unfriendly hands would be a major strategic defeat for the United States. A third security concern was said to be the necessity of continued U.S. and Western access to strategic minerals that are produced in South Africa and Namibia. These minerals include chrome, ferrochrome, nickel, cobalt, beryllium, and other minerals that go into the making of high-performance alloys. To be cut off from the South African source of these minerals was seen to constitute a major threat to U.S. weapons manufacture and to the country's industrial machine.

Economic and strategic concerns were closely linked. The loss of South African strategic minerals would have a significant economic impact as well. In addition to strategic minerals, South Africa is a major producer of such economically important minerals as industrial and gem diamonds and, especially, gold, which is a major factor in international trade. The significance of the economic dimension is clear when it is realized that South Africa possesses a significant proportion of the world's supply of these minerals.

Minerals aside, the Reagan administration saw South Africa as an important trading partner with the United States, an area open to U.S. investments, and an important market for U.S. manufactured and agricultural goods. South Africa is one of Africa's few growth points and U.S. investors have an interest in gaining and keeping access to such a market.

Most importantly, the Southern African region has been significant politically in the U.S. struggle against the Soviet Union and its allies. South Africa, for all of its domestic problems, is an important regional power. Reagan policymakers correctly pointed out that South Africa is the most powerful nation militarily on the African continent. It can and will, like Israel in the Middle East, act independently of U.S. policy interests. For Reagan's advisers, South Africa has played and will play a part in curbing Soviet influence in the region. A continued strong stand against the USSR and Cuba is important both because of tangible U.S. interests in the region and because U.S. credibility is at stake in the post-Vietnam era.

From this perspective the Soviet Union has been concerned with establishing and maintaining permanent diplomatic and military influence in the region. The U.S. concern, therefore, should be to push back Soviet influence where it exists, such as in Angola, or to avoid Soviet dominance in contested areas such as Namibia. Black African states are seen as leaning toward one global pole or another, and U.S. technical assistance is to be used to ensure sympathy toward the United States in such crucial Front Line States as Zambia, Botswana, and Zimbabwe.

Although the overall thrust of the globalist assumptions is shared by most of those who influenced Reagan perspectives of Southern Africa both in and out of government, there are significant differences of strategy and sophistication. On the one extreme are Peter Duigan and L. H. Gann, coauthors of *Why South Africa Will Survive*. For these writers, whose views on South Africa are openly apologist and sympathetic to European imperialism, "The United States should . . . extend the boundaries of the NATO alliance beyond the Tropic of Cancer—an arbitrary boundary that makes no sense in the light of Soviet naval strategy—and associate South Africa with our system of defence."[56]

On the other extreme is Crocker, who is careful not to overstress the globalist influence in the region and who recognizes the domestic origins of many Southern African conflicts. For Crocker, U.S. policy should seek the middle way between the tilt to the south of the Kissinger era and the naïve "fuzzy thinking" of the Africanists who influenced the Carter administration. While the United States is limited in its influence in Southern Africa, Crocker has argued, the actions it takes should bolster U.S. interests, not those of one or another constituency in the Southern African region. Others who influenced Reagan administration thinking on Africa include Raymond Tanter, Uri Ra'anan, Adda Bozeman, and Kenneth Adelman.[57]

Critics of the Reagan policy point to a number of weaknesses of the globalist position. They suggest that the security argument is largely illusory. The Cape route could be circumnavigated even if South Africa fell into hostile hands, and the South African bases would be of little importance either in a limited war in Europe or the Middle East or in a nuclear conflagration. South Africa, because of its racial policies, is a security liability rather than an asset and is likely to be the tinderbox of violence and regional instability well into the 1990s.

Critics of globalism do recognize the economic importance of the region. The overall importance of U.S. investments and trade, however, is downplayed. South Africa purchases only 1.5 percent of U.S. exports and accounts for only 1 percent of overall U.S. foreign trade. Largely because of oil and natural gas, the United States has more overall trade with either Nigeria or Angola than with South Africa. U.S. direct investment accounts for only 1 percent of total U.S. foreign investment. Disinvestment cut the value of U.S. direct investment in South Africa by more than half, from $2.4 billion in 1982 to approximately $1 billion in 1987.[58]

It is the congruence of economic and strategic minerals that is important to the United States. There is "a very real U.S. national interest in maintaining continuous and secure access to African minerals."[59] Globalist strategy risks that access, however, in three ways. First, it overstresses South African mineral production and neglects the importance of black African states as sources of many economically important minerals. Second, it assumes that the ascendancy of a "radical" regime in South Africa would exclude the United States from purchasing minerals when perhaps the export of minerals is so important to South Africa, accounting for some 13 percent of its GNP, that no regime could afford to forgo revenues earned by mineral exports. Finally, U.S. strategy assumes that a tilt toward the south, or even Crocker's neutrality, will provide the United States with access to minerals. While this may be true in the short run, critics suggest the only way that the United States can lose access to minerals in South Africa will be as a result of long and violent racial confrontation in the region that would halt production. U.S. policy, by giving the South Africans a false illusion of time, is leading perhaps to just that scenario.

In sum, suggest the critics, Reagan policymakers, having defined the Southern African region as strategic when most evidence suggests that it is not, contributed to the U.S. loss of credibility. Politically, the U.S. position in Southern Africa is weak because the regional situation remains largely beyond U.S. control. Having predefined national interests within the region as strategic, then having failed to contain revolution and violence in a revolution-prone area of the world, the United States has quite likely weakened its position internationally.

The core of the problem for critics of the globalist approach is a lack of understanding of the forces that make for political change in Africa and the Third World. Critics of Reagan policy suggest that foreign involvement in Africa is important, whether it be Cuban in Angola, French in West Africa, or U.S. involvement in Kenya and Somalia. However, they suggest that historical and structural factors are critical to an understanding of the origins of conflict. Robert Price's summary of the U.S. failure to understand the nature of the Rhodesian crisis applies equally well to Angola, Namibia, and South Africa itself:

> U.S. policymakers, in their search to find a formula that might forestall Soviet involvement, have ignored the historical and structural realities. . . . However unfortunate they may be, these realities create a context within which the otherwise laudable values of non-violence, compromise, and minority rights function to inhibit the reversal of a condition of racial domination and privilege.[60]

A solution to the Namibian question, normalization of relations with Angola, and pressure toward majority rule in South Africa might better serve the long-term interests of the United States in the region. The racial schism in that troubled part of the world will not simply go away.

CONSTRUCTIVE ENGAGEMENT

Although the globalist assumptions of the Reagan administration were apparent from the beginning, it was not until mid-1981 that anything close to a coherent strategy became visible. The mainline thoughts of the Reagan approach appear in the writings and speeches of Chester Crocker among others. His becoming assistant secretary of state for African affairs in June 1981, after considerable delay by right-wing forces in the Senate, marks the beginning of the policy.

Constructive engagement for Crocker assumed the realities of white South Africa and suggested that the United States work through the white power structure as based in the so-called reformist wing of the National Party (the *Verligte* element). Constructive engagement (1) assumed that any power-sharing that occurred would be at the initiative of the ruling National Party; and (2) openly aligned the United States with Nationalist "reform" leaders such as President P. W. Botha who pushed for moderate changes in the apartheid system. To quote Crocker:

> The innovative feature of constructive engagement is its insistence on serious thinking about the sequencing and interrelatedness of change. . . . We must avoid the trap of an indiscriminate attack on all aspects of the [South African system]. . . . Piecemeal power-sharing steps deserve support.[61]

Two main strands became apparent in the South African dimension of the strategy: (1) a series of U.S.-initiated confidence-building steps calculated to reassure South African whites of U.S. good faith and to reestablish Pretoria's trust in U.S. policymakers; and (2) a comprehensive economic, social, and political development program leading to black empowerment. As Seiler pointed out, "Criticism of racism in South Africa must be balanced by an appreciation of the difficulties involved in building stable democratic institutions in that multi-ethnic society and by public appreciation when measurable progress is achieved."[62] Crocker considered education an important element of the black empowerment strand. In his *Foreign Affairs* article he put it this way:

> The case for education as a priority concern (for the U.S.) is powerful because it brings a capacity for participation, self-help, communication, and management. . . . [There should be] a determined external push backed by official and non-governmental facilities and inducements. . . . Ironically, . . . little has been done by Western Governments and educational institutions to focus on upgrading internal opportunities or to support overseas study by persons committed to returning to their country.[63]

At the base of the strategy there remained the overriding preoccupation with a potential Soviet and Cuban challenge to the United States in the region, and the assumption that this challenge would require continued stability in South Africa itself.

In 1981, the United States quietly began to implement the institution-building aspect of constructive engagement. In December, the U.S. Congress, by Sections 303–305 of the Foreign Assistance Act, established a program for the fiscal years 1982 and 1983 that provided help to educate those "legally disadvantaged" South Africans who up to then had been unable, or only with the utmost difficulty been able, to educate themselves. According to a U.S. Agency for International Development (USAID) document that made recommendations for subsequent years' programs, the education program "represents great promise in meeting long felt needs in improving U.S./South African relations [and is] a necessary plank in the policy of Constructive Engagement."[64] Initially, the program was administered by the U.S. Information Agency, though the funding came from USAID. In 1984, USAID opened an office in the Pretoria Embassy, discreetly called the Office of Development Affairs (ODA).

The government program was supplemented by a private program coordinated by the Institute of International Education to provide black South African students access to U.S. colleges and universities, at both the undergraduate and graduate levels.[65] The two programs are jointly coordinated, and students are selected by a single board within South Africa. The two programs have provided scholarships for hundreds of blacks both in the United States and in South Africa. The programs are significant in that they anticipate a generation of African professionals who will have an influence over the affairs in their country. In much the same way as the Tom Mboya airlift in Kenya,[66] they are attempting to influence the attitudes of a generation of Africans toward the United States. A long-range goal of the Reagan foreign policy was to convince a broad spectrum of black South Africans that U.S. policy toward South Africa was influencing socioeconomic change in the region.

The administration also established a human rights program in 1984 under the U.S. Foreign Assistance Act, with the intention of aiding victims of apartheid and promoting justice through social, economic, and political means. More than 200 projects received funding in amounts of less than $10,000 for legal and educational assistance, research in conflict resolution, race relations, promotion of private enterprise, and organizational development. The sum of $1.5 million was committed in 1986 for projects and institutions that address "legal and other constraints to full equal rights and protection of all South Africans' civil liberties."[67]

In a similar vein, the Reagan administration set aside $20 million in FY 1986 for small self-help projects designed to help blacks develop essential leadership skills across the spectrum in labor, education, business, and community development. As Secretary Shultz explained, the goal was to help blacks "take their rightful place as leaders in a democratic post-apartheid South Africa."[68] The Reagan administration argued that U.S. business both within the Southern African region and in South Africa itself is an important catalyst for improving black social welfare and building the foundations of black institutions. For the administration, U.S. business activity was the *force motrice* for change, permitting desegregation of the workplace, following equal and fair employment practices, and promoting blacks to supervisory positions. By September 1986, some 160 of 241 U.S. firms with a South African "presence" had adopted the fair labor code known as the Sullivan Principles. According to a senior Department of State official, U.S. companies spent some $200 million over a ten-year period in improving employee housing, health care, education, and community development. Saving black jobs, improving black living standards, and gradually increasing black political participation in the system was—in the Reagan administration's view—its most compelling argument against disinvestment and sanctions:

> Rising joblessness in South Africa is not a prescription for strengthening the bargaining position of blacks in their efforts to end apartheid. Rising black joblessness is a prescription for apartheid's perpetuation beyond its natural lifespan.
>
> The South African business community has known and said for years that apartheid is the very antithesis of capitalism and that its continuation is inconsistent with the development of a modern economy. That is why the private sector in South Africa has been the principal white voice for the steady dismantling of apartheid.
>
> No section of the business community in South Africa has a prouder record of efforts to break down apartheid and build up black South Africans' role in the economy than American companies.[69]

Critics of the Sullivan Principles argue that the U.S. business presence in South Africa provides only symbolic changes and that continued foreign investment acts as a prop to the South African government and its continued "group approach" to political reform. Significantly, the author of the Sullivan Principles, the Reverend Leon Sullivan, renounced the strategy and called for divestment from South Africa.

CONSTRUCTIVE ENGAGEMENT IN THE REGION

Regionally, the United States recognized the economic and military predominance of South Africa and publicly acknowledged the role that Pretoria would play in the search for regional stability. Persuasion and diplomacy, rather than punishment and isolation, have been the watchwords of constructive engagement. Changes in the region must be acceptable to the republic, and South Africa's security interests have been considered legitimate factors in regional negotiations. The presence of 40,000 Cuban troops in Angola was a prime example of a threat to those security concerns.

With this perspective, U.S. policy sought to increase U.S. military assistance to the neighboring black states under the Security Supporting

Assistance Program (SSA), and technical assistance under regular foreign assistance programs. The bulk of the assistance was to go to African states that were either threatened by the ongoing regional conflicts, such as Zimbabwe, Zaire, Zambia, and Botswana, or to states that have a regional or continental importance such as Nigeria, Kenya, and Senegal. Secretary Shultz stated the U.S. policy objectives for the Southern Africa region:

- To assist the countries in the region to improve the lives of their people
- To end intervention by outside military forces
- To reduce the opportunity and temptation for such intervention to recur[70]

The success of these programs was mixed, partly because of the uneven application of the policy and the continued South African cross-border aggression and destabilization of its neighbors. In Mozambique, the U.S. administration was instrumental in bringing about the Nkomati Accord in 1984, which called for Mozambique and South Africa to end support for insurgency groups on the territory of the other party. (A similar arrangement was signed with Swaziland.) Unfortunately, the agreement, which is considered by some observers to be the high-water mark of constructive engagement, continues to be violated by South Africa.

The Reagan Administration was lavish in its praise for Mozambique for its continued commitment to Nkomati, its openness to dialogue with the South African government, its retreat from socialism, and, perhaps most important, its reduced dependence on Moscow and its new embrace of the West. It fought hard to translate praise into tangible support despite opposition from right-wing politicians in Congress. From the other side, critics such as Howard Wolpe credited the administration for its relief and development effort in Mozambique. In 1987, U.S. commitment to Mozambique in humanitarian relief totaled approximately $75 million.[71]

The record is less laudable in Zimbabwe and other key neighboring states where the tendency to stereotype independent governments as "Marxist" became self-fulfilling prophecies, and thus improved Soviet possibilities in the region. Irked by criticism of its international policies, the administration cut off bilateral support to Zimbabwe when former President Jimmy Carter was insulted by a junior sports minister at a 1986 Fourth of July celebration in Harare. The initiative to cooperate with a promising state model for a postapartheid South Africa was squandered. Critics cite evidence of Zimbabwe's turning to the Soviets in 1987 for possible purchase of MIG-29s.[72]

Nowhere was the contradiction in policy goals more apparent than in Namibia and Angola, where movement on Namibia was to have put into motion the forces for bringing about constructive change, peace, and stability in the region. On April 16, 1981, Chester Crocker met with South African Foreign Minister P. W. Botha and is said to have indicated, "USG [U.S. Government] believes it would be possible to improve U.S.-South African relations if Namibia were no longer an issue."[73] The U.S. approach to Namibia illustrated the problems inherent in the constructive engagement policy.

The Reagan administration came to power just at the time the Geneva talks on Namibia collapsed. After flirting with the idea of a new approach, outside the auspices of the UN, the Reagan administration put its influence and prestige at stake in the search for a settlement. South Africa has a history in the negotiations of agreeing to major conditions but of adding new demands at the eleventh hour. In the mid-1981 Namibia negotiations the pattern held.

By the end of June 1982, it seemed that terms for a settlement had been agreed. Lurking in the background was the question of Cuban troops in Angola. During the June–July 1982 negotiations, Reagan representatives had soft-pedaled the Cuban question, suggesting only that some movement on that issue would speed up the Namibia negotiations. By September 1982, the issue of linkage had been added to the Namibian settlement and was placed on the bargaining table, and by November 1982 Vice President George Bush was publicly stating, during a visit to Africa, that linkage was a U.S. precondition for further mediation on the issue.

Under the Reagan Doctrine, Angola's dependence on Soviet sophisticated military hardware, including an advanced air-defense network, became legendary. The Angolans gained air superiority in the war in early 1988. Cuban troop levels more than doubled. Estimates placed the figure in mid-1988 at approximately 47,500 to 50,000 Cuban troops in Angola.[74] While Angola is second only to Nigeria as the United States' largest trading partner on the continent, the United States is Angola's largest trading partner on the globe. Ironically, U.S. arms and funding permitted UNITA guerrillas to attack U.S.-owned oil installations guarded by the Cuban troops the administration was trying to expel.[75]

For the administration, a settlement to the Namibian problem has often been just around the corner, snagged, for example, on a question of timing for troop withdrawals. Yet, despite perennial optimism, the linkage issue led to seven and a half years of stalled negotiations, thousands of dead, and many more thousands of wounded or maimed soldiers and civilians in Angola. Luanda has become known as the amputee capital of the world. Linkage continued to stalemate the Namibian settlement down to the end of the Reagan administration in 1988.

Perhaps ending the war in Angola will require a delinkage between the United States and its proxy UNITA. In an interview in *Africa Report*, Representative Howard Wolpe put it like this:

[The policy] has reinforced the perception that the U.S. is now a military ally of South Africa and has become party to South African aggression against Angola and the neighboring states. I cannot think of anything that is more counterproductive to American interests in southern Africa than that kind of de facto complicity and alliance with South Africa. It is as though the Soviet Union had written our script![76]

The talks among South Africa, Angola, Cuba, and the United States in August 1988 raised hopes again for a settlement. Chester Crocker found promise for an agreement in the acceptance of a set of fourteen principles by the negotiating parties. Some observers felt South Africa was anxious to reach a settlement before a hostile Democratic administration might reach the White House.[77] On the other hand, the financial costs of the war, estimated in mid-1988 at R4 billion per year, might have compelled the South African government to reach a settlement before a new president was inaugurated in January 1989. A UN peace plan for the independance of Namibia was signed by the United States, Angola, Cuba, and South Africa on December 22, 1988. The UN Transitional Assistance Group (UNTAG) arrived in Namibia on April 1, 1989, with UN-supervised elections scheduled for November 1989.

The Reagan administration's inability for almost eight years to resolve the Namibian question was symptomatic of the underlying contradiction in the policy as well as of divergent strategies that guide policymakers. On the surface is the problem of an administration and a Congress working at cross-purposes. But underneath are opposing factions, both within the administration and within the Congress, whose disparate agendas for progress in the region render policymaking a most arduous and painstaking enterprise.

We are reminded, for example, that a Democratic-led House voted to repeal the Clark Amendment while the Republican-controlled Senate voted for sanctions against South Africa. In the same month—September 1986—the House voted both to continue CIA military assistance to UNITA and to override the president's veto of the Anti-Apartheid Act. The prevailing support for UNITA in the Department of Defense, the CIA, the Defense Intelligence Agency, and the National Security Agency (as well as in Congress) was initially opposed by the Crocker wing of the administration.

The Namibian and Angolan situations are complex and interrelated, and movement on the one will no doubt have an influence upon movement on the other. One can understand the Reagan strategy of searching for concessions in negotiations so that a South African withdrawal from Namibia would not result in a Cuban penetration of the newly independent state. However, it may have been unwise formally to link the two as a precondition to a settlement. The U.S. demand for what it calls parallel progress did not stimulate movement but instead created a virtual deadlock in the negotiations. The South African government, given its fear of a SWAPO victory, was the beneficiary of a lack of movement.

The secretary of state's Advisory Committee on South Africa declared constructive engagement a failure in February 1987. First, none of its central objectives had been achieved, and second, the unmanageable level of violence within the republic invalidated the assumption that the National Party was in control of change. Sullivan renounced his own principles in the report, urging a complete trade embargo and recommending that U.S. companies pull out of South Africa. The report drew this significant conclusion: "US policymakers now face a situation markedly different from that which existed in 1981. A new policy is now urgently required."[78]

The administration however, remained out of touch with reality or unconvinced of the commission's findings. In an October 1987 address, Crocker steered the old course: "Continued vigorous participation by U.S. business in the South African economy, guided by the still-valid Sullivan principles . . . is an important factor in sustaining a climate of economic hope in which black, brown, and white South Africans realize that the politics of negotiation do not need to become a zero-sum game."[79] Like a cat with nine lives, constructive engagement was still alive.

CONTINUITY IN FUTURE POLICY?

The U.S. approach to the conflicts in Southern Africa has shown a surprising degree of consistency given the dramatic changes that have occurred there since 1948. Nor is it likely that the Bush administration will make major changes in the United States' South Africa policy. Increases in concern, particularly after 1974, have been largely reactive and linked to Washington's perception of the region as a center for East–West conflict where U.S. credibility is at stake. Only during the Carter administration was there some attempt to break the mold of the stereotype of East–West confrontation. However, intense public dissatisfaction with constructive engagement and apartheid led to a revolution in U.S. interest in the region after 1984. Wolpe captured the scope of the shift:

> A few years ago, Africa was not even a subject that was discussed in national debates or within the Congress. Now it is very much a part of the overall foreign policy dialogue that is taking place inside the Congress and across this country. I think we will find as we move closer to November that the issue of South Africa and of southern African policy will be much more a part of the presidential debates and considerations than they have been historically.[80]

Constructive engagement may have contributed to the increasing level of political violence in Southern Africa. In addition to South Africa's ongoing military activity in Namibia and Angola, the South African army has invaded Mozambique, Botswana, and Lesotho, attacked Zambia and Zimbabwe by air, and has been involved in subversive activity in Zimbabwe. South Africa has supported opposition elements such as RENAMO in Mozambique and supra-ZAPU in Zimbabwe, and forced the overthrow of the Leabua Jonathan regime in Lesotho. As Jennifer Whitaker has noted, "Pretoria aims . . . to terrorize its neighbors into curbing all ties with South Africa's own broadly backed insurgent movement—the African National Congress."[81] Black African leaders are convinced that South Africa has embarked upon a continuing policy of destabilizing black states that harbor ANC guerrillas and refugees.

With the current policy in confusion, what comes next? Seasoned observers such as Wolpe advise against the myopia and simplicity of the East–West lens. He recommends a balanced program integrating regional and strategic goals in particular, and rapprochement with and development assistance for Pretoria's neighbors, including a serious public dialogue with the ANC and SWAPO. Such a plan would end all covert aid to UNITA and normalize relations with Luanda, as well as provide economic and military support for the SADCC states to counter the regional hegemony of the republic. Wolpe emphasizes that international cooperation in meeting these objectives, backed with the threat of multilateral sanctions, would send a clear message to Pretoria that the status quo at home and in the region is too costly to maintain. A firm believer in the power of sanctions, he intends to push for stronger measures and stricter enforcement:

> Anything that we do that conveys a sense of economic normalcy or an acceptance of continued economic linkages with the regime will serve to delay the time when the Afrikaners will accept the inevitable, namely the necessity of abandoning apartheid and sitting down to negotiate a new political order with the authentic leadership of the black majority. That is an invitation for the prolongation of the struggle, for much greater violence and bloodshed. I think that would be tragic.[82]

The alternative to such a forceful policy risks still greater estrangement from the SADCC states as well as from the Western allies. Wolpe cosponsored the bill by Congressman Ron Dellums that would almost completely stop trade between the United States and South Africa. The bill passed the House of Representatives on August 12, 1988, but did not pass the Senate. The bill was introduced again in both houses of Congress in early 1989.

Clough finds common ground with Wolpe on several points, particularly on: (1) the need to reconcile contradictory policies in the region in order to enhance regional stabilization; and (2) the need for a "broad bipartisan consensus" in Washington. But he differs on a number of key issues, including the effectiveness of blanket sanctions for toppling apartheid. Clough prefers sanctions for specific, limited objectives in last-resort situations where, for example, Pretoria would refuse to negotiate in good faith in spite of Angolan/Cuban cooperation for a regional settlement. He also doubts the likelihood of a repeat sanctions coalition from 1986, citing the fragility of the compact that was held together, not by an abiding faith in sanctions, but by expediency:

> For them [many members of Congress], the act was a political quick fix to get apartheid off the domestic agenda. In the absence of highly publicized violence in SA and renewed domestic protests over apartheid such as occurred in 1984–86, it is doubtful that Congress can be counted on to pass measures that will steadily tighten the screws on South Africa."[83]

Clough's main critique of past policies is that they have not been realistic in terms of time frame, nor have they been in step with the majority of U.S. citizens' expectations for the region. Constructive engagement failed because it overestimated Botha's commitment to reform and the acceptability of piecemeal reform to the U.S. public.

A second fundamental argument advanced by Clough revolves around black empowerment, and what the United States should be doing to promote it:

> One effective black-oriented strategy would be to concentrate on enhancing the black opposition's ability to create autonomous organizations and independent economic and social support networks, thereby reducing black dependence on white-controlled agencies and structures and enabling blacks to challenge the state more effectively.[84]

U.S. churches, labor unions, student and professional groups, and service organizations should be encouraged to communicate with and strengthen ties with black South Africa. Limited U.S. influence in the region means the battle will be decided "not in the halls of Congress or the meeting rooms of the U.N. Security Council, but inside South Africa."[85] The shift in policy, it seems, would be from white to black constructive engagement.

With the future of additional sanctions legislation in doubt, the administration quietly sabotaged the package in place. In Winchester's *Current History* article of May 1988 we read that the Reagan administration reversed the ban on imports of South African uranium intended for reexport, and vetoed a UN Security Council resolution calling for selective sanctions against Pretoria. According to Winchester, "The administration further circumvented implementation of the Anti-Apartheid

Act through inaction and various loopholes and failed to convoke an international conference to consider further sanctions as the law requests."[86] These actions contradicted the president's report to Congress of October 2, 1987: "I am pleased to be able to report that the act has been implemented fully and faithfully. Executive departments and agencies are to be complimented for their excellent work in carrying out this complex piece of legislation."[87]

Chester Crocker, in a speech before the American Legion in August 1981, argued that it was not in the United States' interest to choose between black and white in Southern Africa: "We cannot and will not permit our hand to be forced to align ourselves with one side or another in these disputes."[88] For the black African states, and no doubt for South African blacks as well, this "neutrality" suggested that a choice had been made. Such "neutrality" cannot support majority rule in South Africa and Namibia.

Crocker is his own harshest critic vis-à-vis the eight years of Reagan administration constructive engagement. In his writings and speeches he has placed two caveats on a U.S. strategy of constructive engagement. In testimony before the House subcommittee on Africa he warned that the United States should not become bogged down in protracted high-level negotiations over Namibia if there was a strong likelihood of a deadlock between South Africa and the Front Line States. The United States should not "permit its energies, time and credibility to be frittered away on a drawn out and fruitless diplomatic charade in Southern Africa."[89]

In his *Foreign Affairs* article, Crocker laid down the second warning about constructive engagement. The policy failed, during the Nixon/Ford years, he argues, because

[p]ositive elements of the initial Nixon stance of active communication with Pretoria were soon overshadowed by White House unwillingness to push the policy publicly and energetically. . . . Pressure for change should be a central ingredient in American policy, and that pressure must be credibly maintained if we are not to send misleading signals to South Africa.[90]

Yet, the record shows that the United States under Reagan was willing to apply pressure against Pretoria only when left with no other alternative.

In the early 1970s, the United States assumed the long-term stability of the white minority regimes in Angola, Mozambique, and Zimbabwe. Current assumptions are that the black guerrilla movements will not be able to change the structure of the South African government. South African state violence, which has hurt thousands of innocent people inside the republic and in the region, gets minor play compared to the guerrilla activities of the ANC, directed mainly at military and noncivilian targets. The question might be raised: to what extent do racial stereotypes continue to plague the development of a coherent U.S. foreign policy toward southern Africa? Do members of the National Security Council still pound their fists on the table, jungle-beat style, whenever discussions of African affairs come up? To what extent do cultural and racial stereotypes continue to influence U.S. policy choices?

For Robert Fatton, the answer is clear: "It would be quite wrong to assume that economic and strategic interests are the sole determinants of the Reagan foreign policy toward South Africa. In fact, the role of culture and ethnicity is fundamental in the making of this policy."[91] Fatton's argument hinges on historical events that have shaped the Weltanschauung of the United States. Manifest destiny, the white man's burden, social Darwinism, and the recent colonial past of the West so impinged on Reagan policymakers that only a thin veneer of civilization covered latent, racist passions underneath. "To put it bluntly," he wrote, "affinities of color, race, and culture intrude in the making of the Reagan foreign policy toward South Africa."[92] In his statements, Reagan has alluded to the occidental lineage of the republic and to the common cultural background that South Africa shares with the West. If Fatton is correct, constructive engagement has been an elaborate charade, papering over the administration's desire to clone a reasonable facsimile of the status quo for postapartheid society:

> There is . . . serious ground to believe that the United States under the Reagan administration is at best engaged in trying to guarantee the privileged position of a small white minority within a deracialized but otherwise unreformed social order, and at worst is bent on consolidating the existing structures of white dominance."[93]

Ironically, the failure to take the various actors in southern Africa seriously is *not* a characteristic of South African policy elites. The decade of 1970s began with mistaken assumptions about the nature of political change in Southern Africa. Given apparent U.S. assumptions about the longevity of the Nationalist Party regime in Pretoria, there is every likelihood that Washington policymakers began the decade of the 1980s with a similar misreading of the nature of events in that troubled region. It will be left to a new generation of policymakers in the 1990s to set a foreign policy agenda for U.S. involvement in Southern Africa.

NOTES

1. Henry F. Jackson, *From the Congo to Soweto: U.S. Foreign Policy Toward Africa Since 1960* (New York: William Morrow, 1982), p. 42.

2. R. W. Johnson, *How Long Will South Africa Survive?* (London: Macmillian, 1977), p. 57.

3. See Ofuatey-Kodjoe, "The United States, Southern Africa and International Order," *Journal of Southern African Affairs* 1, Special Issue (October 1976), p. 113.

4. The nations generally included in Southern Africa are the Republic of

South Africa, Namibia, Lesotho, Swaziland, Botswana, Malawi, Mozambique, Zimbabwe, Tanzania, Zambia, and Angola. Sometimes Uganda, Zaire, and Kenya are also included because of their involvement with the core.

5. Robert M. Price, "U.S. Policy Toward Southern Africa: Interests, Choices, and Constraints," in Gwendolen M. Carter and Patrick O'Meara, eds., *International Politics in Southern Africa* (Bloomington: Indiana University Press, 1982); Donald Rothchild, "U.S. Policy Styles in Africa: From Minimal Engagement to Liberal Internationalism," in Kenneth Oye, Donald Rothchild, and Robert J. Lieber, eds., *Eagle Entangled: U.S. Foreign Policy in a Complex World* (New York: Longman, 1979), p. 307; George M. Houser, "U.S. Policy and Southern Africa," in Frederick S. Arkhurst, ed., *U.S. Policy Toward Africa*, (New York: Praeger, 1975), p. 119.

6. As quoted by Rothchild in "U.S. Policy Styles," p. 307.

7. Andrew Nagorski, "U.S. Options vis-à-vis South Africa," in Jennifer Seymour Whitaker, ed., *Africa and the United States: Vital Interests* (New York: New York University Press, 1978), p. 188.

8. George W. Shepard, "Comment," in Arkhurst, *U.S. Policy Toward Africa*, p. 44.

9. Interview with Sir Peter Fawcus, former queen's commissioner, Bechuanaland Protectorate, August 18, 1979.

10. Vernon McKay, "Changing External Pressures on Africa," in Walter Goldschmidt, ed., *The United States and Africa* (New York: Praeger, 1963), p. 102.

11. Rupert Emerson, "The Character of American Interests in Africa," in Goldschmidt, *United States and Africa*, p. 7.

12. Jackson, *From the Congo to Soweto*, p. 42.

13. There was a greater tendency to view African leaders, such as Nkrumah, Nyerere, and Modibo Keita, as "socialist" and as threatening to U.S. foreign policy interests.

14. Thomas Karis, "U.S. Policy Toward South Africa," in Gwendolyn M. Carter and Patrick O'Meara, eds., *Southern Africa: The Continuing Crisis*, 2d ed. (Bloomington: Indiana University Press, 1982), p. 329.

15. See Mohamed A. Khawas and Barry Cohen, eds., *The Kissinger Study of Southern Africa* (Westport, Conn.: Lawrence Hill, 1976), p. 105.

16. Price, "U.S. Policy Toward Southern Africa," p. 47.

17. Clyde Ferguson and William R. Cotter, "South Africa: What Is to Be Done," *Foreign Affairs* 56, no. 2 (January 1978), p. 265.

18. Karis, "U.S. Policy Toward South Africa," p. 337. In English translation, FRELIMO stands for the Front for the Liberation of Mozambique.

19. John Stockwell, *In Search of Enemies* (New York: W. W. Norton, 1978), p. 90. See also John Stockwell, "The Case Against the CIA," *Issue 9*, no. 1 (Spring/Summer 1979), pp. 21–23.

20. FNLA operated in the north of Angola, UNITA operated in the south, and the MPLA controlled the capital and the central provinces.

21. John Spanier, *American Foreign Policy Since World War II*, 8th ed. (New York: Holt, Rinehart and Winston, 1980), p. 205.

22. Rothchild, "U.S. Policy Styles," p. 317.

23. *Ibid*.

24. As quoted by Gwendolen M. Carter, *Which Way Is South Africa Going?* (Bloomington: Indiana University Press, 1980), p. 124.

25. Colin Legum, *Western Crisis Over Southern Africa* (New York: Holmes and Meier, 1979), p. 127.

26. Robert M. Price, *U.S. Foreign Policy in Sub-Saharan Africa: National Interest and Global Strategy* (Berkeley: Institute of International Studies, University of California, 1978), p. 3.

27. At the time, these were Julius Nyerere of Tanzania, Kenneth Kaunda of Zambia, Seretse Khama of Botswana, Samora Machel of Mozambique, and Agostino Neto of Angola.

28. Rothchild, "U.S. Policy Styles," p. 320.

29. The author of the Sullivan Princples, the Reverend Leon Sullivan, a black minister and member of the board of General Motors, proposed a code of nonsegregation and fair employment practices for U.S. firms operating in South Africa.

30. Arthur Gavshon, *Crisis in Africa: Battleground of East and West* (Harmondsworth, England: Penguin, 1981), p. 160.

31. The group was made up of the United States, Great Britain, France, West Germany, and Canada.

32. Attempts after 1979 by conservative legislators in Congress to repeal sanctions against Rhodesia and to get the United States to recognize the Smith-backed prime minister, Bishop Abel Muzorewa, could have had an impact on the British attempts at settlement had they succeeded.

33. Gavshon, *Crisis in Africa*, p. 161.

34. Personal conversation of the author with officials of the Africa Bureau, February 5–9, 1979. Conditions of the interviews and discussions preclude direct attribution.

35. Price, "U.S. Policy Toward Southern Africa," p. 52.

36. Richard Deutsch, "Reagan's African Perspectives," *Africa Report* 25, no. 5 (July–August 1980), p. 4.

37. As quoted by the *Rand Daily Mail* (Johannesburg), March 5, 1981, p. 1.

38. Statement made before the Subcommittee on Africa of the Senate Foreign Relations Committee on June 24, 1987. *Department of State Bulletin*, 1987, p. 19.

39. Pauline Baker, "United States Policy in Southern Africa," *Current History* 86, no. 520 (May 1987), p. 196. For Baker, the U.S. decision to abandon "diplomacy for military intervention" doomed the Namibian initiative, "killing any chance of [the United States'] acting as an honest broker" in the region.

40. A charge made by the American Friends Service Committee, reported in *Congressional Quarterly*, Special Report: South Africa Sanctions, "Capital Hill Taking a New Look at Apartheid," March 9, 1985, p. 443.

41. See J. Gus Liebenow, "American Policy in Africa: The Reagan Years," *Current History* 82, no. 482 (March 1983), pp. 97–100.

42. *Rand Daily Mail*, May 14, 1981, p. 11.

43. *Sunday Times* (Johannesburg), March 29, 1981, p. 2.

44. Quoted in Carl Noffke, "The United States and South Africa," in Calvin A. Woodward, ed., *On the Razor's Edge: Prospects for Political Stability in Southern Africa* (Pretoria: The Africa Institute of South Africa, 1986), p. 46.

45. *Sunday Times* (Johannesburg), May 3, 1981, p. 2.

46. See his December 10 International Human Rights Day speech in *Weekly Report*, 1984, p. 3106.

47. Herbert Howe, "United States Policy in Southern Africa," *Current History* 85, no. 511 (May 1986), p. 207.

48. In "Interview with Howard Wolpe," *Africa Report* (March–April 1988), p. 38.

49. Baker, "United States Policy," p. 194.

50. Cf. Michael Clough, "Southern Africa: Challenges and Choices," *Foreign Affairs* 66, no. 5 (Summer 1988), p. 1067–1090.

51. "Report on Anti-Apartheid Act of 1986," *Department of State Bulletin*, December 1987, p. 35.

52. "Message to the House of Representatives, September 26, 1986," *Department of State Bulletin*, December 1986, pp. 35–36.

53. Clough, "Southern Africa," p. 1086.

54. Cf. Noffke, "The United States and South Africa," pp. 46–49.

55. Chester Crocker, "South Africa: Strategy for Change," *Foreign Affairs* 59, no. 2 (Winter 1980–1981), p. 345. This article and others in a similar vein had an influence on his selection as assistant secretary of state for African affairs.

56. L. H. Gann and Peter Duigan, *Why South Africa Will Survive* (Cape Town: Tafelberg, 1981), p. 272.

57. See Deutsch, "Reagan's African Perspectives," for a detailed discussion of Reagan unofficial advisers on Africa.

58. Cf. "A U.S. Policy Toward South Africa: The Report of the Secretary of State's Advisory Committee on South Africa," U.S. Department of State (January 1987).

59. Price, "U.S. Foreign Policy," p. 14.

60. *Ibid.*, p. 47.

61. Crocker, "South Africa: Strategy for Change," pp. 346–347.

62. John Seiler, "Has Constructive Engagement Died?" *Orbis* 25, no. 4 (Winter 1982), p. 868.

63. Crocker, "South Africa: Strategy for Change," p. 347.

64. USAID Project Review, "Implementation of the FY-1983 ICA Special Scholarship Program for Black South Africans: Recommendations for Subsequent Years' Programs," May 14, 1982, p. 1. Mimeo.

65. Letter, Derek C. Bok, president, Harvard University, to Ronald W. Roskens, president, University of Nebraska, October 1982.

66. The Kenyan leader met with presidential candidate Kennedy in 1960 in order to raise money for 260 Kenyan students who had been offered places in U.S. universities but did not have money for the air fare. Kennedy took up the matter with the Kennedy Foundation, which contributed $100,000 to

transport the students to the United States. See Ali Mazrui, *Africa's International Relations* (London: Heinemann, 1977), p. 156.

67. "U.S. Supported Human Rights Program in South Africa," *Department of State Bulletin*, May 1986, p. 47.

68. "The Democratic Future in South Africa," *Department of State Bulletin*, November 1987, p. 11.

69. Charles W. Freeman, deputy assistant secretary for African affairs, "South Africa: What Are America's Options?" speech of December 9, 1987, *Department of State Bulletin*, March 1988, p. 29.

70. "The Democratic Future in South Africa," *Department of State Bulletin*, November 1987, p. 9.

71. "U.S. Policy Toward Mozambique," *Department of State Bulletin*, September 1987, p. 21.

72. Howard Wolpe, "Seizing South African Opportunities," *Foreign Affairs* 73 (Winter 1988–1989), pp. 60–75.

73. *Rand Daily Mail* (Johannesburg), April 14, 1981, p. 9, reproduced in *African Report* 28, no. 1 (January–February 1983), pp. 39–41.

74. Robert Pear, "U.S. Sees No Bar to Arms in Angola," *New York Times*, July 24, 1988, p. 4.

75. Cf. David Zucchino, "Amid Reports of Peace Talks, Angola's War Goes On," *The Philadelphia Enquirer*, June 26, 1988, p. 3C.

76. Wolpe, "Seizing Opportunities," p. 37. Typescript. See also Clough, "Southern Africa," p. 1086.

77. Pear, "U.S. Sees No Bar to Arms in Angola," p. 4. For linkage issue, see James M. Markham, "Angola and Cuba Rebuff Pretoria on Troop Pullout," *New York Times*, August 4, 1988, pp. 1, 4.

78. Wolpe, "Seizing Opportunities," p. 38. Typescript.

79. Given before the City University of New York conference, "South Africa in Transition." *Department of State Bulletin*, December 1987, p. 32.

80. Wolpe, "Seizing Opportunities," pp. 38, 39. Typescript. For a discussion of U.S. policy for Southern Africa as an issue for the presidential campaign in 1988, see David Rogers, "U.S. Policy on Southern Africa Is Emerging As Potential Flash Point in Presidential Race," *Wall Street Journal*, June 10, 1988, p. 40.

81. Jennifer S. Whitaker, "Pretoria's Wars," *New York Times*, January 21, 1983, reproduced in *AF Press Clips* 18, no. 3 (January 21, 1983), p. 10.

82. Wolpe, "Seizing Opportunities," p. 36. Typescript.

83. Clough, "Southern African," p. 1073.

84. *Ibid.*, p. 1081.

85. *Ibid.*, p. 1082.

86. N. Brian Winchester, "United States Policy Toward Africa," *Current History* 87, no. 525 (May 1988), p. 233.

87. "Report of Anti-Apartheid Act of 1986," *Department of State Bulletin*, December 1987, p. 35.

88. "Crocker on U.S. Policy Toward Africa," U.S. Department of State (August 29, 1981), p. 9. Mimeo.

89. *The Chronicle* (Bulawayo, Zimbabwe), June 19, 1981, p. 12.

90. Crocker, "South Africa: Strategy for Change," p. 325.

91. Robert Fatton, "The Reagan Foreign Policy Toward South Africa: The Ideology of the New Cold War," *African Studies Review* 27, no. 1 (March 1984), pp. 76–77.

92. *Ibid.*, p. 76.

93. *Ibid.*, p. 78.

Index

The Contributors

ABOUT THE EDITORS

Edmond J. Keller is professor of political science at the University of California, Santa Barbara. He is author and editor of many books and articles on African politics, including *Revolutionary Ethiopia: From Empire to People's Republic*, and (with Donald Rothchild) *Afro-Marxist Regimes: Ideology and Public Policy*.

Louis A. Picard is associate professor and associate dean at the Graduate School of Public and International Affairs, University of Pittsburgh. He has written extensively on African politics, including *The Politics of Development in Botswana, The Evolution of Modern Botswana*, and (with Raphael Zariski) *Sub-National Politics in the 1980s*.

ABOUT THE AUTHORS

Heribert Adam is professor of sociology at Simon Fraser University, Burnaby, British Columbia.

Robert Groelsma is a graduate student at the Graduate School of Public and International Affairs, University of Pittsburgh.

C. R. D. Halisi is assistant professor of political science at Indiana University, Bloomington.

C. Tsehloane Keto is professor of African-American studies at Temple University.

Arend Lijphart is professor of political science at the University of California, San Diego.

Pearl-Alice March is coordinator for the Joint Center for African Studies, Stanford University–University of California, Berkeley.

Kogila Moodley is director of the Multicultural Program in the Faculty of Education at the University of British Columbia.

Donald Rothchild is professor of political science at the University of California, Davis.

James R. Scarritt is professor of political science at the University of Colorado, Boulder.

John Sullivan is an analyst with the U.S. Department of Defense.

Richard F. Weisfelder is professor of political science at the University of Toledo.